HIGHER
CONSCIOUSNESS

HIGHER CONSCIOUSNESS

The Responsibility of Soul Freedom

ELIZABETH CLARE PROPHET

Gardiner, Montana

HIGHER CONSCIOUSNESS
The Responsibility of Soul Freedom
Elizabeth Clare Prophet
Copyright © 2021 The Summit Lighthouse, Inc.
All rights reserved.

No part of this book may be reproduced, translated, or electronically stored, posted or transmitted, or used in any format or medium whatsoever without prior written permission, except by a reviewer who may quote brief passages in a review.

For information: The Summit Lighthouse,
63 Summit Way, Gardiner, MT 59030 USA.
1-800-245-5445 / 406-848-9500
TSLinfo@TSL.org
www.SummitLighthouse.org

Library of Congress Control Number: 2021939916
ISBN: 978-1-60988-368-3
ISBN: 978-1-60988-369-0 (eBook)

SUMMIT UNIVERSITY PRESS®
Summit University Press, ☙, Keepers of the Flame® Fraternity, *Pearls of Wisdom*, and The Summit Lighthouse are trademarks registered in the U.S. Patent and Trademark Office and in other countries. All rights reserved.

Image of seagull, page 133: Tim Felce, CC BY-SA 2.0

24 23 22 21   1 2 3 4

LET THE EAGLES GATHER FOR THE ASSIMILATION

Darjeeling, India
May 28, 1976

Chelas on the Path of Higher Consciousness:

I address you in the light of everlasting love. I summon you in the will of the diamond-shining mind of God. I extol your God-identity chaliced forever in the wisdom of the Mother.

Let the eagles gather, for the feast of the Lord's body is nigh. "Except ye eat the flesh of the Son of man and drink his blood, ye have no life in you." The saying of the Lord is for the alchemy of higher consciousness. That which you would become you must assimilate.

The Gurus of the age and of all ages are the ascended masters. We come summoned by the God of all. We are called to the marriage feast; we adorn souls with the bridal veil of native innocence. We are the fathers of the bride. We place the hand of the soul in the right hand of the priest of the flame—the individual Christ Self—that the ritual of the alchemical marriage might be performed, that the soul might be reunited with the flaming Spirit—birthless, deathless, eternal.

Higher consciousness is a ritual of immaculate love. Let those who would enter here wash their hands. We come to assimilate and to be assimilated.

Symbol of infinity, figure eight of flow and Eightfold Path. We release the energies of macrocosmic consciousness.

Come and dine!

Let the eagles gather for the feast of the Lord's body. Let the sheet knit at the four corners be let down to the earth. Let the "four-footed beasts of the earth, the wild beasts, and the creeping things, and the fowl of the air" be lowered into position; for we, the ascended masters, have heard the voice of the Lord to the Vicar of Christ, "Rise, Peter; kill and eat!"

We have heard his reply, "Not so, Lord; for I have never eaten any thing that is common or unclean."

And we have accepted the Lord's rebuke: "What God hath cleansed, that call not thou common."[1]

Yes, the teachings of the ascended masters are to all nations, to all generations and kindreds and peoples. Therefore come!

Come as you are. Come with your untransmuted substance. Come with every aspect of the lesser self, for the Lord has bidden us "kill and eat."

Place upon the altar of the living God and the living flame your sacrifice of the "lower consciousness" with its carnal forces and wearisome, worn-out forcefields; and we, the Gurus, will "kill and eat."

We will pass the flame of our higher consciousness through the density and the debris. We will take in the energy of your microcosmic consciousness to our heart's altar. We shall consume and transmute; and at the conclusion of this gathering, we shall return to you the purified substance, the original innocence that is your higher consciousness.

Let the eagles gather for the assimilation.

I am in the flame of the rebirth of a nation and a people tried in the fire of the will of God.

I AM

Morya

on the Path with my chelas

CONTENTS

1. Higher Consciousness through the Law of Cycles 1
   Elizabeth Clare Prophet

2. Call to Light: Dedication of the Flame 71
   The Goddess of Light

3. America: Ye Shall Know the Truth and the Truth
   Shall Make You Free 75
   Pallas Athena

       The Statue of the Goddess of Freedom 84

4. Releasing the Flame of Freedom Enshrined in the
   Capitals of the Nations 87
   The Goddess of Freedom

5. The Responsibility of Freedom 99
   Elizabeth Clare Prophet

6. Stars and Stripes of Our Cosmic Consciousness 141
   The Elohim Arcturus and Victoria

7. The Rise of the Feminine Ray in America 155
   Lady Master Venus

8. The Disciplines for Higher Consciousness 163
   Serapis Bey, Hierarch of Luxor

9. The Disciplines for Higher Consciousness 175
   The Elohim of Purity

10	The Purification of the Chakras and the Four Lower Bodies: Prerequisites for Higher Consciousness .... 181 *Elizabeth Clare Prophet*	
11	Out of the Flame of Mother .... 207 *Out of the Flame of Mother*	
12	Escape to the Sun .... 215 *Helios of the Sun*	
13	A Thrust and a Roll and a Ho, Ho, Ho! .... 221 *Lord Zadkiel and Holy Amethyst*	
14	We Expect .... 233 *Lanello*	
15	We Expect .... 245 *Godfre*	
16	The Antahkarana of Power .... 255 *El Morya*	
17	The Antahkarana of Power .... 261 *The Elohim Hercules*	
18	We Are One in the Flame of East and West .... 265 *Gautama Buddha and Jesus Christ*	
19	Meditation in the Moment of the Birth of a Nation ....271 *The Great Divine Director*	
20	Our Service in the Next Hundred Years of America's Destiny .... 275 *Saint Germain*	
21	"God Has Decided to Save the Earth" .... 289 *The Goddess of Liberty*	

Notes 293

We scan the centuries and we scan the light of chelas. We scan those who would be chelas but say they cannot. We look for will. We look for the momentum of the will to be. We look for those who have the courage to fling themselves into the majesty of overcoming, into the way of life victorious. We look for those who understand the light of service as the perpetual motion of the lightbearers. We look for those whose heads are not cast down but who look into the skies to see the stars and to see in the stars the hope of life and life everlasting.

—El Morya

1

HIGHER CONSCIOUSNESS THROUGH THE LAW OF CYCLES

Elizabeth Clare Prophet

Why We Are Here

We are gathered here in our nation's capital for the bicentennial to witness and to participate in the rebirth and expansion of higher consciousness in ourselves, in America, and in the nations and peoples of the earth.

We will learn that higher consciousness is dependent upon the law of cycles as that law is operational within the Macrocosm and microcosm of being. We will meditate upon the law of cycles as the controlling factor in the release of higher consciousness within us all. In fact, we will experience this law as it governs the eternal movement of light/energy/consciousness throughout cosmos.

And like awestruck children we will watch in silent wonder the going out of the energy of the soul from Spirit to Matter, from Alpha to Omega, and the coming in of that energy/entity from Matter to Spirit, from Omega to Alpha—both in the nucleus of the atom and in the white-fire core of God's being in man and in woman.

We are going to participate in the law of cycles as it has affected the history of our nation and our movement, and the origin and development of ourselves. We will become aware of the law of cycles as the cycling of our karma and our dharma evidenced in the cause-effect sequences which we have by free will set in motion in our lives.

We are going to examine the how and the why of these sequences as they affect us moment by moment. As types of energy, they cycle from the within to the without and from the without to the within, producing the momentous consequences of bane and blessing, triumph or tragedy in our lives. Here we will consider how we create ourselves, our circumstances, our astrology—yes, even the hereditary and environmental conditions of our birth.

From this point of understanding our co-creative work with the universal Mind, we will reconsider our choices to preserve or to destroy that which we have created—wittingly or unwittingly—by the law of cycles. Then in the power of the Word, spoken and unspoken, we will search the soul's experiences of cycling into the Self that is Reality.

Through conscious rather than unconscious awareness of that Self, we shall spiral into succeeding spheres of our innate higher consciousness. Thence we will, with all due objectivity, survey our ignorant and willful misuses of cosmic law and begin to undo, by the violet flame of the Holy Spirit, by the science of transmutation taught by Saint Germain, all that was done at cross-purposes to the Real Self.

The Teacher and the Teaching Are Ready

If this is your first conference, I would like to tell you that our four days of meditation upon the Word will be based on the great tradition of the teachings of the ascended masters that have already been set forth in this and other activities sponsored by the Great White Brotherhood* since America's last centennial celebration, in 1876.

You who have been searching for the thread of contact with hierarchy—whether the saints of the inner Church of our Lord or the Eastern adepts of the unbroken line of the Himalayan brotherhood—rejoice! For the search is ended. Our cup of good cheer is also that cup of cold water that we offer to you, dear pilgrim, in Christ's name: The teacher and the teaching are ready. Come and dine.

Our conference is sponsored by the Darjeeling Council and its chief, the ascended master El Morya, who comes to define the path of

---

*A spiritual order of Western saints and Eastern adepts who have reunited with the Spirit of the living God and who comprise the heavenly hosts. The word "white" refers not to race but to the aura (halo) of white light surrounding their forms.

initiation for the individual and for America. We give our heartfelt gratitude and obeisance to the Master M—as he has often penned his signature—who presents to each of us, as chelas of the will of God and devotees of the spirit of freedom in this century, a very important opportunity to define both advanced and fundamental steps on the Path.

Increasing Light, Energy, and God Consciousness

Our Summit Lighthouse conferences are for the release of the light, energy, and consciousness of the Great Central Sun to the planetary body through the heart chakras of the ascended masters and their chelas.

This grace of God is stepped down—first through Elohim and solar hierarchies, the hosts of the LORD, thence through the entire Spirit of the Great White Brotherhood, that great company of saints! These beings of immense light transfer this grace to their unascended disciples in the planes of Matter in order that their heart chakras might be focal points for the distribution of energies that flow from heaven to earth with a cyclic regularity according to the law of cycles. This light, energy, and consciousness is for the sustainment of the flow of Creator and creation in earth's evolutions that the birth of higher consciousness—the Christ consciousness—might appear "on earth, as it is in heaven"[1]—as Above, so below, in Matter as in Spirit.

According to his use of the gift of free will, man may elect to fulfill or to abort the law of cycles. Unascended disciples may increase their allotted portion of grace through deeper communion with God. This is accomplished through prayer, meditation, dynamic decrees, and selfless service offered lovingly on the altar of humanity to the glory of God.

The most expedient means of increasing one's light, energy, and God consciousness is through chelaship on the path of initiation under the real Gurus of the Aquarian age—the ascended masters. Within the hallowed circle of the community of the Holy Spirit, they provide, whether directly in the one-to-one encounter or through their embodied messengers and representatives, the soul testings that enable the individual to climb the ladder of attainment and, by his own inner God-mastery, retain more light in his chakras. Their initiations to their chelas are one-pointed—that the chela might play his part in holding the balance of personal and planetary karma during this period of world turmoil and transition.

From the Great Outbreath to the Great Inbreath

Now let us meditate upon the flow of energy from God the Macrocosm to man the microcosm through the frequencies of fire, air, water, and earth. Let's use our imagination to draw in the sky with our mind's eye a giant figure eight within a giant circle. (fig. 3)

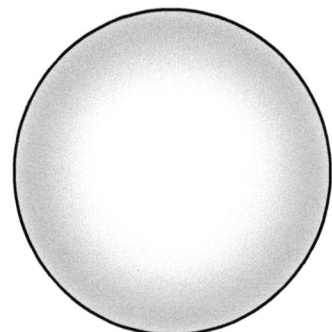

The I AM THAT I AM
Great sphere of higher consciousness
FIGURE 1

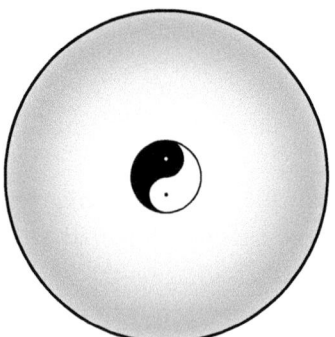

The T'ai Chi plus/minus nucleus, or nexus,
of the great sphere of higher consciousness
FIGURE 2

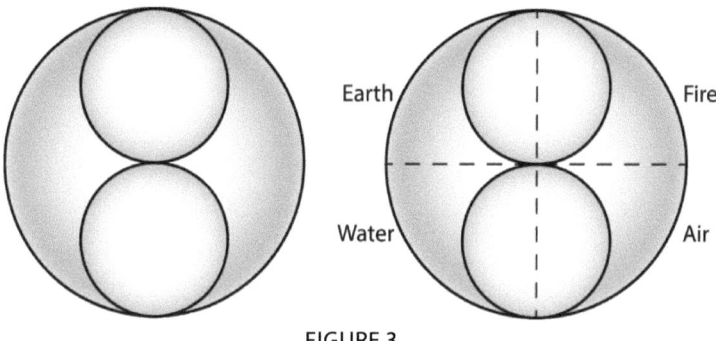

FIGURE 3

Let's trace the circle moving clockwise from zenith to zenith, then let's take the track of the figure eight until it carries us back to where we started from. (fig. 4) This is a cosmic roller coaster! What we're really doing is experiencing infinity becoming more of itself as particles of infinity (that's us) are thrust out of the One (the point in the center of the circle), move through the coordinates of time and space, and return to the One by the law of love.

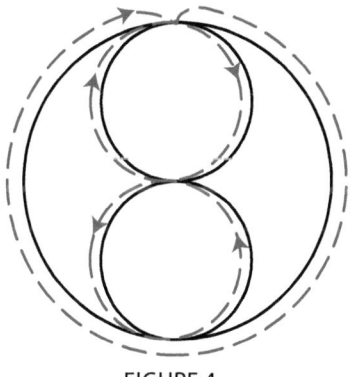

FIGURE 4

Let's go with God as we move with his energy-Self in motion from the point of origin in the center of the circle—the fiery core of life, the sacred AUM—to the circumference. Let's go *be,* as being is thrust from the primordial T'ai Chi over the parabolic curve unto its journey in time and space and returns Home again clothed upon with higher consciousness. (fig. 5) Let's move with him from the Great Outbreath to the Great Inbreath.

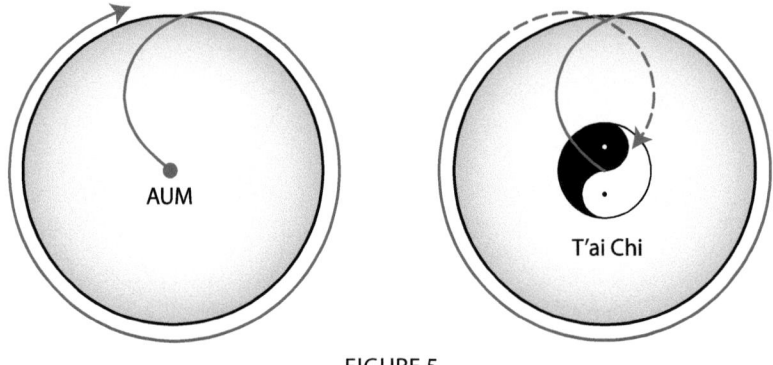

FIGURE 5

On the diagram the initial descent of the soul from Spirit to Matter is shown as an arc of energy from the center through point **A** (Alpha) to point **Ω** (Omega). (fig. 6)

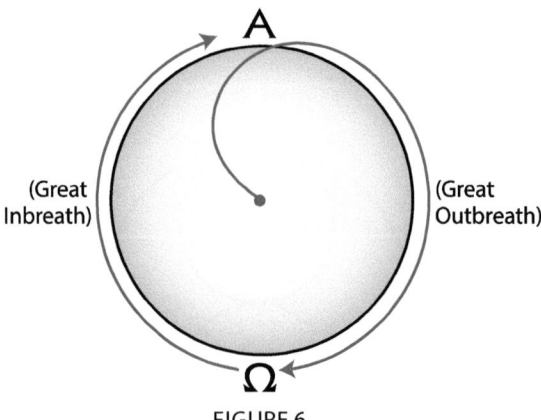

FIGURE 6

This descent from heaven to earth occurs but once within a given cosmic cycle. It is the initiation of the cycles of experiences in the outer Spirit-Matter universes (as opposed to the soul's prior experiences in the inner Spirit-Matter universes). The ascent of the soul from Matter to Spirit is shown as the arc of energy from point **Ω** to point **A** at the top of the circle. The ascent from earth to heaven likewise occurs only once within the given cosmic cycle. It is the consummation of all cycles experienced within the coordinates of time and space.

These two arcs together form the single flame of identity as man consummates the great cycle of becoming. The first arc is the beginning of the Great Outbreath, the last is the ending of the Great Inbreath. All that is in between is the summation of light/energy/consciousness invested by God and man in the joint venture of an individual life. This venture becomes the glorious adventure of the soul called *the crystallization of the God flame.*

As man traverses the great cycle of his being that leads unto the ascension, he experiences the unfoldment of infinite cycles within cycles. In the mystical vision of the prophet Ezekiel, he beheld this reality as the "wheels within wheels."

From the smallest atom to the vast galaxies to the Allness of the Cosmic Egg, cycles interpenetrate cycles. Short cycles compose the essence of long cycles. The cycles of our individual body cells combine to form the biorhythmic cycles of our physical body as a whole. The cycle of a day is made up of twenty-four hourly cycles. One year is composed of 365 daily cycles, and so forth. As we embrace this law of the interdependence of cycles, the realization of the wisdom of God's creation leads us into that sphere of higher consciousness where we can ride the combined crests of our own personal cycles of becoming, to merge with God's ever-transcendent Being.

The course of consciousness noted in fig. 7 is clockwise from point A (Alpha) to point Ω (Omega)—this is called the *thrust*—and from Ω back to A—this is called the *return.*

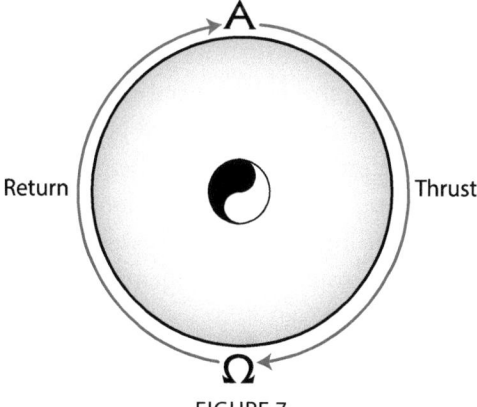

FIGURE 7

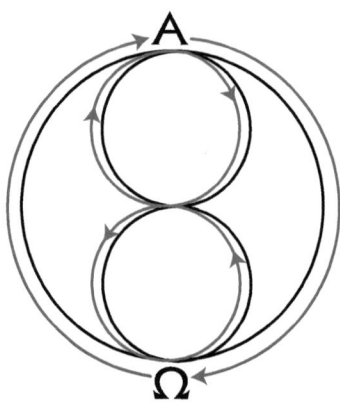

FIGURE 8

After tracing the circle of being once, we reenter the sphere at **A**. (fig. 8)

Following the figure-eight spiral, we descend clockwise-counterclockwise and then ascend counterclockwise-clockwise. In so doing we have passed through the center twice. Returning to point **A**, we repeat the pattern again and again until many cycles consisting of many spirals are completed. Each time we complete a single figure-eight spiral, being advances by microseconds in time and space and in velocity/vibration.

Thus there is no boredom in nature because repetition is not sameness. Rather is it the reinforcement of worlds within worlds. No two spirals are exactly the same—nor do they occupy the same time-space coordinates—when the soul is advancing in its solar and galactic destiny. However, this law is operable in its perfection in man only when there is the daily striving toward perfection—the pressing toward the goal and the pressing harder that bespeaks the will to be that has conquered boredom, sameness, and the looking back to triviality. When the fullness of the inner blueprint is externalized, we reenter the primordial T'ai Chi, the soul (or solar) identity sealed in God—God as quiescence. (fig. 9a)

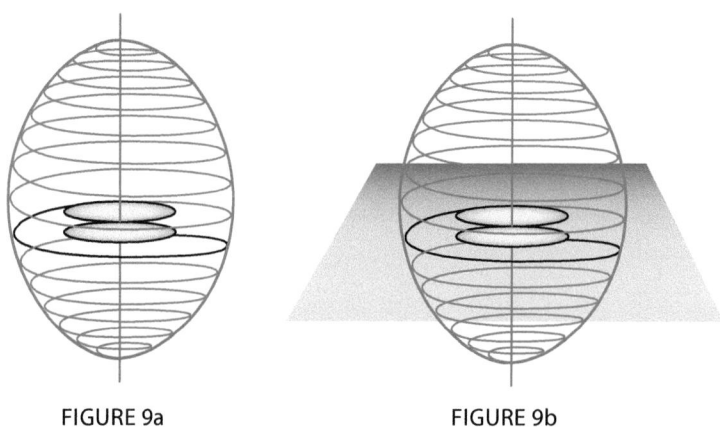

FIGURE 9a   FIGURE 9b

Rest in Motion

There follows the interval of cosmic rest—a "rest in motion" within the central sun of the inner Spirit-Matter universe, called the *pralaya* in the East. This interval precedes and is preparatory to another cycle of the Great Outbreath and the Great Inbreath that will occur in the next slice (spiral) of never ending Be-ness within the cosmic egg. (fig. 9b)

The mystery of this period of going within to the plane of cosmic equilibrium has been described by Mark Prophet in his lecture entitled "The Exhalation and Inhalation of the Breath of God." He says:

> It's the night of Brahma when all of this is drawn back into the Godhead and there is a rest period, and then during the rest period the patterns are being gathered within; it's like a seed. We find that God is functioning now as a seed.
>
> And that during this period of rest, the lacy patterns of the creation [are drawn back to the center]. When I say lacy patterns, I'm referring to all of the whole divine DNA chain, if you will—the patterns that God makes by which stars will be born and spiral nebulae and whole systems, galaxies....
>
> And we have to recognize that during this period of rest that there is an actual manifestation of divine intelligence—the stirring, the shaking of divine intelligence in the seed, and that

this shaking is the drawing by the fingers of God of the various graphs and patterns and hieroglyphs that are going to manifest in the various systems of worlds.

When the whole is complete, which is supposed to be during the night of Brahma, during the period of rest . . . then once again comes the dawn of creation and the exhalation of the breath of God—and the whole system is repeated over again.[2]

On the path of higher consciousness, we understand the need for cyclic periods of rest in motion as we go within the inner chamber of our hearts to find the point of peace midst the turmoil of the outer world. This is not rest in the sense of stopping our forward motion, but rather we cycle our consciousness through the balance point of God's heart, where his harmony can resonate upon the inner walls of our being. We can then give forth that vibration of harmony to troubled souls and to a waiting world.

A Circle of Spiral

Now let us look at the line in the diagram as though it were a free atom—a free particle of energy, verily a part of God that has elected to do God's will in fulfilling the law of cycles in order to sustain the whole Spirit-Matter creation. Born in the cradle of the T'ai Chi, the atom—a soul, if you will—is thrust from the nucleus charged with the wholeness of the plus-minus polarity of the whirling sun center called the Father-Mother God. (fig. 10a)

As it descends the Alpha curve, the soul-atom, a Spirit-Matter particle, is stripped, so to speak, of its Alpha (Spirit) charge through the deceleration of its momentum. Moving like a fiery comet apparently consumed by its fiery passion to fulfill "the will of him that sent me,"[3] it is actually endowing the Matter universe with its Alpha current. Having divested itself of its Alpha, or plus, charge in the planes of Matter, it has now become endowed with the Omega, or minus, charge. As it ascends the Omega curve of return, it is stripped of its Omega polarity as it accelerates its momentum, thus endowing the Matter universe with its Omega current by a love that is the utter givingness of the self in "the laying down of one's life for one's friends."[4]

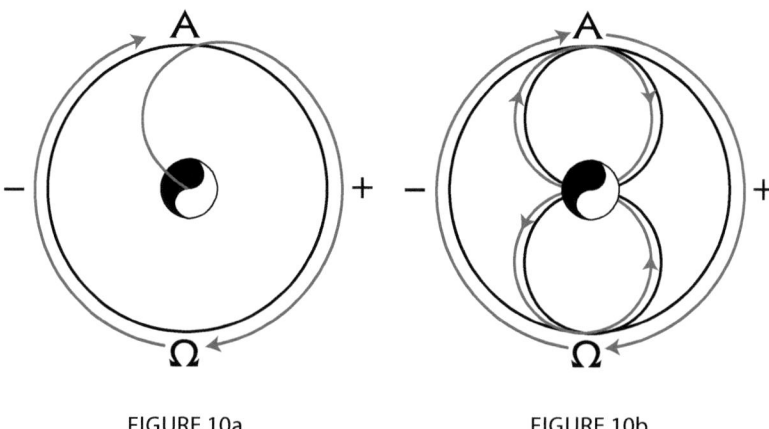

FIGURE 10a   FIGURE 10b

Having followed its course on the circumference of the circle, the soul returns to the nucleus to be born again—first to be recharged with the Alpha thrust as it descends the figure eight, then to be recharged with the Omega return as it ascends the figure eight. (fig. 10b) Thus each completed round is a cycle fulfilled. It is, as Gautama Buddha has called it, "a circle of spiral." This is the path of our meditation upon the soul's involutionary-evolutionary cyclings in the Spirit-Matter cosmos from the moment of the Great Outbreath to the culmination of the Great Inbreath.

The energy flow of the circle of spiral is sustained by the law of the Three in One, or the Trinity. The original thrust of the atom of the soul is in the name of the Father-Mother God. It is sent from God to do the will of Alpha and Omega for the fulfillment of the beginning and the ending of cycles in Spirit and in Matter.[5]

This phase of its journey—the thrust and return of Alpha and Omega—is experienced by the soul on the outer surface of the sphere of life in the four quadrants of Matter. It is noted as steps 1 and 2 on the diagram of initiations into the Personhood of the Godhead. (fig. 11) It may require several million "years" (cycles or, in Biblical parlance, "days" or "times"), plus or minus, for the soul's experiments with free will in the uses of light/energy/consciousness to net the desired gain of higher consciousness.

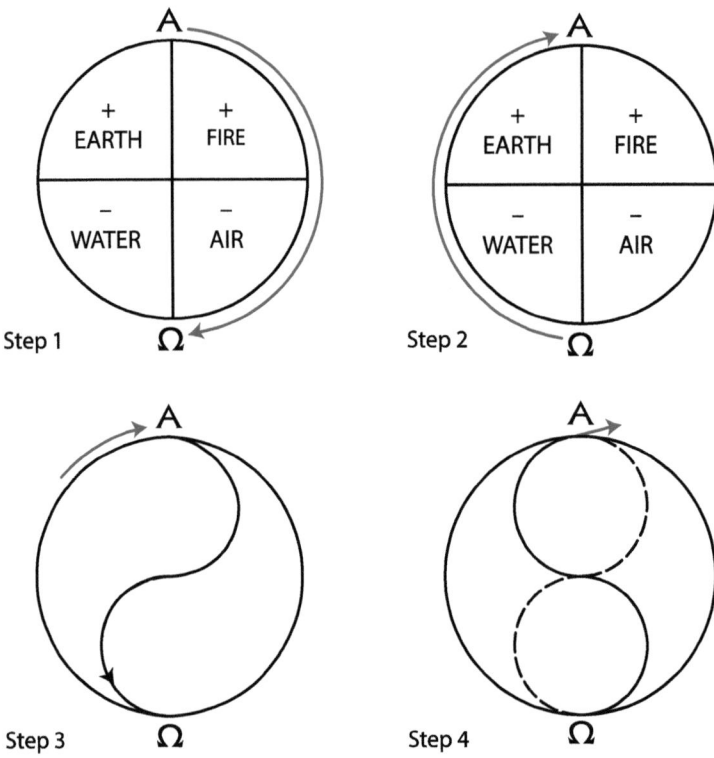

Initiations into the Personhood of the Godhead
FIGURE 11

The Completion of the Spiral through Acceleration— the Intensification of the Velocity of Love

The entire process noted as steps 1 and 2 is one of acceleration on the path of initiation (discipleship under the law of the Christ and the Buddha). And without acceleration—defined as the intensification of the velocity of love—this cycle cannot be completed.

We can gauge our progress on the path of higher consciousness by the ratio of Spirit-to-Matter essence we embody and outpicture. As our souls journey into the progressively denser planes of matter, our challenge is to retain the impulse of Spirit while submerged in the veils and nets of outer manifestation. We must guard against losing so much momentum on the descending arc that we grind to a halt at that point, stuck in the mire of our own karmic creations.

Paul knew the law of total self-givingness to be the law governing the going out and the coming in of the atom. He also knew that the mechanical, rote performance of this law in the ritualism of doctrine and dogma, whether in science or religion, would not suffice as grace for the soul's coming into its joint heirship with the Son: "And though I bestow all my goods to feed the poor, and though I give my body to be burned, and have not charity [love], it profiteth me nothing."[6]

Two men may perform the same good works with the same good smiles—one with hatred, the other with love; one for political ambition and economic gain, the other in the sheer joy of self-giving for the impartial blessing of all. Vibration is the proof of the pudding and the real profit (i.e., grace). Without love there is no acceleration; without acceleration there is no coming into higher consciousness. The motive in self-giving must be pure. Therefore the motive will be tested time and time again—yes, according to the law of the cycles of love.

The Soul that Merges with the Christ Self by the Law of the Cycles of Love

When steps 1 and 2 have thus been victoriously completed, the soul is ready for steps 3 and 4, the dual passage by love's acceleration through the white-fire core of being over the sine wave of the figure eight. This phase of the soul's journey is usually experienced simultaneously in the Spirit-Matter universes, whether in the physical (outer) octaves or in the etheric (inner) retreats of the Great White Brotherhood. Having the inner life reflected in the outer, such a soul is among the saints who walk with God. Fearing no one, no thing, they are in heaven while they are in earth.

As we learn from Paul's testimony, the early Christians, charged with the love of the Holy Ghost, had no fear of the soul's free flight traversing the Spirit-Matter octaves. Nor did they label as heretical or Satanic those "visions and revelations of the Lord" so feared by their unfruitful—and quite often fanatical—counterparts of succeeding centuries:

> I knew a man in Christ above fourteen years ago, (whether in the body, I cannot tell; or whether out of the body, I cannot tell: God knoweth;) such an one caught up to the third heaven.
> And I knew such a man, (whether in the body, or out of the body, I cannot tell: God knoweth;)

How that he was caught up into paradise, and heard unspeakable words, which it is not lawful for a man to utter.
(II Corinthians 12:2–4)

The first passage (step 3) through the nucleus is accomplished by freewill election in the name of (in the attainment of) the Son who has fulfilled the requirement of the Law in the Alpha and the Omega rounds of the will of the I AM THAT I AM and now passes through the white-fire core to put on the garment of the Lord (the Word). The soul who has become congruent with the Son—the triangle of the Trinity personified—now declares: "I AM the Way, the Truth, and the Life: no man cometh unto the Father, but by me."[7]

In other words, the "I AM" in me, who is the Christ in me—the nucleus or sun center of my being, the Real Person that I AM who remains after I have freely given to life the all of my plus-minus charge—is the *only* Way, the *only* Truth, the *only* Life that I AM. No man cometh unto the Father (no man may approach the white-fire core of God's Being, the I AM THAT I AM) but by me (except through the path of becoming this Christ, this higher consciousness that endures the peripheral comings and goings of the soul and is, in fact, its Real Self). Only that soul that has merged with the Christ Self by the law of the cycles of love may spiral through the Great Central Sun of Being.

Without love, existence is an endless merry-go-round on the surface of the great sphere of Being. Round and round she goes and where she stops nobody knows. But stop she must because it's in the nature of the Alpha thrust and the Omega return to "spend and be spent,"[8] as Paul said.

When the cup of life's energy is empty, having been drunk by the self to save the self, that self is self-consumed. Having not the acceleration of *Self/Love,* she can't get on the track of the figure eight that carries her back to the Central Sun/Son. "He who seeks to save his life (lesser self) shall lose it.[9]. . . He that denieth me (the Greater Self) him (the lesser self) will I deny before my Father (will I deny entry into the Central Sun)."[10]

The second passage (step 4) through the nucleus is in the return to wholeness in the name of the Holy Spirit (the Whole-I-Spirit). At this moment the soul of the Christed One (the one anointed with the sacred fire of the Sun behind the sun, endued with that Holy Spirit who is the force behind all actualities) declares: "All power is given unto me in heaven and in earth."[11] In other words, "The all-power of the AUM in the inner Spirit-Matter universe and the all-power of the I AM THAT I AM in the outer Spirit-Matter universe is given unto me—unto the Son, the Trinity or Word incarnate, that I have become."

It was the law of this power-wisdom-love in perpetual motion from the inner to the outer court of the being of God in man, matter, and molecule—truly the law of cosmic cycles—to which Jesus the Christ, great Guru of the Piscean age, attained. Therefore he had the authority of his own higher consciousness to transfer this law to his apostles in his final admonishment recorded by Matthew: "Go ye therefore, and teach all nations, baptizing them in the name of the Father, and of the Son, and of the Holy Ghost"[12] (in the name of the cycles of the Great Outbreath and the Great Inbreath, which I have demonstrated for you, so that you, too, might go and be the example of my love).

Planes of Higher Consciousness Follow the Alchemy of the Signs and the Seasons

Now let us intensify our meditation with the saturation of our soul (i.e., *solar* awareness) in the dimensions of fire, air, water, and earth. Signifying rites of initiation to the ancient alchemists, these terms designate the quadrants of the great sphere of higher consciousness and the flow of the signs and seasons through which the soul journeys in its initiations on the Path to wholeness (holiness). (fig. 12)

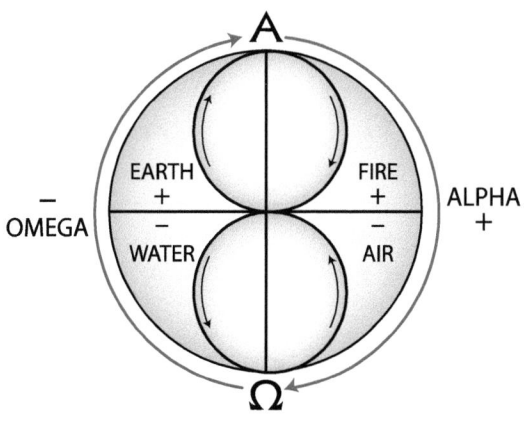

FIGURE 12

From out the Great Central Sun, the Hub of life in the center of cosmos, the Great White Brotherhood—composed of solar hierarchies, cosmic beings, Elohim, archangels, and ascended masters—release to their representatives in all planes of Spirit and Matter the energy of Alpha and Omega, the Father-Mother God. The heart chakras, centers of Christ Self-awareness, of sons and daughters of God ascended and unascended are the nexus, or focal point, for the transfer of God's energy from the "inner" worlds to the "outer" worlds.

The cosmic caduceus is the flow of energy from God to man and from man to God. In this Alpha-to-Omega action-reaction-interaction, Alpha becomes Omega and Omega becomes Alpha over the figure-eight spiral again and again all the way from the Great Central Sun to the nucleus of the atom—from the heart of God to the heart of man. This flow, illustrated in figure 13, is truly infinity in motion, an endless chain of self-awareness in higher consciousness. It is life becoming life that God may truly be the All-in-all.

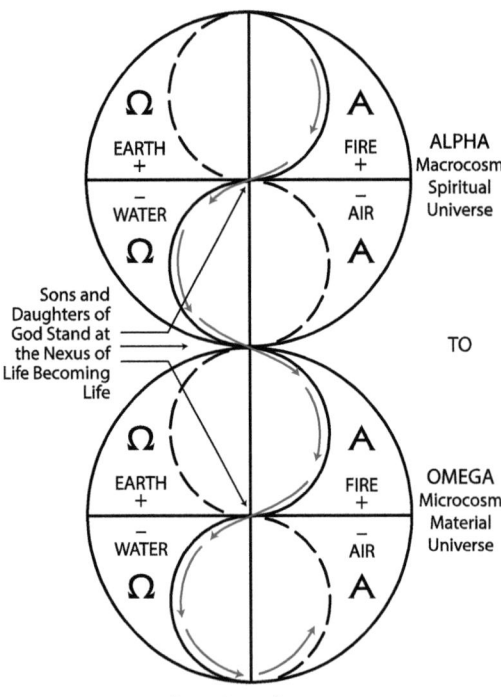

Cosmic caduceus
The flow of energy from God to man
FIGURE 13

As we enter into this flow, we participate in the movement of the energy that is God throughout all creation. And we discover that every ray of light that originates in God and culminates in man consists of this endless spiraling caduceus of the figure eight.

Oh, wonder of joyous relief! Each circle is a sphere of wholeness, of identity within itself; yet by law it acts, reacts, and interacts with the cycles that precede and follow it in the vast chain of being we call life. Now in the awe of the Great Silence, we behold over this ongoing spiral-within-spiral of energy a veritable chain of hierarchy—God imparting to his sons and daughters his own higher consciousness.

Seasons and Cycles of the Year

The ascended master El Morya, beloved teacher of my late husband Mark L. Prophet and myself, founded The Summit Lighthouse here in our nation's capital in 1958 and commenced the spiral of the publishing of the teachings of the ascended masters through Mark, using the format of weekly letters called *Pearls of Wisdom,* which were sent to a bold band of eager chelas. Since then, the *Pearls* have never skipped a beat of Morya's devotion to the diamond heart of God's will. These precious *Pearls,* profound in the intimacy of the Guru-chela (i.e., Master-disciple) relationship, are the table prepared for those who are called to be the true shepherds of the lambs of God.

In 1960, El Morya also appealed to the Lords of Karma for the dispensation that was granted for the holding of our quarterly conferences. He has thus stated their purpose:

> Our conferences are held for the turning of the cycles of the year—winter solstice, spring equinox, summer solstice, and autumn equinox. The physical changes occur prior to the conference and the light released from the hierarchies of the Sun at the change of the seasons is then expanded by ascended and unascended beings serving together at the conferences for the fulfillment of a cosmic purpose on earth as it is in heaven.[13]

In the light of this profound understanding of the law of cycles and the cosmic caduceus that beloved El Morya has released in these diagrams, we see that the coming together of the ascended masters and their unascended chelas at quarterly intervals is for the reenactment of the great drama of the Spirit-Matter cosmos: the ritual of God becoming God through the polarity of Alpha and Omega actualized in his sons and daughters. Thus we have come together for four days to be the instruments for the stepping down of the light of the Great Central Sun released to earth and her evolutions at summer solstice.

Entering the planes of higher consciousness, we follow the flow of the season. We put on the sense of the awareness of God originating in the sun center, then cycling through the moment of winter solstice as the sacred fire in winter penetrates the etheric, or memory body of being, the inner matrix establishing the blueprint of life through the flame of our Father. (fig. 14)

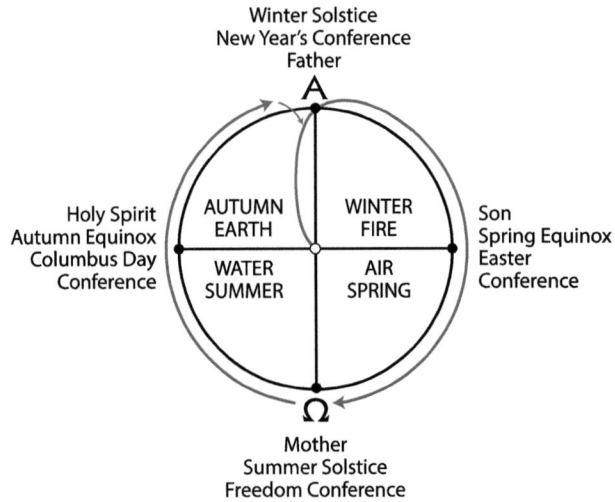

Quarterly conferences for the turning of the cycles of the year
FIGURE 14

Now at spring equinox we experience the flame of the Son in the bursting forth of the mind, the mental body, as deep from within the dormant subconscious come forth buds of Self-awareness—*Buddhi,* the awareness of the Self as the Christ or the enlightened Buddha in the spirit of the resurrection.

We move from the cycles of rebirth and resurrection in spring to God's energy in motion, *e-motion,* at summer solstice when the soul must master the flow of water in the feeling, or emotional body. Now we learn the Law governing the harmonious interchange of the harmony of the octaves. This is the flow of the energies of the Mother—of life begetting life. It is the time for the deeper feelings of God, for communing with him through the movement of the elements of life, truth, and love in nature and through actually feeling, in a most awesome and humble way, *God desiring to be God within us.*

Through the flame of Mother there is an acceleration of God consciousness in summer, whereas the autumn is the time of the resolution of energies within the physical body for the gathering of the harvest of the Holy Spirit—replete with all of the challenges of a new freedom and its attendant responsibilities to maintain harmony and wholeness. Now we are the channels for the release of light into the "earth, earthy."[14] Now the physical consciousness of a work well done begets the enjoyment of the fruit of the sacred labor made manifest (in earth) through the trinity of heart (fire), head (air), and hand (water).

Our Initiation in the Great Game of Life
Vehicles of Self-Expression

After the perfecting of works is accomplished in the ritual of autumn, the soul ascending (coming in) to the AUM meditates upon the fiery blueprint of life within the crucible of Being. (fig. 15)

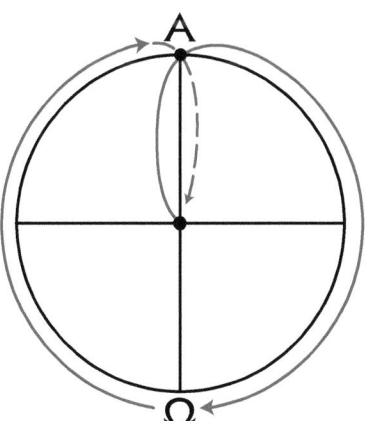

The soul coming into the AUM
FIGURE 15

It centers itself in the law of the One in preparation for another round on the periphery of the circle of spiral through (1) the conscious and subconscious memory, (2) the active mind, (3) the feelings and the desire body, and (4) the physical body. (fig. 16) These are the "lower" vehicles whereby in the planes of Matter the soul gains self-mastery in its own higher consciousness.

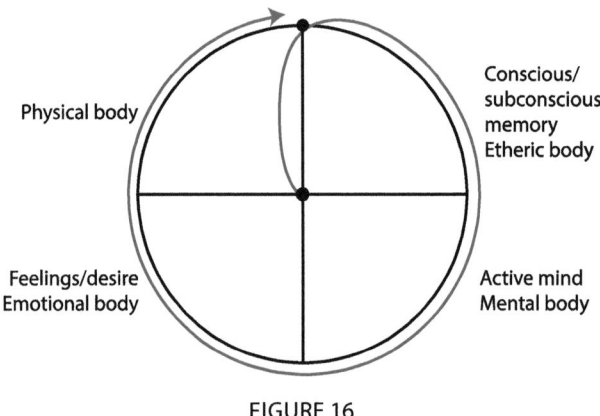

FIGURE 16

Higher consciousness, as illustrated on the Chart of your Divine Self actually consists of the three higher vehicles. Accelerating from the plane of the soul into the white-fire core of being, one contacts these vehicles of Self-expression in the following order: (1) the Christ Self, or Christ consciousness called the Higher Mental Body (the Person of the Son); (2) the I AM Presence, the I AM THAT I AM or God consciousness—the Great God Self (the Father in whom the Mother is Self-contained) whose secret place of the Most High is surrounded by (3) the rings of the causal body consisting of concentric spheres of cosmic consciousness (the Holy Spirit). These spheres provide the soul with extensions of solar awareness through the Father and the Son into the Spirit-Matter universes.

The seven archangels are the guardians of the signs and the seasons. They stand at the quadrants of Spirit and Matter and at the twelve portals of the zodiac guarding the consciousness of the twelve tribes of Israel as they enter the New Jerusalem through the twelve pearly gates.[15]

Our conferences follow the seasons of the year because these focus

The Chart of Your Divine Self

the personal and planetary cycles of the unfoldment of the great triad of higher consciousness through humanity as a whole as we pass through our individual initiations in the frequencies of fire, air, water, and earth, affecting the four lower bodies of a planet and a people.

These initiations are the testing of our souls by the I AM Presence and the cosmic hierarchies in order to determine what portion of cosmic energy we are capable of holding at our link in the chain of being. It is the holding of harmony and the harmonious flow of energy winter-spring-summer-autumn in the etheric, mental, emotional, and physical planes of consciousness that is the deciding factor in this our initiation in the great game of life.

At each conference the ascended masters lower into the heart chakras of their disciples a certain portion of energy from the Great Central Sun as well as the necessary instruction in cosmic law which, when applied, enables us both to hold the energy in harmony and to transfer it in harmony to the children of God on earth. This just portion is that grace of the master which is "sufficient for thee,"[16] the disciple, in the next three-month cycle as soul nourishment for the four lower bodies.

If we break our harmony at any level—etheric, mental, emotional, physical—we break our link in the chain of being. And the broken link—until it is reconnected by a call to the law (LORD) of forgiveness—prevents the flow of energy from God above to man below. While persistent inharmony (the sin of the unrepentant sinner) causes us to be removed entirely from the chain of hierarchy—i.e., from the Master-disciple interchange—persistent harmony not only enables us to sustain and strengthen the relationship of all within the chain, but it also enables us to advance or accelerate link by link over the chain of being.

The Cosmic Caduceus

We are proceeding, then, from the beginning to the ending of God's Being, "I AM Alpha and Omega, the beginning and the ending, saith the Lord, which is, and which was, and which is to come, the Almighty."[17]

In this yearly pilgrimage as the cycles of God's consciousness unwind as coiled ribbons of light, the atom of energy moves from the point of origin in the white-fire core of the T'ai Chi to the beginning at winter solstice. From this point of the Alpha thrust, it decelerates through spring equinox to summer solstice; there at the point of the ending, the Omega return, the particle of energy moves on to the consummation of the journey of love, accelerating through autumn equinox to the victory of winter solstice whence it reenters the fiery core, the Great Silence of nonduality, nonpolarization.

As the Alpha thrust proceeds from winter solstice through spring equinox, the highest energy of Spirit is being stepped down by solar hierarchies in what is known as the crystallization from the etheric to the mental planes of consciousness. When the Alpha thrust becomes the Omega return at summer solstice, the momentum of Spirit crystallizes in Matter as solar hierarchies continue to step down the currents from summer solstice through autumn equinox in the emotional and physical planes of consciousness. (fig. 17)

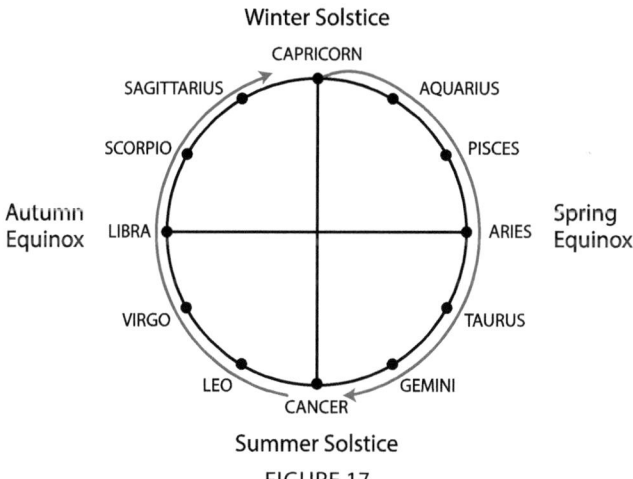

FIGURE 17

Each year (or corresponding cosmic cycle) every planetary body, sun or star center, solar system, galaxy, and the universe of cosmos (the Macrocosm) receives from the Great Central Sun a quotient of energy to be released from its own nucleus, or white-fire core. This energy allotment is sealed in the sun of even pressure within the core of the earth's body and is released in four equal increments at the solstices and equinoxes for the turning of the cycles of Alpha to Omega in each of the four quadrants—fire, air, water, earth.

Simultaneously as the energies of God are being crystallized (stepped down) in the four planes of consciousness through the four seasons, the energies of man are being etherealized (stepped up) for his soul's reunion with the I AM THAT I AM. The energies of the descent of God (deceleration) and the ascent of man (acceleration) intertwine to form the cosmic caduceus. This is the rhythm of the stars and the perpetual flow of life becoming life that is the dance of Brahma, Vishnu, and Shiva.

At the beginning of every century, the Solar Logoi (the masculine-feminine polarity of the Logos, or Word) release cosmic dispensations to the evolutions of this planet Earth. They release dispensations of the Lords of Karma of what can be accomplished in that century in science, in religion, in education, in culture, in the revelations of God, and in the expansion of the abundant life through the governments and the economies of the nations. These dispensations are released in multifaceted forms of light, energy, and consciousness as the opportunities of life—decade by decade, year by year, cycles within cycles.

Thus God proposes and man disposes. It is God's will to give to man his abundant life. It is man's will to accept or reject—to use wisely or unwisely the gifts at hand. God preordains the blueprint of life and the cycles of cosmos. Man ordains what, if any, part of that blueprint and the cycles of cosmic destiny will manifest in his individual world. Jesus chose to make his will one with the will of God in the cycles of creation. He said, "My Father worketh hitherto, *and I work.*"[18]

The Ritual of the Ascension

Moving from God to man, then, is a deceleration of consciousness. Moving from man to God is an acceleration of consciousness. (fig. 18) The two in one are another definition of the wholeness, or oneness, of Alpha and Omega. There really is not God and man as manifestation, but there is only God, God, God. If we understood that—if we were liberated from our sense of separation from God—we would not be *here.* Yet we would be *here.*

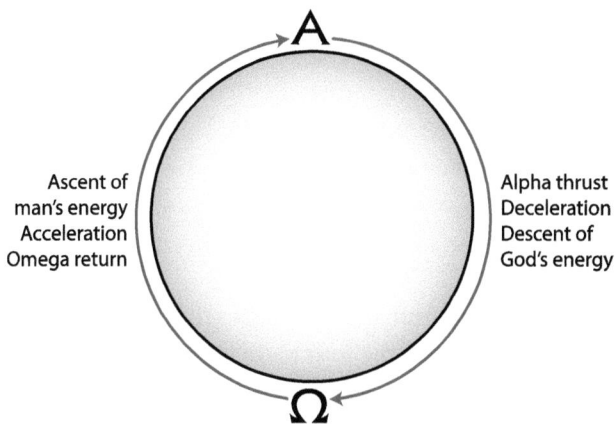

Energy in motion from God to man and man to God
FIGURE 18

Now we are here *dependent* upon time and space as the coordinates of our consciousness. Without time and space and the necessary vehicles of consciousness (the four lower bodies) our souls would cease to evolve either spiritually or materially. With the attainment of higher consciousness—our soul's reintegration with the Christ Self, the I AM Presence, and the causal body—we would still be *here*. But we would be *independent* of time and space.

In the fullness of our own higher consciousness, we *are* the coordinates of infinity. Now we interpenetrate time and space from the plane of cause rather than effect. Should time and space collapse, and with it the laws of mortality and limitation, we would remain God-identified in the Great Central Sun of Being. Such is the condition of the ascended masters. They are the immortals moving in our midst. They are in the world of time and space but not of it. They have reentered the white-fire core of being through the ritual of the ascension. They are not *here*. But they are *here*.

And what is the ritual of the ascension? It's the dance of the soul who is come to do God's will—now gone, gone, gone into higher consciousness. It's the song of the Buddha: *Gate gate paragate parasamgate bodhi svaha*—"Gone, gone, gone beyond. Gone beyond the Beyond. O Enlightenment. So be it!" It is the law of cycles come full circle in you. The ritual of the ascension is everything we've been talking about and more. It's the life process that leads to the goal of the soul's integration with God instead of to its disintegration and death.

The ascension is the goal of this life we now live in time and space. And the path of initiation according to the law of cycles is the proven method to achieve that goal—yes! proven by the ascended masters and now being demonstrated cycle by cycle by their daring chelas.

The Cross of Alpha and Omega

Being is the cross of Alpha and Omega. The cross forms the lines of initiation for the mastery of the four planes of consciousness in Matter. The cross is made up of the vertical bar, symbolizing the energies of Spirit, or Infinity, descending; and the horizontal bar, symbolizing the energies of the planes of Matter, defined by time and space. (fig. 19)

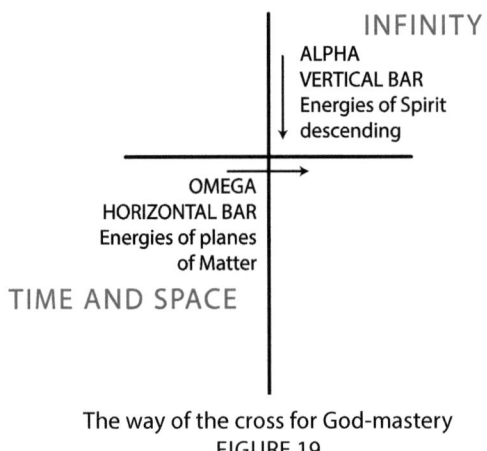

The way of the cross for God-mastery
FIGURE 19

The cross is the symbol of the crucifixion. The term *crucifixion* is taken from the Latin *crux* meaning "cross" and *figere*, "to fasten"—literally, the act of fastening to the cross. The crucifixion is an initiation given to every son and daughter of God on the path of higher consciousness by the Cosmic Christ, personified in the "Coming Buddha who has come," Lord Maitreya. Step by step, the crucifixion teaches us the God-mastery of the energies of Spirit and Matter even as we master the flow of the cosmic caduceus. Thus, by the way of the cross, scientifically demonstrated by Jesus Christ and Gautama Buddha, we learn the discipline of energy at the nexus where the vertical and horizontal bars converge.

The nexus of the cross marks the point in the center of the circle of being where we realize higher consciousness. This higher consciousness is the Real Self—the anointed one, the inner Christ, the inner Buddha. The nexus marks the point where the energies of Spirit and Matter have been disciplined in the four planes of consciousness by the soul who has thereby attained the awareness of the Self as the totality of God within the sphere of wholeness. The lines of the cross divide the circle into halves and then quadrants, each having a unique frequency according to its position in the circle.

Energies of Spirit descend on the Alpha (vertical) bar and meet the energies of the planes of Matter, Omega (horizontal) bar, at the nexus where qualification through the heart center (chakra) occurs. The nexus is the altar of being where the alchemy of change as *alter*ation, both positive and negative, takes place.

Our sowings (the Alpha thrust on the circle or the vertical bar of the cross) are our correct or incorrect qualification of the energies of Spirit (love/hatred, joy/sorrow, life/death, etc.), which are distributed in the four planes of Matter according to their frequencies. Our reapings (the Omega return on the circle or the horizontal bar of the cross) are the return of these sowings as positive or negative karma for transmutation or "sublimation" in the ascension process. (fig. 20)

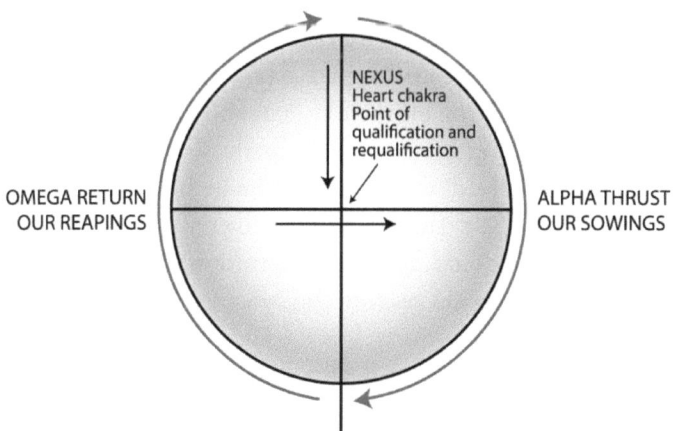

The cross in the cosmic clock illustrates the cycles
of our sowings and our reapings.
"Whatsoever a man soweth, that shall he also reap."
FIGURE 20

And so the cross presents the dividing line for the release of the frequencies of God's consciousness. We call them frequencies, we call them vibrations, because currents of God Self-awareness are experienced in the four lower bodies in Matter. And our ability to define the Self depends on our ability to anchor and focalize vibration at will through the flame of God-mastery. These frequencies transmit a certain qualification of the energy of the Whole, of God, and they key the transfer of energies of acceleration and deceleration point by point around the circle. Thus the cross, visually and mathematically, is the basis for the diagramming of the cosmic clock taught to me by Mother Mary.

The Cosmic Clock

The cosmic clock illustrates the flow of God's energy both in the Macrocosm and the microcosm of the Self—in higher consciousness and lower consciousness, in Spirit and in Matter. Our individual cosmic clock, which we diagram according to our cosmic astrology (also taught by Mother Mary), reveals our individual path of initiation—the cycles of our sowings and our reapings of positive and negative karma as well as the challenges of the fulfillment of our dharma. The more we know about the cosmic clock, the more we know about ourselves—what is Real and what is unreal—and the better we understand how the law of cycles and the cosmic caduceus are functional in our daily lives.

Through the cosmic clock we learn how to individualize, personalize, and crystallize our higher consciousness day by day until we move from glory unto glory,[19] putting off the old man and putting on the new,[20] transcending cycle after cycle until the path of our initiation under the ascended masters leads to the soul's ultimate liberation in the great sphere of the Higher Self. This liberation is the reunion of the soul with the Spirit of the living God. It is the acceleration from Matter back to Spirit, from the microcosm back to the Macrocosm.

This is the ascension process. It is the Path whereby, cycle by cycle, the soul penetrates its ultimate Reality and thus attains the all-power of heaven and earth that dissolves all duality and finds itself one with the One by the law of the One. Yes, this is the ritual of the ascension.

Superimposing the clock on the four seasons, we begin to define that cosmic clock as the teaching of the Divine Mother. (fig. 21) It is a very important teaching because it enables us to define the path of initiation, which is the path of attainment. Without understanding the law of cycles and their logical sequence and unfoldment, we are not prepared in time and space for the passing of the torch of energies from God to man, from the hierarchies of the Macrocosm to those of the microcosm, and, as in this conference, from ascended masters to their unascended chelas.

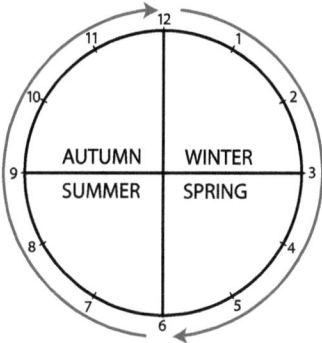

The energies of the four seasons flow in the cosmic clock
Figure 21

Initiation: The Transfer of Light for the Stepping up of Consciousness

When the energies of cosmic beings—who are known as the Elohim, archangels, solar lords and Solar Logoi, and hierarchies of the zodiac—are released to us, it is for the stepping up of consciousness. This step-up is brought about through the intensification of light within the sacred centers (chakras). It is marked by successive stages of attainment denoted by steps on the ladder of initiation.

The stepping up of consciousness necessitates initiation. Now we see that the entire purpose of initiation is to increase our self-discipline in the qualification of God's energy so that we may hold the reins of the mastery of the God Self to retain greater and greater increments of light within the chakras and the auric forcefield.

In order to contain the greater light of God's greater consciousness, we must not only gain greater mastery in the qualification of God's energy but also we must have an expanded chalice, or cup, to contain both the light and the consciousness bestowed from on high. That light and consciousness that we can contain—i.e., hold in harmony—and make our own becomes our own individual self-awareness. This in turn is what determines the degree of our self-mastery, which we call attainment.

If the cup is not expanded by exercises in meditation, visualization, self-purification, prayers and fastings coupled with dynamic decrees—affirmations of life and denials of the death cult—then when the new light and the new consciousness is released to us by the members of the Great White Brotherhood, we will not be able either to contain it or to retain it—it will spill upon the ground and we will suffer the loss that our impoverished sense of sin, struggle, and shame has decreed.

To thus forfeit the light and the consciousness of higher planes is to forfeit the initiations of higher planes. Therefore the preparation for the giving and the receiving of light and consciousness is one of the most important parts of the path of initiation. The lectures and the dictations that are scheduled for this and every conference are designed by the ascended masters, working with the messengers, to give us the understanding so necessary for our success on the homeward (*AUM*ward) path.

Charting the Cycles of One's Individualization of the God Flame

As God transcends himself, cycle by cycle, his sons and daughters do the same. And so we chart our initiations on the cosmic clock according to the individualization of the God flame.

What does this mean? It means that God individualizes himself as Father, as Mother, as Son, and as Holy Spirit. It means that as we move through the cycles of our life, our karma and our dharma, God will initiate us so that we, too, may realize the Great God Self within us *as* Father, *as* Mother, *as* Son, and *as* the Holy Spirit. (fig. 22)

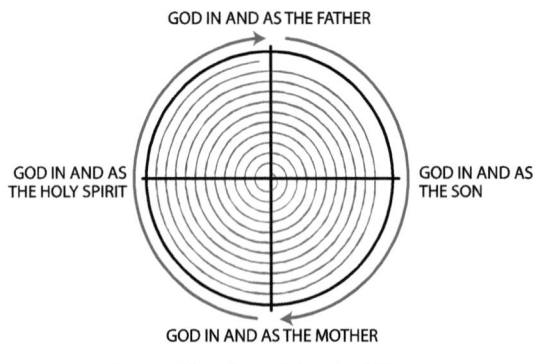

Personification of the God flame
FIGURE 22

These initiations occur over many lifetimes as we fulfill our various roles on the stage of life, but they may also occur within a given lifetime as we become aware of the Great God Self within us simultaneously fulfilling the law of cycles in and as all of these personifications of the One.

The degrees of one's awareness of the self as the Greater Self in one or all of these relationships is another way of defining one's light, one's consciousness, and hence one's level of initiation on the Path. With each successive spiral of living on earth as in heaven, we realize more and more how we are one with God in and as the Father, one with God in and as the Son, one with God in and as the Mother, and one with God in and as the Holy Spirit.

Each of the signs of the zodiac is actually the name in the cosmic hierarchy of an order of 144,000 cosmic beings who personify the frequencies of God's cosmic consciousness on each of the twelve points of the cosmic clock. (fig. 23) Each hierarchy is responsible for stepping down the energies of God in the great circle of God's awareness to lesser evolutions in the human, angelic, and elemental kingdoms and in the animal, vegetable, and mineral kingdoms as well.

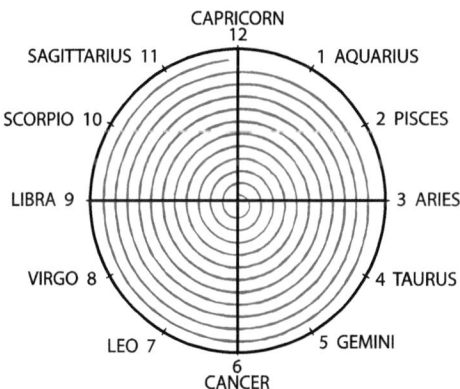

Each cycle is an opportunity for initiation
under the twelve cosmic hierarchies
FIGURE 23

Each of the twelve points marks thirty degrees within the 360-degree circle. Ten times three degrees (between each point) denotes the initiations of the threefold flame of the Trinity (or tri-unity) of life,

East and West. Because this three is an infinite three, the multiplication of its light within the soul by the test of the ten results in a soul magnitude of calculable, though seemingly incalculable, brilliance.

Given its spiral in the cosmic cycles, the maximum light which the chalice of the soul can hold and still remain within that spiral can be, believe it or not, mathematically determined. When it exceeds the mathematical bounds of its habitation, it accelerates into the next slice of the spiral of self-transcending life.

The number ten signifies the initiation of sacrifice, surrender, selflessness, and service known as "the test of the ten." It is this test that the initiate of the Great White Brotherhood must pass victoriously under Brahma, Vishnu, and Shiva—Father, Son, and Holy Spirit—as the personification of power, wisdom, and love, under each of the twelve solar hierarchies.

The testings under each hierarchy differ because the frequency of the God consciousness ensouled by the hierarchy differs. Each frequency is noted by a mathematical formula; but we note them here by the distinguishing virtue, or God-quality, that manifests as both the cause and the effect of that frequency in all sons and daughters of God, ascended or unascended, who choose by free will to ensoul it. (fig. 24)

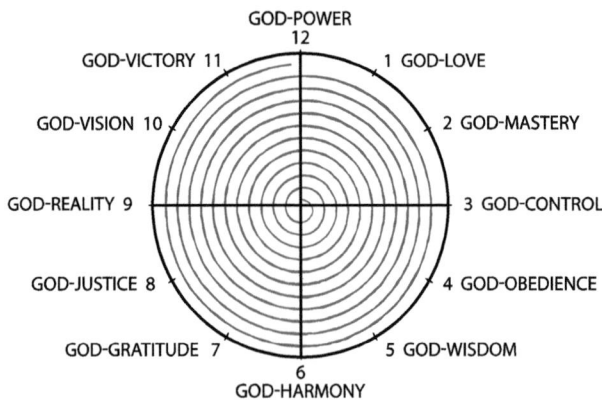

Each line of the cosmic clock denotes
another sphere of God's consciousness
FIGURE 24

Each spiral around the clock represents a cycle of our life—a day, a week, a month, a year, a century, or more. Each cycle is an opportunity for initiation under the twelve solar hierarchies (designated under the names of the signs of the zodiac) who test our souls in their evolution both in time and space (Matter) and in eternity (Spirit). (fig. 23)

Each test or series of tests we pass qualifies us for step-by-step initiations on the path of the ascension (the path of the accelerating spiral) of higher consciousness. With each initiation, our awareness of God increases and intensifies not only as Father, Mother, Son, and Holy Spirit but also as the twelve qualities of God on the twelve lines of the cosmic clock. (fig. 24) These lines mark each of the twelve major frequencies experienced in the four quadrants under the twelve solar hierarchies.

The diagrams of the cosmic clock reveal God as the spherical being whose consciousness ensouls a spherical cosmos. Within, without, everywhere—God is the great unity of life. (I have actually seen the cosmos as an egg and the sphere we are dealing with as the yolk suspended within the white light.)

The lines of initiation drawn by the cycles of cosmic hierarchies who ensoul and are ensouled by the great sphere of God's wholeness tend to make us think of existence in terms of duality ad infinitum, but this is the result of the long human habit of linear thinking and feeling. Transcending the modes and models of plane geometry and the three dimensions that compartmentalize our existence in time and space, we comprehend the oneness of God in the infinitude of his expression. Thus thousands, millions, and billions of God-free beings ensouling a cosmos still add up to one God, one Lord, one Israel—one consciousness that *Is Real*.

Within the great sphere of cosmic consciousness that he is, God is daily realizing more and more of himself, thus ever transcending himself in order that we, his sons and daughters ordained as co-creators with him, may also fulfill the law of cosmic cycles. Thus each of the twelve points of the cosmic clock denotes another plane, or shall we say *sphere,* of God's consciousness that he intends us to become as one by one we fulfill the law of the One.

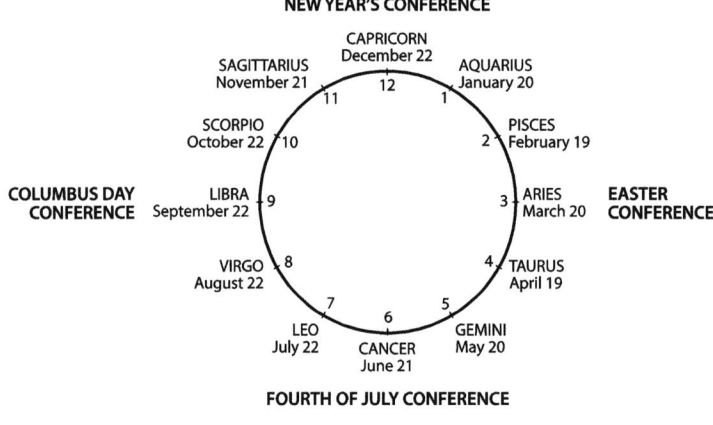

FIGURE 25

Ascended Master Conferences: The Passing of a Torch of Hierarchy

Each of the conferences is for the passing of a torch of hierarchy. There is a cosmic ritual that occurs at the four seasons wherein hierarchies pass to one another the flame of their God Self-awareness. We have seen that from the Great Central Sun a giant sphere of white fire is released and actually focalized in the white-fire core of the earth at winter solstice. These are the energies we consecrate at our New Year's conference.

The first fourth of that energy is spent by mankind during the first quadrant of the year under the hierarchies of Capricorn, Aquarius, and Pisces. As these energies are qualified, they build a foundation of the fire element in the etheric plane. At spring equinox, the second increment of energy is released and spent by mankind during the second quadrant of the year under the hierarchies of Aries, Taurus, and Gemini. As these energies—which we consecrate at the Easter conference—are qualified, they build the foundation of the air element in the mental plane.

At summer solstice, the third increment of energy is released and spent by mankind during the third quadrant of the year under the hierarchies of Cancer, Leo, and Virgo. These energies are consecrated at the summer conference held over the Fourth of July weekend. As they are qualified, they build the foundation of the water element in the emotional plane.

At autumn equinox, the fourth increment of energy is released and spent by mankind during the fourth quadrant of the year under the hierarchies of Libra, Scorpio, and Sagittarius. We consecrate these energies at the autumn conference, held over the Columbus Day weekend in honor of Saint Germain in his incarnation as Christopher Columbus. As they are qualified, they build the foundation of the earth element in the physical plane. Thus each increment of sacred fire released from the white-fire core of the earth provides us with three months of initiations.

Not a living soul on the planetary body is excluded from these initiations. It is not a question of choosing to be on the Path or choosing not to be on the Path. The very fact that we are in incarnation indicates that our souls have already chosen to separate from God and to define identity by the gift of free will and the grace of the Triunity of life. Because we have asked for free will, our souls have come forth into material manifestation clothed upon with four lower bodies as vehicles through which we experience and evolve.

Now in order for our souls to reunite with God, we must choose to be God here and now that we might be one in God in eternity. In order to accomplish this, we must set about mastering our use of God's energy, God's consciousness, and God's being in time and space. This we do according to the cycles of the cosmic clock as they are released to us by the solar hierarchies on the path of initiation.

And so the path of initiation is not for the few. It is a torch that up to the present has been upheld by the few and is now passed to the many by the hand of the World Mother. Our government, our economy, our culture, our religion, the cycles of war and peace on the planet, the phases that we go through as nations, all are governed by the solar initiations that are released according to the cycles of our planetary karma and planetary dharma.

The First Summit Lighthouse Conference

The first Summit Lighthouse conference was held during the Fourth of July weekend, 1960. As we follow the clock from that point of origin to the present (1976), we see that we are marking the cycles of sixteen years of Summit Lighthouse conferences. Please note that within each year there are four conferences. Because the 1960 summer conference was the first public quarterly conference ever held, we place it on the twelve o'clock line of the cosmic clock.

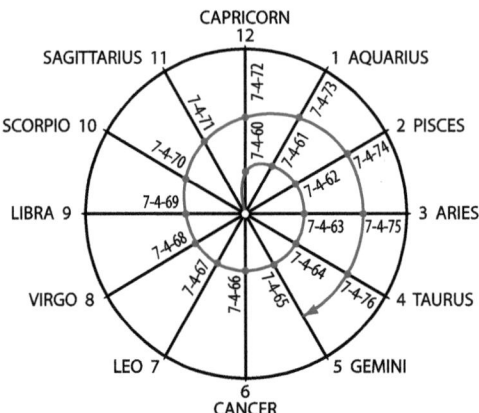

Sixteen years of Summit Lighthouse conferences
FIGURE 26

In charting the cycles of the events of one's life, we always begin with the hierarchy of Capricorn, positioned on the twelve o'clock line. Capricorn is the first hierarchy to receive the Alpha-Omega energies from the white-fire core of being, the point of the origin of spirals whereby the energies of God cycle from Spirit to Matter, from Matter to Spirit. This point of origin is marked by the dot in the center of the circle, symbolical of the nucleus of the atom, the Sun behind the sun—the inner cause behind the outer effect. It is in fact the nexus where the cause becomes the effect, the Creator becomes the creation.

Each succeeding Freedom conference is positioned on the cosmic clock moving in a clockwise direction point by point from Capricorn to Aquarius to Pisces, etc.—from the twelve o'clock line to the eleven o'clock line and then beginning again at the twelve as the circle becomes a spiral of never-ending cycles of experience in God Self-awareness. And so we find that in 1976, the spiral has reached the four o'clock line, and thus our action in this summer conference is for the release of the energies of God through the hierarchy of Taurus.

The spiral returns to the four o'clock line, and this shows us what our initiation is in this year. It is a year whose thrust will be taken from the essential qualities of Taurus as these are revealed on the cosmic clock: Taurus is an earth sign in the air quadrant. It represents the master builders who build the temple on the foundation of the Christ mind. Its God-quality, the summation of the inner and outer frequencies, is God-obedience. Its essential energy is love.

This means that by loving obedience to the law of our innermost being, we will use the energies released by the solar hierarchies at this conference to lay the foundation for the new temple that is necessary to contain our higher consciousness. Perhaps it is a temple "made without hands" (the integration of the inner Self); perhaps it is one made with hands (the outer sign and symbol of the inner mastery of the soul). Taurus teaches us how to make concrete, both in Spirit and in Matter, the vision of the New Jerusalem that we behold through the all-seeing eye of the Christ mind.

Three Centuries of America's Destiny on the Cosmic Clock

Now let us take a look at the larger cycles of America's destiny as these appear on the cosmic clock. Three centuries unwind from the central sun of purpose that ordained the founding of the thirteen original colonies and the Declaration of Independence, which spiral was initiated July 4, 1776.

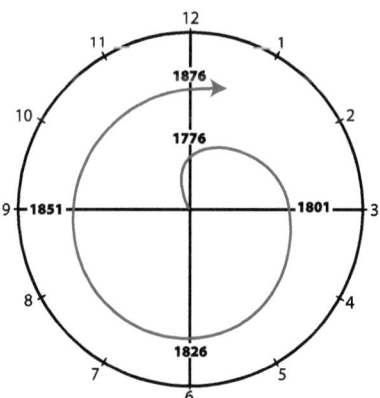

The first century:
The Alpha spiral of America's destiny
FIGURE 27

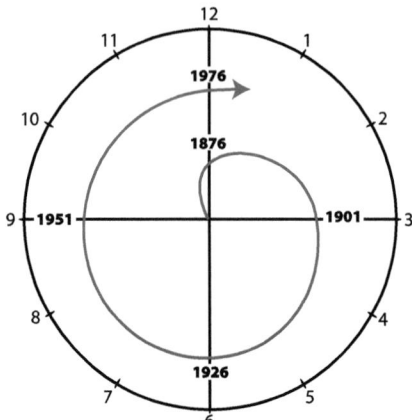

The second century:
The Omega spiral of America's destiny
FIGURE 28

The first century—from 1776 to 1876—represents the Alpha spiral, or the Alpha thrust. The second century—from 1876 to 1976—represents the Omega spiral, or the Omega return. The two together form the white-fire core of Alpha and Omega, the sponsorship of America's destiny by the Father-Mother God. Alpha and Omega are the Father-Mother God who give birth to the Christ consciousness in America and in every nation. The bicentennial is the birthday of the Manchild—the day and the year, the cycle when sons and daughters of God in America realize one by one that their own Real Self is the eternal Christ and hear the lost Word of our God: "Thou art my Son; this day have I begotten thee."

The first two centuries of America's progress are marked in the first by the movement from the pilgrim to the pioneer era, the defining and the refining of the boundaries of both the land and the consciousness of the people in the law of the Father; the second by the flowering of a culture and a technology, the expansion of the cities as the Mother has tutored her children in the materialization of the God flame for the building of a civilization.

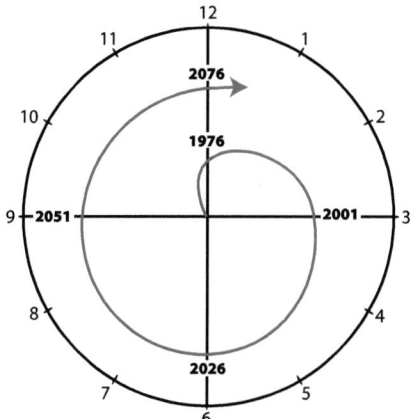

The third century:
The fusion of twin flames of Alpha and Omega for the birth of the
Divine Manchild and America's destiny in the Holy Spirit
FIGURE 29

It is out of this collective and cumulative experience in the building of a nation that America as a people come to realize their identity. Thus for the third century—1976 to 2076—we are destined to expand our individual awareness as sons and daughters of the Father-Mother God who gave us birth through the Holy Spirit.

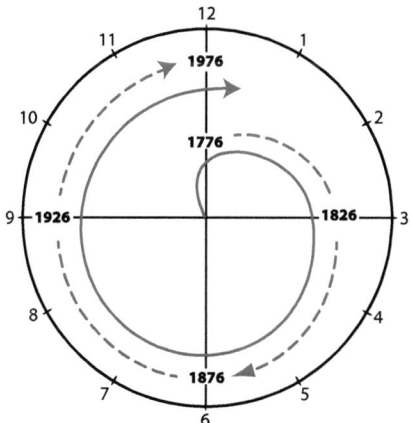

Two centuries as a single Alpha-Omega spiral
FIGURE 30

The first two centuries, when diagrammed as a single spiral, illustrate the energies of God the Father and God the Mother as America is born out of the white-fire core of God's being. The fruit of the divine union is always the Christ consciousness. As the energies of two hundred years of America's destiny polarize on the cosmic clock as the Alpha thrust and the Omega return (dissecting the circle) so the energies of three hundred years of America's destiny become the Trinity in motion.

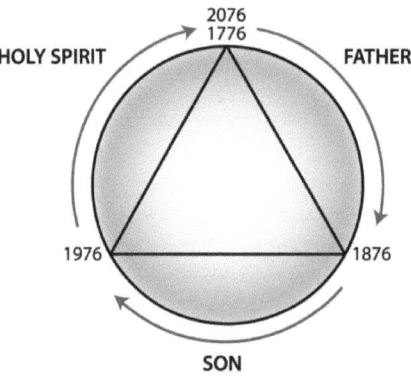

Analyzing three centuries of America's destiny, the energies of Alpha and Omega polarize as the Three-in-One, the Trinity of life.
FIGURE 31

We diagram the Trinity as a triangle within the circle (trisecting the circle). The triangle represents the omnipotence, the omniscience, and the omnipresence of Father, Son, and Holy Spirit suspended in the white-fire core of the Mother flame. And this configuration of our destiny brings us to the Great Seal of the United States. It is a pyramid, symbol of the Trinity incarnate in her sons and daughters, suspended in the spheres of the Mother, or Matter, cosmos. This Woman, America, symbolized in the Statue of Liberty, comes to the wilderness land to give birth to the Manchild, depicted as the eagle.

This Trinity is repeated in the triangles that form each of the four sides of the Great Pyramid that appears on the reverse of the Great Seal. When we, through the Christ Self of all, form one great brotherhood under the Father-Mother God and through the community of the Holy Spirit that America is intended to be—and when we collectively pass our initiations under the solar hierarchies of Father, Son, and

Holy Spirit (and under the fourteen ascended masters who govern the destiny of *America,* i.e., the *I AM Race*), we will have laid the foundation for the restoration of the true culture of the Mother in the City Foursquare (the four-sided base of the Great Pyramid) through the All-Seeing Eye of God.

The Great Seal of the United States of America
FIGURE 32

Annuit Coeptis
"He Has Smiled on Our Undertakings"

Truly, the All-Seeing Eye of God is upon us. And the culture and the civilization that sons and daughters of God will build upon the geometry of this eye, this Logos, is the *Novus Ordo Seclorum*—the new order of the Aquarian age. It will be the capstone upon the Great Pyramid of our achievement, stone upon stone, life upon life. It will be the culmination of the sacred labor of love of all who have preceded us since the LORD God, the Ancient of Days,[21] made his covenant with our father Abraham and with his seed—with Isaac and Jacob and his sons who established the twelve tribes of Israel and Judah.

The All-Seeing Eye of God centered in the capstone is the symbol of America's collective Self-realization of higher consciousness. It is the reminder of our Founding Fathers that this nation was founded under God in order that we and succeeding generations might have the opportunity to realize this goal—as individuals, through the wisdom of Christ, and as a community, through the love of the Holy Spirit. Our vision of God will be the measure of our attainment as we perfect our perceptions of life through the religion and the science of our Father and our Mother.

Our ability to effectively deal with our personal problems and the problems of the American community in the next century will arise out of our meditation upon this eye, this Logos, and our focusing of its energy/light/consciousness in the sacred centers (chakras) of being. A brief examination of the mystical symbolism sealed within the Great Seal by early initiates of the Brotherhood will provide us with keys to unlock the energies of the chakras and to use these centers as transformers to store the light of Elohim.

Mystical Symbolism of the Great Seal

The Divine Manchild of America's self-awareness as a nation is symbolized in the obverse of the Great Seal of the United States. The eagle is the ancient symbol of spiritual vision. Archetype of the Christ, he is the only creature said to be able to gaze directly into the sun. Only the Christed One, the anointed one, can look into the face of God and live.

The olive branch held in the right talon indicates the rule of the Prince of Peace by the authority of Jehovah. Jehovah is taken from the Hebrew letters of the tetragrammaton *YOD HE VAU HE*—"that which was, is, and will be," or "I AM THAT I AM"—the name through which God revealed himself to Moses.[22] The revelation of the sacred name to Moses was the dispensation of the Ancient of Days to the twelve tribes of Israel—their souls now reincarnated throughout the earth—who should follow the freedom flame of the prophet Samuel (Saint Germain) to America, the promised land, through their realization of the Christ consciousness.

The thirteen arrows in the left talon are the power of the defense of peace by the law of the One—the law of love. The red, white, and blue shield symbolizes the perfectionment of the soul of humanity by the white stone through the alchemy of the Christ Self (red, or ruby, being the symbol of the blood or essence) under the sponsorship of the Ancient of Days and the wise master builders, the sons and daughters of God who serve under his aegis in a confraternity of heaven and earth. That organization of the ascended masters and their unascended disciples is known as the Great White Brotherhood.

E Pluribus Unum
"One out of Many"

The feathers of the right and left wings indicate the path of wisdom and the path of the ascension respectively. These initiations culminate in the realization that (1) I am the Christ, the Son of God, individualized as a son or daughter of God, and (2) I am the Holy Spirit, the fullness of the Father-Mother God, the Whole-I-Spirit of Alpha and Omega.

The brotherhood of the I AM Race of America is founded upon the Christ consciousness through the path of wisdom. The community of the Holy Spirit that is the culmination of America's destiny is founded upon the realization of wholeness through the Father-Mother God and the collective awareness of the Christed ones that "I am my brother's keeper." Both paths are necessary for the realization of America's destiny stated in the motto *E Pluribus Unum,* "one out of many," or one consciousness of the Holy Spirit out of many Self-realized sons and daughters whose identity is sealed in Christ.

The crest above the eagle's head symbolizes the I AM Presence out of which the individualization of the Christ comes forth. Out of Alpha and Omega in this great sphere of higher consciousness are brought forth the mystical thirteen of Christ and his apostles and the twelve paths of initiation of the Cosmic Christ directed by the twelve solar hierarchies. The I AM THAT I AM in the center of the twelve spheres of the Great Causal Body contains the inner blueprint of the Christ consciousness for America that shall evolve the one universal God consciousness out of the many individualizations of himself.

Five-Pointed Star: Symbol of the Word Made Flesh

The thirteen five-pointed stars are arranged in the pattern of the hexagram, or six-pointed star. This is the shield of David, the standard of the twelve tribes of Israel who are to reunite on the virgin soil of America as they discover their real identity through the Mother flame, demonstrated in the sacred-fire teaching of the Woman clothed with the Sun.

The interlaced triangles that form the six-pointed star symbolize the rise of civilization through the mastery of the rising Matter triangle on the path of wisdom and the descent of the Holy Ghost through the descending Spirit triangle for the spiritualization of consciousness on the path of the ascension. Thus the five-pointed star, symbol of man perfected in God, is realized through the pattern of the six-pointed star. The six points show the initiations of the three-times-three—the Trinity in Spirit, the Trinity in Matter—focused in the threefold flame within the heart.

The five-pointed star, then, symbol of the universal synthesis, becomes the focal point for the realization of the Christ consciousness in each of the fifty states according to the ancient maxim, "Nature is to man as man is to God." This indicates that, by the alchemy of the five-pointed star, sons and daughters of God in America are to take dominion over the elements of nature even as they allow God to take dominion over their souls. And the goal of this alchemy must be according to the Hermetic axiom, "That which is above is as that which is below and that which is below is as that which is above." In other words, the five-pointed star is the symbol of the Word that is made flesh.

The twenty-four divisions of the golden glory are the cycling of the twenty-four hours in service to God, the Brotherhood, and the community through Jehovah. When written as the *YHVH* and infused with the Holy Spirit, it becomes the mystical rendering of the name Jesus. Thus when the Spirit of the Lord, the I AM THAT I AM, is personified in the Word made flesh, it is for the purpose of soul liberation.

The literal meaning of the name of the Saviour is "that which is liberates" or "the nature of reality is to set free."[23] Thus the Christ in his incarnations as Joshua (the son of Nun), Joseph (the son of Jacob), and Jesus came for one purpose—to liberate his brothers and sisters on the Path (that they might come to know, even as he knew, the one true God as their own true Self) and to found the community of the Holy Spirit as that union of souls who would realize their true Self as God.

The Sign of Aquarius and the Alchemy of the Mother

The nineteen clouds around the golden glory are the symbol of Eve, the Mother, whose energies show forth, declare, and manifest the power of the Spirit in manifestation. It is through the Mother within us that the Logos, or the Christ, is clothed with the physical temple and the material universe. Eve, "the mother of all living," whose body is mystically taken from Adam, her twin flame, provides in turn the vehicle whereby the spirit of Adam and his seed is made flesh. Through the Mother of the World, the energies of Spirit spiral into Matter; and through the veiling of the light in flesh, clothed upon with "coats of skins"[24] (the four lower bodies), the eternal Son is made manifest.

The sign of Aquarius is the sign of the redemption of Eve, of that Woman who now stands before her sons and daughters clothed with the Sun of the I AM THAT I AM. The redemptive process must always precede the Self-liberating process of the soul. And the soul—as the feminine principle of both man and woman—requires liberation in order to realize the fullness of its potential.

Americans are destined to be doers of the Word. This they accomplish in the mystical power of the three-times-three, symbolized in the nine feathers of the eagle's tail. The tail, the symbol of the base chakra, is also the light of the Mother that, when raised up, culminates in the release of the energies of the crown chakra. It is the Mother who teaches her children the God-control of the life-force (threefold in its root at the base of the spine) by the power of the Trinity within the Father, the Son, and the Holy Spirit—the *three-times-three.*

In God-harmony the Mother teaches her children to subdue the energies of war and the warring in the members, the discordant energies between the four lower bodies. Through the Mother flame, the children of God redeem the warlike energies of Mars that have burdened the earth for thousands of years. And by the alchemy of Mother, Mars becomes the white sphere of *Ma* in the *r*ay personified in the radiance of the *s*un (symbol of the one God). Through the Mother, the energies of generation in Mars become the energies of regeneration through the resurrection of the eagles (the sons and daughters of God) in Scorpio.

America's Destiny:
To Unfold the Cycles of Love as Creativity

Scorpio is the sign of creative love. America's destiny in the next hundred years is to unfold the cycles of love as creativity. It will be the opportunity for the completion of a Trinity of manifestation. Our opportunity, then, as initiates on the path of attainment, as Americans, and as citizens of planet Earth is to define love.

Love is the most difficult of all tests. It is much more difficult than the setting of the will and the blueprint or even of the manifestation of wisdom. When it comes to love, we enter into states of confusion. We do not understand what love is or how we are to regulate our lives according to love.

Love is a powerful energy, but it is a free energy. It is an energy of flow. It is an energy of polarity. And so it requires interaction between people. And people, you know, are supposed to be individualizations of the God flame of love. Love demands maximum cooperation, understanding, flexibility—all of these we must experience within the family, the community, the nation, and the planet.

The great initiator, Serapis Bey, whose love of the World Mother inspired him to dedicate his ascension retreat to the victory of her sons and daughters defines love in this way:

> Love is not just a feeling, an "emoting" that desires to swallow up the object of its affection.... True love is love for the God flame and holds no other desire save the expectation of the amplification of that flame as a tangible, divine feeling that sweeps the world pure and clean "with the washing of the water by the Word" invincible.[25]

The Trinity for the Building of the Person and the Nation

We are dividing, then, this experience into the first three rays: the first, second, and third—the blue, yellow, and pink; and there are seven rays on the path of initiation of Christ-reality. These three rays are the paths of the initiations of the soul in the three vehicles of our higher consciousness: (1) the path of the Father personified in the I AM Presence (God consciousness), (2) the path of the Son—the teacher and the teaching personified in the Christ Self, the Real Self (Christ consciousness), and (3) the path of the Holy Spirit, the life and the bestower of life—love and the beloved, comfort and the blessed Comforter.

These attributes are personified in the soul who realizes cosmic consciousness through the spheres of the causal body. These concentric rings record the aura of each one's higher consciousness; and they shew forth the handiwork, the sacred labor, of God wrought by his sons and daughters. The paths of the Father, the Son, and the Holy Spirit unfold the Way, the Truth, and the Life of the I AM THAT I AM. They unfold that God-realization that is necessary for the building of the person and the collective person—the nation.

If we cannot get through the cycle of love and the definition of love, we will have failed the test of the ten and the nation will cease to exist as a nation that has an identity on the world scene. If we fail it as an individual, we lose our consciousness; we are absorbed into the plot of mass mechanization and we do not have an identity, a blueprint, a mandala for the externalization of the God flame.

What happens within the individual happens among the nations; and all of the nations as a whole, as individuals, comprise the planetary consciousness. Love, then, becomes the challenge of this conference and the challenge of the balance of this lifetime and this third century of America's destiny unto the fulfillment of our individual and collective reunion with God.

Paul the Venetian is the chohan of the third ray of love, and he comes to the fore from his retreat in southern France, the Château de Liberté, to teach us the meaning of freedom in love. We all know that in the past decade our attention has been on love—defining love, all kinds of love in America, all kinds of responses to love, the molding of domestic and foreign policy according to the principles of love.

The Laying Down of Lesser Consciousness and the Taking Up of the Greater Self

One of the world's great leaders, Mohandas Gandhi, set forth the teaching of love for the Aquarian age in his nonviolent resistance to injustice, which kindled the torch of a free India. That love is manifest also as the ultimate sacrifice of one's willingness to lay down one's life for one's friends.

The laying down of our life as a nation and as an individual does not mean death or annihilation; it means the laying down of the lesser consciousness in the ritual of surrender to the Higher Self: "Not my will, but thine be done." The purpose of this ritual is that the Greater Self may be glorified in the one who has come out of the many to sacrifice for and on behalf of the many *(E Pluribus Unum)*. Once we have vanquished the lower nature by the higher consciousness, then that Greater Self, that Christ in us all, lays down its life that it "might take it again."[26]

When we have the courage to plunge into cosmic consciousness, knowing that we will lose the self as we have known the self, when we are willing to take that step and we take it, we gain the Greater Self. But there is a moment when we do not know what that Greater Self is, because we have not yet experienced it, because we have not yet made the decision to take the plunge. And so this is the test of love: to give all of the self for the greater good that all selves may realize the Greater Self.

We know that if we do not take the plunge into the higher consciousness of love, there will be no path, no footsteps in the sands of time and space for others to follow. Taking the plunge into higher consciousness demands great courage. We cannot have fear—fear of our own inadequacies. We cannot have doubt—doubt in the Creator's existence, doubt in the path of initiation, doubt in the great Gurus who are the ascended masters. We find that perfect love casts out fear. We need to bring to that plunge enough love—the love of not fearing to lose ourselves in God, the God that is love.

The Revolution of Love: Movement toward the Source of Creativity

Paul the Venetian has said:

> We who serve on the third ray look for the revolution of love. We look for love as art and as the discipline of art to take command of civilization, to draw mankind away from their anxieties and their tensions, to heal hearts that beat out of rhythm with the cosmic heart, to heal the bodies where cells are in rebellion to the divine blueprint.
>
> We look to art and music coming forth out of the genius of souls now and in incarnation and coming. We look to this to restore a planetary momentum of movement toward the Source, of creativity and all that leads mankind into that Source—the noble, the true, and the virtuous. This is that which will usher in the golden age.[27]

Love is the birth of the Saviour. "For God so loved the world, that he gave his only begotten Son, that whosoever believeth in him should not perish, but have everlasting life. For God sent not his Son into the world to condemn the world; but that the world through him might be saved."[28]

What more could he give than the portion of himself that is the Word incarnate? What we have not understood is that Christ is born again and again and again. The Spirit of the Christ Mass is the point of contact of higher consciousness within us all.

Jesus Christ, the Piscean Conqueror and the Lamb of Aries

Jesus was the Piscean conqueror. We are told that he was born in the spring of the year, but that the celebration of Christmas in winter is and was designed by the Brotherhood for the celebration of the coming of the great light of the Christ in the darkest period of mankind's consciousness—and also to counteract the pagan festivals that had been continually carried on at winter solstice for the purpose of seizing the light from the solar hierarchies and misqualifying it in the "way that seemeth right unto a man," which is the way of death.[29]

When we study the chart of the cycles and the cosmic clock, we realize that Christmas is our celebration of the four seasons—that in each of the four seasons Christ is born. We realize then that Jesus, being born at the spring of the year, was actually born at that point where Pisces becomes Aries at the spring equinox. As the Piscean conqueror, he came to set the cycles of the two thousand years of the Piscean age. But he is also the Lamb of Aries; and he is prophesied as that Lamb of God who was slain from the foundation of the world[30] because when the Christ consciousness appears in Aries, it appears in the mental belt, where it is first recognized. It is not recognized in the subconscious in the period of the winter.

The coming of the Christ as the celebration of the Christ Mass within us—within planetary, solar, and galactic cycles—follows according to the release of energy from the Great Central Sun. We can say, then, that at winter solstice Christ is born in the etheric body, and the Bethlehem babe within us all is the experience of the child innocence mastering the element of fire. This is the initiation for the first quadrant of our birth year and of the planetary year—individual and planetary initiations going on simultaneously.

The initiation for the mastery of Christ in the mental body comes with the spring; Christ is born in the mind. In the summer, Christ is born in the desire body—the opportunity to master desire not as attachment or possessiveness but as that God simply desiring to be God within us. The autumn is the opportunity to experience the birth, the Christmas, of Christ in the physical body.

The ascended master El Morya says:

> If you could behold our quarterly conferences from the inner planes, you would observe how the chelas build the forcefield in the physical plane by their devotions and by their oneness and how hierarchy lowers a grid that is the mandala for that class in the etheric plane over the physical place where the class is held. . . .
>
> This geometric design suspended over the group is the focal point in which the energies of the group coalesce to magnetize, as a magnet of light, the releases of the ascended masters that are planned by the Karmic Board for that particular conference. Each lecture that is scheduled and each dictation that is given fills in a portion of the mandala.[31]

The Soul and the Spirit

We come, then, to the purpose of the cosmic clock as an assist to the individual soul. The soul must be defined because the soul and the Spirit are two different concepts. We read in *The Path of the Higher Self*:

> God is a Spirit and the soul is the living potential of God. The soul's demand for free will and its separation from God resulted in the descent of this potential into the lowly estate of the flesh. Sown in dishonor, the soul is destined to be raised in honor to the fullness of that God-estate which is the one Spirit of all life. The soul can be lost; Spirit can never die.[32]

The Spirit is deathless and eternal. It always is and it always was because it is the I AM THAT I AM—the cause, the core of being. It is the permanent atom of Self. The soul is the potential of that Spirit that went forth to claim an identity, to master time and space—that portion of God that demanded free will and was given that free will. We are called unascended beings because our souls having descended from the One have not yet ascended to the plane of the I AM THAT I AM.

The soul, then, comes forth out of Spirit. Spirit, as a charge of energy, is a masculine charge, masculine/Spirit; and this is why Spirit, as God the Father, has been adored principally as Father. Soul, then, coming forth from Spirit, becomes the feminine frequency, the feminine aspect. The two, then, are again the two of the whole clock, Alpha and Omega. Alpha and Omega exist in the white-fire core as the wholeness of masculine and feminine principle. When there is a separation out, the soul goes forth; and therefore the soul becomes the feminine potential of the masculine being.

The soul is not permanent. It is written: "The soul that sinneth, it shall die."[33] We seem to be under the illusion, through a misunderstanding of the teachings of the great avatars of the ages, that the soul is permanent—that we can do anything we want to do in time and space but the soul will live on forever.

This is not true. The soul has cycles—cosmic cycles—and they unfold according to the cosmic clock. The soul, then, is in time and space for a certain series of cycles on this clock, a certain given number of turns—thousands, millions. Ages pass; the soul goes through many incarnations. But there comes a period when there is the harvest—the time when the soul must show forth its fruits and its works.

The Judgment:
To Confirm Wholeness in the Cycles of Being

This brings us to the teaching on the Last Judgment, the judgment when the soul is weighed in the great balance and every man is judged according to his works.[34] If he is found wanting, having had no part in the first resurrection, and his name not found written in the Book of Life,[35] then the judgment rendered by the Ancient of Days from the great white throne is the second death.[36]

This is the canceling out of the soul's identity by the great white flame of Alpha and Omega. It is the exercise of the mercy of God not to perpetuate the existence of souls who by free will have chosen to be outside of God—the Father, the Son, and the Holy Spirit—souls who have elected to be the "not self," the "synthetic self" that has no part with the reality of God's kingdom (i.e., God's higher consciousness).

If the soul that has gone forth from God has not correctly used free will, it cannot be made a permanent part of God. The soul who by free will elects to qualify God's energy in light and harmony, in wisdom and love according to God's will (and most especially in the grace of our Lord and his own Christ consciousness), earns through the path of initiation the right both to return to that Spirit from whence it came and to preserve its immortal identity as the son or daughter of God.

Souls who have incarnated on earth or these several systems and who have undergone the initiatic process through the various religions and mystery schools of the Great White Brotherhood are the immortals. We call them ascended masters because this term aptly translates the meaning of their acceleration into God consciousness through the path of self-mastery individually won by freewill election and by application of the laws of the Spirit-Matter science. This science revealed to us today by the Holy Spirit governs the soul's descent from God for the purpose of gaining experience in the freewill uses of his energy and consciousness and its ascent to God via the white light, or the ascension flame.

In the Bible these overcomers are referred to as kings and priests unto God,[37] showing their self-mastery in service in both Church and State. They are also observed by John the Revelator as the saints robed in white[38] and the ten thousand times ten thousand who worship at the throne of God.[39] Our quarterly conferences are for the direct communion with this company of saints—angels and ascended masters—which God Almighty has ordained by his Holy Spirit unto all who believe on the Word of God and bear witness to its incarnation in Christ Jesus.

This is where we are. We are souls gathered and gathering for the notable day of the Lord's coming into our temple. We are gathered here in Washington on the occasion of the bicentennial because we realize that we as souls and as a nation have to get back to wholeness; i.e., to our own awareness of wholeness. We need to confirm that wholeness in the four cycles of being. We need to pass the tests of initiation so that once again we can live forevermore in the I AM THAT I AM and so that the Spirit may dwell in us bodily as it did in our Piscean Guru.

Mary Magdalene

Mary Magdalene: Personification of the Soul of America

I see Mary Magdalene as the personification of the soul of America. In her we see all aspects of our own soul awareness. We see that feminine potential all the way from the point of Eve—I, *Eva*—"the mother of all living creatures,"[40] to Mary who became the Mother of God. We see woman's consciousness from her descent to the testings and temptations of Eve to her ascent through the initiations of Mary.

It is the blessed Mother who summons women of this century to their own revolution in higher consciousness. By following in her footsteps, women set the standards for a way of life in America that protects the rights of the soul within the family and the community to pursue the path of a creative Self-realization. She teaches woman to mother the Christ consciousness in her children and in her beloved. For it is the privilege of every woman to give birth to the potential of the Real Self—first in herself, second in her husband, third in her children, and fourth in her community.

And so the soul of the individual and the soul of America moves from that point of Eve creating anything and everything, releasing any kind of vibration whatsoever, to that point of Mary's Christly discrimination, creating only after the inner blueprint of that only begotten Son of God, that Christ-potential that is the gift not to one but to all sons and daughters of God.

The Need for Forgiveness as a Nation and as a People

In defining love, the love that must be realized through the soul, we consider three episodes in the life of Mary Magdalene. And they represent three episodes in our own life that we also must experience as individuals and as a nation. To get from the place of Eve's soul awareness to the soul awareness of Mary the Mother, we must reinstate within ourselves conformity to the inner blueprint. In order to do this, we require forgiveness.

Never before have we had a greater need for forgiveness as a nation and as a people. We are guilt-ridden. We are self-condemned. We are condemned by the nations of the world. And this condemnation divides and demoralizes us. It weakens our will and our self-esteem.

We have forgotten the meaning of grace. We know not the scientific use of the law of Christ: the law of forgiveness. Without it we cannot pursue our fiery destiny. We cannot define our individual and national goals. We don't know where we're going because we don't know where we've come from. We are not correctly defining our policies within or our policies without. We do not know how to release the flow of love because love, as pure love, cannot come forth until we are cleansed by Christ.

There has been a great rejection of organized religion. The concept of confession and forgiveness of sins is repugnant to many. Many say, "Why should we go through a human being to experience forgiveness? We can go directly to God. How can a man and a mortal who is a sinner himself be the instrument of forgiveness?" We experience many dilemmas: the challenging of the authority of Church and State, and the demand for greater standards of morality, honor, and integration in both.

Come, let us reason together, saith the LORD. We have much to consider in this conference. We find that many of our woes and our wants concerning authority around us are resolved in the teachings of the Great White Brotherhood. Let us consider the law of forgiveness as Jesus taught and demonstrated it. For this is the point of beginning as we pass through the open door to the third century of America's independence.

Who Is the Great Forgiver of All? Who Is Christ?

Who is the great forgiver of all? It is Christ. We must know, then, who Christ is. Christ is not Jesus alone; Christ is the potential of the Real Self in us all. It is the potential toward which the soul is moving. And therefore, we have a priest of the sacred fire within ourselves—our own Christ Self. And to that Christ Self we run for forgiveness. In this, the Beloved's name, we cry out to the Father and he answers us through his Son.

Let us consider, then, how Jesus defined what the Father would forgive and what the Father would not forgive. It is made very clear in the teachings that are set forth in the New Testament. "Forgive us our trespasses against the law of thy Being in the same manner in which we forgive (or do not forgive) those who trespass against the law of our own being."

The First Episode: "Thy Sins Are Forgiven"

The law of forgiveness is first taught by Jesus at the house of Simon, a Pharisee. The sinful woman (though unnamed she is generally thought to be Magdalene) stood at Jesus' feet "behind him weeping, and began to wash his feet with tears, and did wipe them with the hairs of her head, and kissed his feet, and anointed them with the ointment."[41] When in his heart Simon challenged Jesus' authority because he allowed the sinner to touch him, Jesus taught him the law: She who loves much is forgiven much; she who loves little is forgiven little.[42]

The Law is plain. The penitent heart of society's condemned sinner was moved to intense love for Christ. This love became a prayer of deeds. Her first deed—an act of faith—was her unconditional acceptance of the One Sent, the Messiah come, as her personal Saviour (Guru). Her second deed—an act of loving obedience—was personal service to the Master. Her devotion to the Person of Christ was her way of calling upon the law of forgiveness; she understood that Jesus was the embodiment of the Law come in the person of the teacher.

In this instance Jesus clarifies the requirements of the law of forgiveness—the law of grace that is sent by the Father and mediated by the Son. He gives the teaching of the first ray embodying the principle of the will of the Father by faith in and obedience to his living Word. Here faith has become love and love has increased faith.

The master pronounces his benediction upon woman's first initiation: "Thy faith hath saved thee; go in peace."[43] Likewise this is America's first initiation as she enters the century of her soul's testing in love: believe on the Lord Christ who lives in one another and serve him by serving each other in love according to the greatest needs of the hour.

The Second Episode: "Go and Sin No More"

"The scribes and Pharisees brought unto him a woman taken in adultery."[44]

The scribes and the Pharisees represent the previous two-thousand-year dispensation under the cycle of Aries. They had received the Law from Moses. They were in the consciousness of the Law and the interpretation of the Law. They did not understand the identity of their prophets and teachers in Christ. They didn't see the Christ in their teachers, therefore they could not accept the Christ in themselves or in Jesus. They did not understand grace, the grace of the Person of the Son of God that is the mitigating factor of the Law.

And so they challenged him: "This woman was taken in adultery, *in the very act.*"[45] They sought to trap Jesus. They wanted to be sure he understood.

"Now Moses in the law commanded us, that such should be stoned: but what sayest thou? This they said, tempting him, that they might have to accuse him. But Jesus stooped down and with his finger wrote on the ground as though he heard them not. So when they continued asking him, he lifted up himself, and said unto them, He that is without sin among you, let him first cast a stone at her. And again he stooped down, and wrote on the ground."[46]

What was he writing on the ground? He was writing the Law. He was writing the record of their own adulterous consciousness and their own sin and the sins committed in previous incarnations. They saw what he wrote on the ground. They saw that he knew the Law, that he perceived the record which he read in *akasha*. "And they which heard it, being convicted by their own conscience, went out one by one, beginning at the eldest, even unto the last: and Jesus was left alone, and the woman standing in the midst."[47]

Jesus the Christ, the Great Mediator of the Law

Jesus *the Christ*, the Christ Self of Jesus and the Christ as your Real Self, is the great Mediator of the Law. Without the Christ as the Saviour of us all, nothing stands between us and the absolute Law of the absolute Lawgiver. We are under the absolute Law; and if we sin against that Law, without him we have no recourse. Because we stepped out of the way of the garden of cosmic consciousness, God provided that intermediary, that Christ Self. And so the Christ Self becomes the interpreter of the Law. The Christ Self, then, is the aspect of the Great God Self that can extend forgiveness.

Jesus Christ was a priest after the order of Melchizedek.[48] He came to reestablish the Melchizedekian order. He has ordained your own Christ Self as the representative of his own priesthood. You may therefore in his name confess your sins before the inner priest, the hidden man of the heart[49] who dwells forever in your own Holy of holies.

"When Jesus had lifted up himself, and saw none but the woman, he said unto her, Woman, where are those thine accusers? hath no man condemned thee? She said, No man, Lord. And Jesus said unto her, Neither do I condemn thee: go, and sin no more."[50]

Jesus was also aware of the vulnerability of the lesser self to err. He was aware of his own past incarnations when he manifested less than the totality of the Christ consciousness. How could he condemn in another what he himself could be subject to or may have been subject to? Furthermore it is written: "For God sent not his Son into the world to condemn the world; but that the world through him might be saved."[51] Jesus is much more concerned with the saving of the soul of America than with her condemnation. So should we be.

This is the illumination of the Great Law that comes to the disciples of the enlightened ones—Jesus, Gautama, Maitreya, Kuthumi, Lanto,

Confucius, Meru, and Padma Sambhava to name a few—who have taught that the law of forgiveness necessitates the forsaking of sin through understanding the self and the Self. This, the second episode, illustrates the teaching of the World Teachers and avatars on the second ray, which embodies the principle of the wisdom of the Son.

Just following this episode recorded by John, Jesus makes the revolutionary statement of the one anointed to the office of World Christ for the Piscean age: "I AM the light of the world: he that followeth me shall not walk in darkness, but shall have the light of life."[52] His teaching to Mary Magdalene is: "Because I have realized the I AM He consciousness, because the I AM THAT I AM is where I AM—as Above, so below, Being is congruent where I AM—this Word incarnate in me is the I AM who sustains the light of God on behalf of all of earth's evolutions, I AM the embodied authority of the Law, hence the forgiver of sin—i.e., the one who transmutes the law of sin that you yourself have set in motion and that now binds you. You may retain this forgiveness only so long as you maintain that level of my Christ consciousness which is required of my disciples. In the heightened awareness of your Real Self, go and sin no more."

Under the initiations of the second ray, the individual assumes greater responsibility to personify the Law. To retain the grace of the Guru, he must be willing to make the sacrifices necessary to embody a portion of that grace. No longer does he walk by faith alone or even by trusting, loving obedience—the requirements of the first ray. Now he must integrate with the Law and the Lawgiver through understanding and through acceptance of a personal commitment to witness both to his teacher and to the teaching by his words and his works.

America and the Adulterous Generation

We see then that the soul of America is also involved in what I call the adulterous generation[53]—the generation of adultery that has set itself apart from the wholeness of God. This adultery is mass whoredom of the people who have gone after the gods of materialism, money, pleasure, and the cult of success and death.

We speak about the casting of the seven devils out of Mary Magdalene. The seven devils represent the seven deadly sins, or compromises of the energy of the seven chakras. We as a nation have compromised that feminine principle in each of the chakras. We have misused the light of the seven rays of God, the seven planes of the Christ consciousness, that are intended to be anchored in these chakras.

We as individual souls have sinned also. Paul said: "All have sinned, and come short of the glory of God."[54] This is not condemnation. This is not the wrath of God. This is a necessary understanding of our present state of evolution—so self-limiting—in order that we may take the necessary steps for our soul's restoration to the state of grace—i.e., oneness with God through Christ Jesus, the mediator of our personal Christhood.

The very first step, then, on the path of initiation—unless you are a perfected one, unless you have balanced 100 percent of your karma—is the call for forgiveness. The soul must be rescued from the self-made laws of sin and death by the Christ or it cannot begin the Path.

Forgiveness is the setting aside by the law of individual Christhood of the energies misqualified in the misuse of the sacred fire that is God. When that energy is set aside, then the soul is free to move Godward, to move toward the Christ consciousness. When the soul grows in stature and in the wisdom of the Christ, then with that self-mastery it is free to balance the karma that has been temporarily set aside by the grace of our Lord. And our Lord is our Christ Self, personified in Jesus and many other ascended masters who have walked in his footsteps and fulfilled the requirement for personal Christhood and the ascension.

Forgiveness, then, is not the wiping out of sin (karma); it is the setting aside of sin (karma) for the purpose of allowing our souls to expand in grace and understanding of the law of transmutation. When we reach a certain level of soul attainment, we are required to stand, face, and conquer the weight of karma that has been temporarily held in abeyance while we attained a certain spiritual maturity.

The great gift of salvation through Jesus Christ is that he, as the Piscean avatar, took upon himself the sins of the world—i.e., world karma—until the world through him might accept the Christ within as the individual redeemer. ("I know that *my* redeemer liveth."[55]) Through that inner Christ, or Logos, the creative Word incarnate in all sons and daughters of God, the individual invokes the sacred fire of the Holy

Ghost that now consumes the sin set aside, transmuting the darkness of our misqualified energy of previous incarnations into the illuminating light that now becomes the Word made flesh[56] in us all.

Mary Magdalene and Jesus

The Third Episode: The Recognition of the Risen Christ

The third episode of Mary Magdalene is the initiation on the third ray, embodying the principle of the love of the Holy Spirit. It is the meeting on Easter morning of Mary, the chela, with her Guru. She is the first to see him out of the tomb because she has, at this point, that development of the feminine principle that enables her to see the risen Christ.

She is weeping. She is looking for her Lord. He comes forth and he says unto her, "Mary." And with that word, he calls her "Mother ray" —*Ma-ray*. And when he ignites in her the flame of Mother, she then has the awareness to exclaim in profound recognition of his person, "Rabboni"[57]—to acknowledge him as her teacher and her master. As we in this conference define love and the action of love, we will come to an understanding of these relationships.

Here we see Jesus the Christ now representing the risen Christ, his soul risen to the plane of Christ Self-awareness about to ascend to "your Father and my Father," to "your God and my God"[58]—*to the one God individualized as your I AM Presence and my I AM Presence.*

We see depicted here our relationship to the Spirit. Here is the soul kneeling before the Spirit. The soul has come to the threefold embodiment of the virtues of the Trinity: faith, enlightened hope, and love. The soul will no longer be part of the adulterous generation, but it will be the manifestation of the abundant regeneration, giving birth to the Christ light.

America, Call on the Law of Forgiveness!

What we must do, then, as we begin this conference, is to call upon the law of forgiveness. It is a legitimate law. We understand that in asking for forgiveness, we are asking for a cleansing—the cleansing of the chakras of the individual and the cleansing of the chakras of the nation.

I would like to ask you to join me in calling on the law of forgiveness for the soul of America—to call for forgiveness for America as a nation for all misuses of the grace of God; to call upon the law of forgiveness for all that we have been accused of, even the accusations of the one known as the accuser of the brethren,[59] and for all that we have actually abused of our fiery destiny; to call upon the law of forgiveness so that we can be free from conscious and subconscious hatred, from divisions within our members, from self-condemnation and the condemnation of one another, from the sense of guilt and shame that binds us to our sense of sin and sinfulness.

Until Christ has forgiven us, we constantly stand in fear of our accusers. Who are our accusers? Our accusers are the nations of the world and individuals within our own society who do not understand grace. They are still in the consciousness of the Pharisees: "America has done wrong; she must be punished. She must go down because she has done wrong. She must go down as a second, a third-rate power. She can no longer rise, because she has abused her place in the family of nations. We will no longer defend her, but we will allow the enemy to destroy her from within and from without. We will stand by and watch the desolation of a mighty people and a mighty nation because they have sinned and now they deserve to be stoned—by nuclear holocaust; by international political and economic blackmail; by the great giveaway of grain, gold, and technology; by the murder of her children (through abortion and oblivion in hard drugs and hard rock)."

Yes, this is why we, as Americans, don't fight any more for life, liberty, and the pursuit of happiness—because we've accepted the condemnation of the Pharisees who say America has sinned and she must die. Caiaphas says in our time: "It is expedient that one nation should die for the people."[60] This is the subconscious reason we have accepted the psychology of death and its frivolous preoccupations.

Wake up, America! Accept the grace of God through the indwelling Christ! Hear his Word spoken unto thee: "Thy faith hath saved thee; go in peace.... Neither do I condemn thee, Go and sin no more.... Mother ray of the world, enter into the abundant life and heal thyself and the nations of the earth as I have healed thee!"

We have to realize that the Christ consciousness of America, the Christ Self whom we see personified in Jesus and in Saint Germain, in order to forgive must unsee the wrong, must realize that every misqualification of energy can be transmuted by the sacred fire of the Holy Ghost, whose very Person appears to us in the violet flame. This transmutation can take place—which means that all that is created in time and space, when it is passed through the violet flame (the veritable flame of forgiveness) can be transmuted into love and into the Christ consciousness by the release of that sacred fire of the heart.

America Is Mother
America Must Walk the Path as Mary Magdalene

America is Mother. America is a feminine principle. America is the place prepared for the coming of the Woman with the crown of twelve stars into the wilderness,[61] the virgin territory, to give birth to the Christ consciousness in the twelve tribes of Israel—who reincarnate in this land promised unto the seed of Abraham—and to the multitudes of God's children who gather from every continent under the aegis of Mother Liberty, the ascended lady master who sponsors the initiation of every soul come to these shores. With her torch of freedom and her book of the Law, she offers a new life through enlightened self-effort to the "huddled masses" who greet her as their Guru Mother.

The Statue of Liberty

America, then, must begin with forgiveness so that she can get on with self-mastery in the levels of the chakras, so she can anoint the feet and the head of Christ—i.e., prepare the blessed sons and daughters of God for their initiations of the crucifixion, the resurrection, and the ascension. America must walk this path as Mary Magdalene. America must believe that she can be purified, that she can become whole, that she can be restored and be regenerated.

And what is the key to this? It is the acceptance of forgiveness and the fact that there is a principle, a person, a God, a Christ, a flame, an energy, the Holy Spirit. It is a mathematics and it is a science. It is a consciousness. And when we make contact with it, He releases the light of God for the clearing and the cleansing. And this, too, is the fulfillment of prophecy of Isaiah that "though your sins be as scarlet, they shall be as white as snow; though they be red like crimson, they shall be as wool."[62] White as snow, white as wool, white as the sacred fire of the noonday sun—this is the promise of the prophets of the Old Testament to America today.

We cannot rise, we cannot hold our heads high, we cannot look ahead to define love in the next century until we get through this crux, this nexus, of the law of forgiveness. Because we have rejected mortals as the instruments of forgiveness, we have failed to seek forgiveness.

But beyond the mortal is the immortal, the Shining One.

Do you know how good it feels when you go to a friend and tell that friend that you have done something wrong that you are ashamed of, and the friend says to you, "That's all right; we're still friends"? That's the action of the Christ in that friend. And when you can confide something that is of great shame and a source of great self-condemnation to someone that you love and that someone can still love you, it makes you feel that there is hope, that God still loves you, and you can pick up the pieces and you can carry on. So the Christ of each of us is able to forgive not only sin in ourselves but in all, when we appeal to that Christ.

America, We Can Rise as Mary Magdalene

The three experiences of Mary Magdalene are yet to be experienced by us as a nation. I find that this is a tremendous experience for me—to look at the life of Mary Magdalene—because until we come into the love of Christ, there is yet the carnal-minded side of us that takes the side of the Pharisees, that sees her as a woman of ill repute, that does not equate her with Mary, the Mother of Jesus, or other holy women. And we tend to tie into the mass consciousness of condemnation—and of course that condemnation is then heaped on our own heads.

And so in order for ourselves even to experience the forgiveness of Mary Magdalene, we have to grow in love. We have to realize that she was worthy to be equal with the Christ—yes, this position of coequality he gave to her as a soul, as a woman, and as his disciple and dear friend! Because she accepted the Christ in him, he acknowledged the Mother flame in her as not only the soul forgiven but now as the initiate on the same path that he was walking. We have to realize that we can rise as Mary Magdalene. America, we can rise in the name of the Lord who is risen within us!

Prayer for Forgiveness to the Christ Self of the Nation

And now, in the name of the Christ, in the name of Jesus the Christ, I call for the drawing nigh to these souls of the individual potential, the Christ Self. As we assemble together, we kneel in the spirit of humility before the risen Jesus Christ, before our own Christ

Self-awareness, our own higher consciousness, and we call upon the law of forgiveness for ourselves and for America as a nation. We call upon that law of forgiveness. And we ask the Cosmic Christ, Lord Maitreya, and all who have attained the Christ consciousness to intercede this day that we might enter the path of initiation, individually and collectively, as a people dedicated to freedom in all mankind.

I call directly to the heart of the Lords of Karma. In the name of the I AM Presence and in the name of the Christ Self of each one, we call forth forgiveness. We do confess our sins, our errors, our misuses of the sacred fire. All of this we lay upon the altar of the Lord, and we beseech the intercession of the Christ who will stand with us, who will rebuke the adversaries in their blind miscalculated judgment and their blind misunderstanding of the Law.

We ask for the defense of the Christ consciousness through the entire Spirit of the Great White Brotherhood and the Divine Father and the Divine Mother. We ask for this intercession for all people who call for forgiveness and for every nation. We direct our call for and on behalf of America because this nation, this people under God is the responsibility of our calling in life. In the spirit of asking for forgiveness and accepting that forgiveness in answer to our call, we release the energies for the establishment of the path of initiation. And the path of initiation is truly, O Lord, the battle of Armageddon.

So the battle of Armageddon and the putting down of the carnal mind by the action of the Christ—this is our calling to higher consciousness, and this is the calling that we accept in the name of the Father and of the Mother, of the Son and of the Holy Spirit.

Steps of Initiation for America Outlined in "The Battle Hymn of the Republic"

I would like, then, in that spirit of this understanding, to sing together "The Battle Hymn of the Republic." I would like to point out the steps of initiation for America that are outlined in this song.

Mine Eyes Have Seen the Glory

"Mine eyes have seen the glory of the coming of the Lord." That is the word of Mary Magdalene as she sees Christ coming out from the tomb.

Mine eyes have *seen* that glory. I have been able to perceive it because I have been able to rise to the level of the Christ consciousness.

"He is trampling out the vintage where the grapes of wrath are stored." This is taken from the Book of Revelation, chapter 14, verse 19: "And the angel thrust in his sickle into the earth, and gathered the vine of the earth, and cast it into the great winepress of the wrath of God." Immediately upon seeing the Lord, we see him as the sword of the sacred Word that cleaves asunder the Real from the unreal. For the Christ becomes the instrument of judgment, for only through the judgment do we understand what requires forgiveness. He is gathering the vine of the earth—and the vine represents the sons and daughters. The great winepress is the balance, the scales of judgment.

So the moment we perceive Christ, we perceive that the path of initiation is a continual sifting, a continual weighing, a continual understanding of what is in God and what is outside of God, a continual measuring of vibration, an examination of cycles, an examination of vibrations in our seven chakras, an examination of where we have gone wrong, of where we have misused this feminine aspect of our being—our very own soul.

The judgment is always more swift with the sons and daughters of God because they are chastened, for they are on the path of initiation. God is very quick to show us our errors when we are on the Path, whereas for those who are not on the Path it may take many years, decades, or embodiments for them to understand what it means to depart from the Law and the blueprint of life.

So the judgment is an action of love. The ascended masters give to us their understanding of love as it is expressed in all human relationships. Jesus defined this love as a total commitment when he gave us the commandment: "That ye love one another as I have loved you."[63]

The Fateful Lightning and the Swift Sword

We need to understand, then, that the judgment is something we welcome; for unless we are judged, we cannot advance. So it is the very next cycle: "He hath loosed the fateful lightning of his terrible swift sword." It is the action of the white light and the flame of the will of God that descends upon the consciousness of the people, upon the nations, for this judgment of love, for this sifting process, so that we can refine and remove the gold, separate it out from the impurities. The "swift sword" is the certain sword of the *sacred Word* separating, separating.

Sacred Word is the inner meaning of *sword*. The sword is for the alignment of energies, the separation of darkness and light, rallying our energies to the invincible flame of truth. This conference is dedicated to truth, and the truth is the coming of Christ—"I came not to send peace, but a sword."[64] The "Battle Hymn," then, becomes the rallying of the forces of light, the hierarchies of heaven, for the defense of the flame of the Christ on the altar of the heart. The heart is the seat of the Christ consciousness.

The Watchfires of a Hundred Circling Camps

"The watchfires of a hundred circling camps" are the chakras in the four lower bodies of the microcosm of being and in the macrocosm of the nation. Those altars are the place for alteration, for change. The sacred fire is the point of change, the point of alchemy. The key altar is the altar of the heart where the threefold flame burns.

When we look into the sky, we see the same "watchfires of a hundred circling camps"—the circle, the symbol of initiation of the disciples gathered around the Christ, who is the consuming fire of God in the center of every initiatic school. The stars in the heavens reveal the same action of focalizing the flame of the Christ consciousness in the chakras of the body of God.

His Righteous Sentence, the Fiery Gospel, and the Burnished Rows of Steel

"His righteous sentence" is that man was born to be free—that man shall know the truth and that the truth shall make him free.[65] The righteous sentence is the descent, increment by increment according to the cosmic clock, of the cycles of karma.

The "fiery gospel writ in burnished rows of steel"—we think of the words of Jeremiah, "I will put my law in their inward parts, and write it in their hearts; and will be their God, and they shall be my people."[66] This is the prophecy for the soul of America, for the souls of all nations.

The true Israelites, the true ones who have the consciousness of the Spirit as the I AM THAT I AM, have the Law written in their chakras, in their hearts. And that "fiery gospel" is the sacred fire of the Law sealed in every nucleus of life. And the "burnished rows of steel" are the activation—line by line, decision by decision—of when to release that energy as power, when to release it as wisdom, when to release it as love.

As Ye Deal with My Contemners

And so the law of karma: God promises that as we deal righteously in the law of karma, "as ye deal with my contemners [condemners], so with you my grace shall deal." This is the law of karma—the putting down of the erroneous consciousness of those who are contemptuous of the Law.

As we challenge those who are the challengers of the law of God, so God will assist us in putting down the carnal mind by the action of the Christ within us. As we determine how we will deal with the wrong decisions we have made and with the manifestations of our decisions, so the grace of God will be upon us to go forward. Therefore, let the Christ Self of each one now consume every aspect of the carnal mind that the flame of God's own higher consciousness, his truth, might march on through the temple of being.

Sounding Forth the Trumpet

The sounding forth of the trumpet is the release of the fire of the Word of God coming into this age in the teachings of the Great White Brotherhood. And they come forth in every age through the understanding of the path of the Christ and the Buddha.

God—through his emissaries, prophets, messengers, and through devotees of the flame, gurus and chelas—establishes righteousness and judgment and sifts the hearts of mankind, drawing out their motives, their pride and their prejudice, that they might be judged whether they are of the light or of the darkness. When our subconscious is played out before us and we are forced to make a choice, then we are reenacting the judgment within us.

God Is Marching On

So let the soul rise to answer the call of the Christ Self and the power of the spoken Word, for "God is marching on." God is rising in the chakras. From the base chakra of the feminine to the crown chakra of the masculine, God is marching on.

If we will look, then, at the great mystery of love that is a part of all of our history and our culture and our religion, we will see that even this hymn in itself is not simply something we sing on the basis of nationalism. *Hallelujah,* taken from the Hebrew, means "praise Jehovah," or "praise I AM THAT I AM." Thus it is a hymn that all nations can sing because it is a hymn to the path of initiation under each one's I AM Presence.

Blessed friends of light, this is our challenge in America today: that we not only enter the path of initiation as individuals but that we also put down our separation, our division, and realize that as one people and as one soul, we must pass the solar initiations that the planet is undergoing. If we can make that choice to be initiated as one body, one heart, one soul, one mind, we will set the example of freedom to the nations.

Let us stand and sing "The Battle Hymn of the Republic."

The Battle Hymn of the Republic

1. Mine eyes have seen the glory
    of the coming of the Lord
   He is trampling out the vintage
    where the grapes of wrath are stored
   He hath loosed the fateful lightning
    of His terrible swift sword
   His truth is marching on.

Refrain: Glory! Glory! Hallelujah!
   Glory! Glory! Hallelujah!
   Glory! Glory! Hallelujah!
   His truth is marching on.

2. I have seen Him in the watchfires
    of a hundred circling camps
  They have builded Him an altar
    in the evening dews and damps
  I can read His righteous sentence
    by the dim and flaring lamps
  His day is marching on.

3. I have read a fiery gospel
    writ in burnished rows of steel
  "As ye deal with my contemners
    so with you my grace shall deal:"
  Let the hero, born of woman
    crush the serpent with his heel
  Since God is marching on.

4. He has sounded forth the trumpet
    that shall never call retreat
  He is sifting out the hearts of men
    before His judgment seat
  O be swift, my soul to answer Him!
    be jubilant my feet!
  Our God is marching on.

5. In the beauty of the lilies
    Christ was born across the sea
  With a glory of His bosom
    that transfigures you and me
  As He died to make men holy
    let us live to make men free
  While God is marching on.

Julia Ward Howe

2

CALL TO LIGHT: DEDICATION OF THE FLAME

A Dictation by the Goddess of Light

Good morning, sons and daughters of flame. I come at the behest of Saint Germain, even as you have come in answer to the call of the Knight Commander. I salute you one and all in light. I come to dedicate this conference, as I have dedicated civilizations in the past, by the light of the rising feminine ray.

I am so privileged to be called to come with my taper of light to ignite a torch of freedom, a torch that each one of you will then carry through this conference day by day by the action of the five secret rays. Those of you who have come to find yourselves this day in the right place at the right time have the privilege of carrying an inner action of the white-fire core, the five secret rays of God-mastery of the mighty Elohim in the Christ consciousness. And those who come on the morrow will carry the taper of the four aspects of the four lower bodies. And so those who come for five days will carry the action of the inner rays and those who come for four will carry the action of their manifestation in the four quadrants of the Mother flame.

Let it be, then, that sons and daughters of flame who have come together again and again in civilizations rising, rising with the spirals, undulating and rising again—so let these Keepers of the Flame who have known the face of the Ancient of Days[1] and the face of the lady master of Venus, let them also know the face of one another that this body of lightbearers may recognize each other as brother, as sister of light, as the indomitable light of the will of God and the will of freedom carried in the heart that is for the victory of an age.

I come, then, to endow with light, to dedicate with light, and I bring with me the full-gathered momentum of my service to light on the continent of South America, through North America, and through all of the ages past when light, as the apex of the rising of Omega to the flame of Alpha, has been the apex of civilization. It is therefore to the feminine potential of man and woman and child that I dedicate this conference. I dedicate this flame of freedom to the freeing of the soul potential of each one. I dedicate this conference to Saint Germain, our noble king, to Portia, our lady, our queen.

Angelic Reinforcements of Cosmic Consciousness

With me are the reinforcements of the angels of light who serve in all of the retreats of the Great White Brotherhood. For did you know, O precious hearts of light, that our angels are called upon to tarry and to reinforce the light, light, light momentum of every action of every ascended master and Elohim and cosmic being?

We are legions transparent and our garments come. We are the ones who filter the air, the land, the sea, the sky. We filter all elemental life. Our garments of light are charged with cosmic consciousness of fire and air and water and earth, and our awareness of that flame is for the balance of all of the beings of the elements.

I give you this insight into the service of the angels of my bands that you might understand that in this cosmos, in each of the consciousness of the ascended masters, there are bands of angels who serve in a very specific way, in a very specific calling to make life on earth and in these planetary systems a balanced manifestation of Father, Son, and Holy Spirit that can only be released in Mater[2] by the action of Mother light in you and in me, in the masters ascended and unascended, in the entire Spirit of the Great White Brotherhood, in all of the chelas and devotees of the flame.

Let Your Heart Be That Place for the Release of Light

So let the Mother fire within you release the full potential of the kindling spark of threefold flame! And now let the mighty Elohim, let the Queen of Light and the Goddess of Purity, let the entire Spirit of the Great White Brotherhood, the causal body of the World Mother, the light of Alpha and Omega now touch your heart as a kindling fire. Let it burst aflame as the sparklers of the Fourth of July, and let your heart be that place for the release of the light of Columbia, the name of Portia, the name of the flame of opportunity—Columbia!

Let each one be the gem of the ocean of God's being! Let that gem be the jewel in the heart of the lotus! Let that gem-fire be for the igniting of a world!

We are not dismayed by the darkness, for the darkness has never in all eternity displaced the light of God. The light of God always puts out the darkness, and the farthest star, the farthest causal body, illumines the heavens. And so the single candle of the Keeper of the Flame keeping the flame of life, of freedom, and of the Holy Spirit suffices to illumine a world. All of the darkness of the world cannot silence the single flame of devotion.

Our Oneness Is One God, One Christ, One Cosmic Consciousness

I AM the flame within you! I release the light of the Great Central Sun for the inauguration of the spirals of freedom! I AM the flame of fire and of light within you! Let us then vow together that we be not separate but that we be one, that there is the converging in the heart of all hearts, that the one heart is the heart of the many, is the heart of God and Christ and of all elemental life.

Therefore if I AM and if you are, then we are one. Then I AM where you are in my Electronic Presence. And therefore I stand where you are that our heart chakras might be one, that you might understand that defeat is in division and separation, and victory is in our oneness.

Our oneness is the understanding of one God, one Christ. And in that fire of cosmic consciousness, I release the energies of the fiery core of the earth, of Mother Earth. O Virgo and Pelleur, send forth thy light! Oromasis and Diana, send forth thy light! Aries and Thor, send forth thy light! Neptune and Luara, send forth thy light! I AM light, light, light! There is one light—universal light! And in the moment of your God-realization, death is swallowed up in victory![3]

Homage to the God of Freedom

Freedom is the fulfillment of all who have ever overcome bondage and tyranny. Freedom is the flame, freedom is the joy, freedom is the beholding of the light! Now as I stand with you, I desire to pay homage to the God of Freedom to all of this galaxy and these many galaxies and systems of worlds, for by his flame there is hope and hope of freedom on Terra.

May I, then, sing with you in this moment of the glory of Saint Germain, may I sing with you to his blessed name? And may your voices echo across the cosmos that every cosmic being and cosmic council might hear the breath of joy and of the Spirit that ascends from your heart this day in gratitude for the gift of freedom.

In the name of the flame that we are, I salute you! In the name of the entire Spirit of the Great White Brotherhood, in the name of the Father and of the Mother, of the Son and of the Holy Spirit— All hail, Saint Germain!

3

AMERICA: YE SHALL KNOW THE TRUTH AND THE TRUTH SHALL MAKE YOU FREE

A Dictation by Pallas Athena

Sons and daughters of flame, I am grateful for your presence in the light of truth. Your vision is the open door for the coming of the messengers of truth. Hierarchy cannot speak in a vacuum. Hierarchy cannot speak where there is not the chalice of Matter to receive the precious flame of Spirit that is the living Word of truth.

I AM the light of truth. I come bearing the lamp of truth of the ages, truth that was exalted in the golden age of Pericles, truth that wrought the mighty city-states, truth that was the testing ground of souls—your souls and many souls who live in America this day who lived in ancient Greece, who lived in ancient Rome and who have come forth to claim the culture of the Mother once again.

The materialization of the God flame in America is for the testing, the testing, the testing of souls of ancient Atlantis. Atlantis, light of Mother in Matter! Atlanta, light of a free people, a people proud in their freedom who carried their freedom to the nth, to the place where the freedom of the light of truth reached a culmination and then, through misuse, began to decline.

There is a wave, a cosmic wave that comes in every civilization. And the cresting of that wave by the people at the high peak is not that they will go under the wave but that the breaking of the wave might release the energies of the desire of God, of the water quadrant, for the focalization in the physical plane of all attainment that has gone before.

But there is a requirement, you see. In order to carry the mastery of fire and air and water into the physical earth, there is a pause, there is a moment before the breaking of the wave. It is the moment of alchemy. It is the moment of transmutation. It is the moment when all that has been misqualified in fire and air and water must be surrendered that it might be consumed by the sacred-fire action of the cosmic wave.

This moment is known as a cosmic interval; and at that moment of the interval, there is turmoil, there is a disruption in society, in the nature kingdom. There is the moment when all mankind wait with bated breath, waiting for the Redeemer and the Saviour, waiting for the light of the Holy of holies, waiting for the rescue team of the cosmos, failing to understand that the Redeemer and the Saviour and the light of the rescue team is the fire of the heart within, and that those at that moment who receive the prophet in the name of the prophet will receive the prophet's reward.[1]

The Timing of Cosmic Cycles Is upon Us

Understand that the timing of cosmic cycles is upon us—upon us as Lords of Karma, upon you as Keepers of the Flame, upon America where the drama of the flame of freedom is outplayed for a planet and a people. America is on stage and all the world waits to see what America will do.

The enemy is testing, testing the fire of freedom and the determination of a free people to guard the bastions of freedom for the earth; and the watching, watching by the friends—friends who call themselves friends and allies and yet who silently send that jealousy and that hatred, that condescending glance, that condemnation. So then, whether friend or foe alike, their attention must be dealt with through the science of the spoken Word.

This is the land of a free people—a people who are free, not unto themselves, but a people who are the guardians of freedom to the earth. You cannot keep that which you would possess; you can only keep that which you give away. Freedom, then, is a torch that must be passed, and you are all the Greek runners in the race, a race that is unto life and unto victory.

My Proclamation to America

I come then to address America, and rightly I address Keepers of the Flame; for unto the Lords of Karma and to the Brotherhood ascended, *you* are America. You are the hope of America. You are the leaders of the dharma and the group mandala of America. Your vote of confidence for Saint Germain, manifest by your presence here, is a vote for freedom that counts for tens of thousands of souls. The soul that carries the flame of life is the soul that has the right to represent the people in the republican form of government founded by the Knight Commander whereby all mankind might be free.

And therefore, to each one of you I impart the scroll of my fervor, my dictation, my proclamation to America. And the scroll is as an electrode to be carried, to be unwound, to be released in your cities and in your homes. Without Keepers of the Flame in America, I can surely say to you that the Lords of Karma would have an altogether different dispensation to release to America and to Terra this Fourth of July. Because Keepers of the Flame have sounded the word and the voice of freedom and liberty and of peace only with honor, so hierarchy stands and still stands in America today.

We then applaud Keepers of the Flame and we say, Keep on keeping on! For the crest of the wave is not yet fulfilled, and the breaking of the wave is yet to come. And in this moment of the interval, you are the hope not only of the nation but of the world.

Americans Do Not Know the Truth

I come then with the focalization of my message: America, ye shall know the truth, and the truth shall make you free![2] I come with a report that I have researched with the Keeper of the Scrolls and with the angels of truth and the angels of record. I bring to you this report that Americans do not know the truth—the truth of who they are, the truth of the fiery core of the destiny of the individual and of the nation and of its cosmic purpose.

Americans are ignorant of the truth of the power and the wisdom and the love within the heart that is theirs to release for the action of planetary freedom. Americans have forgotten the ancient heritage of

Greece and the lessons of Rome, the lessons of Atlantis. They have forgotten the lessons of Maldek and Hedron, of self-destruction in selfishness, the ways of the pleasure cult, the ways of the drug culture and the ends thereof, which are the ways of the death of the soul.

Locked within their causal bodies, locked within the etheric memory is the knowledge of the truth that shall make them free. Americans do not know the truth, and therefore consequences are parading across the screen of manifestation. Americans have not caught the vision of being the I AM honor guard of truth on Terra. Because they have not known the truth, they have accepted the lie of the fallen ones. They have walked in the way of compromise, of relativity, and have not known their compromise or the state of their consciousness. Because they have not known the truth, they have remained in a pocket of indecision and of self-condemnation, perverting the life of Alpha and Omega.

Without Vision the People Will Surely Perish

Do you understand that without vision the people will surely perish?[3] For the vision is the definition of the lines of consciousness directing internal affairs and external affairs, creating a strong foreign policy as well as a strong domestic policy. Truth known and manifest, crystallized in consciousness, would enable the American people to see the darkness in their leaders, to call them back from office and to support lightbearers whose consciousness is in alignment with the Great White Brotherhood.

Americans in this hour of the bicentennial are in a state of confusion. They are at a loss to know whether they have an identity as a people, as a nation. Americans standing in the way of overcoming have upon them then the dark, the dank, the humidity, and the heat that denotes untransmuted energies in the astral plane. Therefore, our focus in this conference will be to show you how to deal with these energies of the emotional quadrant that are used by the manipulators for the manipulation of America and her government.

Let us understand that even Keepers of the Flame do not always have a clear-cut and concise definition of the principles they ought to espouse, nor do they recognize the Christ consciousness when they see it. Precious ones, it is truth and truth alone that will make known in this land the way—the way that ye ought to know, the way that will make men and women and children free, staunch, upright, noble in the defense of a heritage that comes forth from the very Ancient of Days.

For you are of the lineage of Sanat Kumara. You are of the lineage of those orders of celestial beings. You are sons and daughters of God. You are outstanding as a people prepared by the Holy One of Israel for this calling, for this moment in a cosmic destiny that is to affect millions of lifewaves even beyond this system of worlds.

How often do you remember your worth and the truth of your cosmic worth and cosmic purpose? Even Keepers of the Flame when they are outside of our presence or the aura of the Mother tend to forget their worth as gems and crystals in the mind of God. You tend to enter into spirals of self-deprecation, taking on the belittlement that emanates from the fallen ones who surround you on every side.

Remember, you are mighty conquerors! And the flame of life within you and the science of the spoken Word—this is enough! This is enough, I say, to coalesce that fire of the great cosmic wave and to reverse the tide of civilization.

I Dedicate This Conference to the Coming Revolution

I dedicate this conference to the coming revolution. Call me a revolutionary if you will, and I will say, Yes, I AM! I AM the Goddess of Truth! I AM the incarnation of the feminine ray! I AM at the front of the battle! I AM in the image of Joan of Arc and the great patronesses of the Law, the great mothers who have gone before to enshrine in the womb of time and space your Christ-identity. I AM in this land the fervor of truth! I AM touching the spectrum of consciousness from the left unto the right. I AM touching all who love freedom and truth and those who do not, for I will not be turned back.

And I wish you would understand this day that when I say I AM truth incarnate, I must rely upon your body, your flesh and your blood, your mind and your soul to be the incarnation of the Word of truth that I AM. And when I say that I go forth in this land to spark truth, it is as Christ talking to Peter, saying, "I go to Rome to be crucified again."[4]

The ascended masters come. We appear to our chelas. We declare our fiery destiny and our mission. We want you to understand that that destiny and that mission can be accomplished only through your materialization of the God flame. We need to work through you, and yet we also have the dispensation of the Lords of Karma that our angels of truth and freedom might go before you to clear the way, the way of receptivity and truth.

The Ascended Masters Are Everywhere in the Consciousness of God

You know well that the ascended masters do not engage in the polemics of politics, that they do not side with the left or the right wing or with any political party. We must be everywhere in the consciousness of God, and most of all we must be where humanity has forsaken the blueprint of truth.

Therefore I say to you, do not leave those forcefields and those organizations who do *not* espouse the teachings of the Great White Brotherhood. Yes, I said, who do *not* espouse the teachings of the Great White Brotherhood. You must be unto them that pillar of fire by night and that cloud by day.[5] And if their platform and their party consciousness is anti-Christ, then be the silent sentinel in the midst making silent invocation, holding the flame of truth and freedom, keeping the flame with beloved Igor, keeping the flame of truth.

One Keeper of the Flame in any and every organization politically oriented in America, through the making of the calls to the Great White Brotherhood, can be the leaven that the woman took and hid in three measures of meal until it leavened the whole lump.[6] Truth is the leaven of the Mother. Truth is the fire of the geometrization of the God flame. *Truth,* I say!

One candle of truth at the strategic points where decisions are being made can turn the tide. And you will see before your very eyes the alchemy of consciousness. You will see how in silence that flame of truth will turn the consciousness of the people 180 degrees.

Now you must realize that a thousand may fall at thy side and ten thousand at thy right hand, but it shall not come nigh thee.[7] This is the promise of Lord Michael, the Prince of the Archangels. This is the promise of protection. It is also the promise of the perfecting action of the flame of truth that where you are, there must be the alchemy for the reversing of consciousness.

Jesus Taught the Science of the Spoken Word

All that is outside of God may be committed to the flame by your calls made silently in the midst of darkness, made vocally in the secret place of the Most High when you return to your closet to pray.

Why do you think Jesus admonished the disciples to pray in secret? Do you think it was only to teach them the lesson of humility? We expect that disciples of Christ who have come this far on the Path understand humility; therefore the teaching is for the understanding of the necessity of secrecy when you are applying the alchemical laws of the great masters of the White Brotherhood, which were vouchsafed even then to the disciples.

Jesus knew well of the Sanhedrin and of the Pharisees and the Sadducees lurking, waiting to take him, waiting to also take the disciples who would be identified with him. And therefore he taught them the science of the spoken Word. He taught them how to pray, but he said, "Pray in secret; and thy Father which seeth in secret shall reward thee openly."[8] Openly in manifestation in the marts of the world you will see the results of your alchemy.

Saint Germain On Alchemy, the bible of the Keeper of the Flame! Saint Germain wrote that dissertation on alchemy[9] that you would read and reread and inculcate in your consciousness, precept by precept, the formulas of alchemy so that you might transform the waters of the astral quadrant into the wine of the Spirit, that you might be the action of the Maltese cross and the holy amethyst, that you yourself might be that holy precipitator of will—the will to be truth.

Legions of the Cosmic Christ Fill Washington, D.C.

I come by your authority, and the authority of your invocation fulfills the Law—as Above, so below. You, then, have widened the opening for the entering into the planes of Matter of legions of the Cosmic Christ. You have bored a hole through that density of mankind's selfishness and self-indulgence, and we will pass through that opening and we will take our stand.

We will fill this city as the throat chakra of America! We will fill this city with millions of angels who will stand guard to strip mankind of all that is less than the Christ consciousness. And I tell you this: of a truth, some of you, ere these days have passed, will look into the streets of the city as though you beheld the hillsides of the world encamped roundabout with the hosts of the Lord. And your vision will be transferred into a new level, and you will suddenly look up and see the warriors of Peace, legions of Victory, legions of the Faithful and True.[10]

And do not be surprised if they are dressed according to the dress of the revolutionaries of America, for the hosts of the Lord come identifying with the way of freedom. They come to celebrate the freedom charged from the heart of Saint Germain two hundred years ago. They come, for they have identified themselves as Americans of the Spirit—Americans as a term that means far more than the narrowness of a nationalism that does not look beyond itself. [They are] Americans in the sense that they know the fiery destiny of the children of Israel who have gathered on this soil to forge an identity in the I AM THAT I AM.

The I AM Race

Know ye not that ye are of the twelve tribes of the house of Israel? When these twelve tribes were scattered and went forth to the four corners of the earth, their incarnation was among all peoples. These peoples are numbered among those who are in England and Scandinavia, the Germanic peoples, those of the Mediterranean, the Russian people and those who have covered the face of the earth with the very special vibration of the understanding of ascended master law that was written in their inward parts long ago when they were with Moses, and long before that when they were with Sanat Kumara.

The children of Israel are of every race and nation and religion. They are not confined to any one race. This is the I AM Race. The I AM Race is one with every Keeper of the Flame; there is no distinction. The children of Israel are the sons and daughters of God who have appeared again and again throughout the ages.

We look upon your profiles. We look into your auras. We see you as you came out of Egypt, out of the land of bondage, as you compromised not the flame of freedom, as you were willing to surrender all possessions, all comfortability, all way of life that was known to move toward the unknown. That record is within you.

Thus, this is the new nation of the people of Israel conceived in liberty. This is liberty: to know the truth that the truth might make you free.

I AM Pallas Athena. I AM Greek. I AM Roman. I AM freeborn. I AM a member of every nation. I AM an American. From this day and forevermore, I claim you for the cause of truth because you have made that cause your own. In the living flame of truth, I am grateful for your love of truth, of liberty, for your courage and your self-sacrifice. I am grateful, and I bow before the flame of truth within you. And I will use that flame to light a nation and to light a world!

Messenger's Comments:

Our joy is very great in the presence of one so devoted to truth. I feel redeemed, for as I walked among our people in these days and looked into their faces, I have seen the record in many faces of the compromise of truth. I have seen people whose lives are comfortable rather than truthful, who would sooner compromise truth than become uncomfortable. Many of you have made yourselves uncomfortable for truth. As Morya says, "The trek upward is worth the inconvenience." It is not always convenient to be a Keeper of the Flame.

THE STATUE OF
THE GODDESS OF FREEDOM

Armed Freedom, a statue depicting the Goddess of Freedom, crowns the dome of the United States Capitol. The statue, which has come to be known as the Statue of Freedom, portrays the goddess dressed in flowing robes, her right hand upon a sheathed sword, her left hand holding a wreath and a shield. Her head is covered by a helmet encircled with stars and surmounted by a crest composed of an eagle's head and feathers.

Few details are available about the inception of this remarkable work of American art. The artist, Thomas Crawford, sometime between 1855 and 1856 received "an invitation" from Captain Montgomery Meigs, chief engineer of the Capitol, to design the statue. Crawford, one of the foremost American sculptors of his time, had already been commissioned by Meigs to design other works in the Capitol, the most notable of which is the pediment in the Senate wing, which portrays the emergence of a great civilization in America triumphant over a barbaric way of life.

In 1855 Crawford was at work on the doors for the entrance to the House and the Senate wings of the Capitol; but before the doors were completed, the artist had begun sketching an "Armed Freedom" at the invitation of Meigs. His sketch eventually resulted in the 19-foot bronze figure that stands upon the Capitol dome.

Though the particular impetus of inspiration for *Armed Freedom* is not known, Crawford, in general, was a highly inspired artist. He is reported to have kept a room above his studio full of small clay sketches and sculptural ideas that came to him while he was working on larger projects. "The flow of his ideas was of such force and insistence that he often had to stop work on his monuments to dash off these little models. Sculptural ideas seemed 'to rise spontaneously and intuitively at Crawford's bidding. He hit off his marble epics as a poet would turn a graceful stanza,'" wrote historian Albert G. Gardner. And he himself wrote, "I regret that I have not a hundred hands to keep pace with the workings of my mind."

His inspiration saw him through at least two bouts with an eye tumor, which eventually led to his death in 1857, just shortly after he completed the model of *Armed Freedom*. He is said to have been in "severe agony" during the final months of his work. The statue was cast between 1860 and 1863 by Clark Mills, another American artist, in a foundry just three miles from the Capitol. Though the Civil War had broken out in 1861, President Lincoln is known to have insisted that work on the Capitol dome—to him a symbol of national solidarity—continue.

Finally, on December 2, 1863, *Armed Freedom* was enshrined atop the Capitol dome. The president watched as the last section of the statue was raised into place, and the event was heralded by a 35-gun salute.

On November 23, 1975, Saint Germain placed the flame of freedom in the heart of this statue. He said: "I select the monument, the focal point for the enshrining of freedom; and I place that focus of freedom in the heart of America, in the very heart chakra of the Goddess of Freedom reigning over the Capitol building of the United States. And there the heart chakra of the Divine Mother shall broadcast the fires of freedom from the crystal of the heart, from the twelve fiery focal points of the mandala of her crystal. So shall freedom from the twelve hierarchies of the Sun go forth and beam that arc of light to the heart of the Statue of Liberty."

4

RELEASING THE FLAME OF FREEDOM ENSHRINED IN THE CAPITALS OF THE NATIONS

A Dictation by the Goddess of Freedom

I come in the flaming presence of the hosts of the Lord! I come surrounded by the forces of freedom! I AM the flame of freedom! I AM the Goddess of Freedom! I AM the consciousness of the fullness of the feminine potential of the freedom of the Godhead. I travel through the cosmos surrounded by legions of freedom.

Armed Freedom I am called. When one has the flame of cosmic accountability for cosmic freedom, one does not remain unarmed. I come bearing in my right hand the sheathed sword and in my left the shield of armour and the laurel wreath of victory. Upon my head, the five-pointed stars I carry are for the victory of evolutions and lifewaves, testing in the fire of the secret rays that flame of freedom that must first be disciplined within ere it can be the disciplined manifestation of life without. The eagle of Sirius is my signet and my crown, feathers as flames of fire from the God Star, adornment of the feminine ray, protection of the crown chakra of the Mother who has realized the flame of Father.

In my heart there burns a fire, a fire augmented by the fires of Saint Germain. And I stand in the presence of this land. I stand with the hosts of the Lord encamped round about, intensifying the action of the light of freedom enshrined by Saint Germain in the capitals of the nations.[1] Therefore my cosmic momentum of freedom reigns as the love fires of a nation and every nation. And from that sun of even pressure within my heart, a million rays of light [go forth], a million billion rays of light contacting souls evolving on Terra, contacting the focuses in the capitals of the nations.

I Release the Energy of Mother

I come to release the light of Saint Germain by the thrust of the power of the feminine ray. For I, too, am the Shakti of the God of Freedom. I release the energy of Mother for every ascended and cosmic being who has espoused the flame of freedom and who has mastered the masculine ray of freedom and is releasing that ray of the Spirit into Mater in this hour of the grand culmination of life in so many systems of worlds.

Brothers and sisters of freedom, be the equals of the Gods—not out of pride but out of humility. Because you are conceived in God, you have a claim to the flame which I AM; therefore, in potential, you have equality with all of the sons and daughters of God of a cosmos. In actuality, there is no equality in hierarchy. Neither can there be equality in the evolutions of any lifewave, for all are fitted by the Master Planner of life into this blueprint of the gems and diadems that compose the armour of the Goddess of Freedom.

And the laurel wreath—it is the crown of the victors, the victors who have conquered their selfishness, their sensuality, their darkness and their self-deception. It is the flow of fire of the crown of twelve stars of the Divine Mother.[2] I come carrying that laurel wreath, and I am ready to place it upon the heads of the sons and daughters of God in this age who have made their calling and their election sure[3] in the victory of the sacred fire of the twelve solar hierarchies.

Single Souls Who Turn the Tide

I AM Mother. I AM Mother in all of life. I came to be enshrined in America upon the insistence of the great patriarch, exponent of the Father and the Law and the principle, your own Abraham Lincoln. It was he who determined that the statue of *Armed Freedom* should be erected even in the dark hours of the Civil War. So he saw that "the hand that rocks the cradle is the hand that rules the world."[4] He saw in Mother the liberation of a mighty people. He saw in Mother the synthesis of all of the separatists, of all of those who cannot find the way to converge in the flame of Liberty. Great champion of all peoples, in the heart of this president of the United States of America there yet burns the flame, the flame for the resolution of the division of the Union.

What gratitude from hierarchy above and below to those single individuals who have stood and stood through all and have yet been found standing, defending freedom, defending a concept of principle, of Christhood, of nationhood, of the mandala of the thirteen. These individuals are not numberless, but they are single souls who come forth at the calling of the Great White Brotherhood in every age, in every dark night of the soul of nations and kingdoms and continents—single souls who turn the tide in the entire evolution and generation of darkness that hangs over the land.

Many Souls to Whom the Calling Is Given

Now we enter into the company of many souls to whom the calling is given. We come in the midst of many who have in the heart the flame of love, the flame of devotion and, above all, an understanding of cosmic law. For mankind have formulated laws. Yes, they have evolved systems and ideologies, but these will fail when they are not in conformity to cosmic law, to the will of God, and to the inner blueprint of the soul of individuals and nations. Build as they will, build as they will, the empire builders will stand to see all of their creations come to naught when that fire that tries every man's work is released; and that work that is not the work of God must be burned,[5] must be leveled, and mankind are called to begin again.

I survey the future. I survey the opportunities of mankind and I say to you, Do you think that the ascended masters' concepts are limited to those ideologies and political and economic theories that are evolved by your current intellectuals and the elite of science and government? Do you think that the Great White Brotherhood must be confined to such idiocy? Do you think that we do not know the Law, that we do not see the handwriting upon the wall?

Do you think that the principles taught by the Lord Buddha and the Lord Christ do not remain to the present hour as the foundation of all government and the flow of abundance in the economies of the nations? Do you think that because mankind have the backing of millions of souls and of supply for their theories that this makes them more powerful than the hosts of the LORD and the edicts of the Lords of Karma?

Factor No. 1: The Force of the Lightbearers in This Age

The question is, will those individuals who are taking mankind on the course, the juggernaut course, of their own karmic self-destruction be challenged, or will they be allowed to take yet other millions of souls down the path to that self-destruction? Well I tell you, with all of their planning for world takeover, world government, world religion and expansion beyond the stars, with all of their planning and their plots, they have not taken into account a number of factors, which I would call to your attention, not the least of which is the force, the very real force of the lightbearers in this age, of the sons and daughters of God who will not be limited by their doctrines and their dogmas, who will not be separated into separate camps, who will remember the words of the Angel of Unity, "Remember, ye are brethren!"

Sons and daughters of God who will not forget the flame of love, which is the crux of overcoming in this age, have you noticed that they have forgotten love—love of the people, love of one another, love of Christ, love of the culture of the Mother, love of the holy children? Love is glaringly absent from the dry formulas of the theoreticians of the day, and therefore they will be as tinkling cymbal and sounding brass[6]; they will be as naught. For without the flame of love, they will be self-consumed by the cancer of hatred that they have spawned over the nations of the earth.

One, then: The force of the lightbearers has not been reckoned with; it is not even spoken of in this land. The Great White Brotherhood, the teachings of the ascended masters, the messengers and the chelas of the Law are not identified as a force—political, religious, economic or cultural. So let it be. The Darjeeling Council will announce one of these days its plan for the spreading abroad of mankind's awareness of this force.

Factor No. 2: The Earth Is a Finite Sphere

Second: They have not reckoned with the fact that the earth is a finite sphere. In their unquenchable greed for conquest, economic conquest, and the building of the empire of Nimrod and the Tower of Babel,[7] they have not reckoned with the fact that there are finite resources, finite land, finite air and waters and all energies accessible to every nation on earth.

Projections have been made by the Club of Rome,[8] by other scientists and bodies of those who have studied this situation, even using their computers to project the fate of the earth. They have all concluded that after the year 2000, in the coming decades, the resources will be exhausted. Whether or not their conclusions are accurate depends on vital decisions that must be made by those who have the flame of hierarchy and of the Law and an understanding of cosmic purpose. The race of arms is a futile race, for by the time anyone is ready to use nuclear power, that power will indeed be obsolete.

O mankind, the collision course of the blind leaders of the blind in East and West is such an obvious folly that if we were not cosmic beings with the all-seeing eye, we would wonder why the intelligent people, the citizens, the educated citizens of the world would not rise up to overthrow these insane leaders who have not reckoned with the teaching of the Buddha.

Factor No. 3: The Purpose of Existence and Life

And this, my third point: They have not reckoned with the purpose of existence and life—not economic escalation, not the continuation of the production of goods and more goods, not the continuation of a conquest of lands and peoples, but the development of the Christ consciousness, the development of the Buddhic light. And therefore they are wrong, one and all, because they yet retain desire that is not the desire of God to be God, which is the only legitimate desire. They retain that attachment of which Lord Buddha spoke: attachment to the fruit of action.

They are attached by greed, by gluttony, by the beast that ascends out of the bottomless pit of carnal desire for more and more, failing to nourish the souls of the people, failing to train mankind in the development of the heart. Even your own historian Toynbee predicted the rise and fall of civilizations on the basis of the fact that when the material expansion reaches a certain point, unless the people go within for spiritual development that civilization is doomed.[9] And this, *this,* my friends, is the cause of the failure of every civilization that has gone down since the early days of Atlantis, this fact: that the greed for material conquest and materialism overtakes and strangles the hunger of souls for reality, for freedom and for the flame of freedom.

Youth of the Aquarian Age—Future Leaders of the Land

Do you not understand, then, that few among the American people, the youth of the Aquarian age who are turning to the things of the Spirit, to the development of self-mastery and the discipline of the path of initiation—these are the ones who have tuned in to the delicate winds of the age of Aquarius? These are on the track. These are the future leaders of the land if they themselves can be rescued from the false ideologies of the fallen ones, if they can be separated out from the false teachers, who also are motivated. Their motive is manipulation; and manipulation in any form is never freedom, but bondage.

Therefore, ask yourself, are you the object of someone's manipulation? Or are you at the mercy of your own carnal mind and are you powerless to stand in defense of Saint Germain because you are in bondage in one form or another to the carnal mind and its greed and its endless desires to acquire, to achieve in the cult of success?

Do you think that the cult of success is only in the West? You have only to look at the grab for land and territory by those who follow the Marxist doctrine. See, then, how the Communist world is also besieged by the cult of success—which they decry—and they go hither and there to claim lands and peoples for the camp of World Communism.

The evils in society are widespread. They are not confined to East or West. They are simply on the opposite sides of vibration: in the West, the perversion of the Christ consciousness; in the East, the perversion of the Holy Spirit. And therefore polemics, endless political polemics, and never the release of soul freedom.

This Is the Moment for the Development of the Within

And so I say to you this: that unless all the nations of the world will make an about-face and cease their struggling for control of one another and of peoples and masses and wealth and the ecology and the resources, unless one and all they turn within to realize that this is the moment for the development of the Within...

This is the moment to let materialism be. Let economic progress be. Let there be a leveling-off. Let there be a return to the life that is humble, that is simple, that is without so many needs to continually gratify the senses.

I appeal, then, to Keepers of the Flame. For unless this occur, you see, the world, East and West, is headed for that collision course when the resources will run out, when the landed areas for which the political powers are vying will be no more, when the finite world will suddenly come to a screeching halt. But mankind's desires will not come to a halt, and a sudden stopping of the collision course at that moment will not be possible. Unless, then, there be the reversing of the tide of goals and aims, there can only be the futility and the failure of civilizations.

The Fate of the Human Race

The fallen ones have projected the degeneration and the fall of America. Well, they themselves are not far behind, for in the history of all the great powers of the world, the rise and fall is over a mere few centuries. Let them look, then, to their own internal weaknesses. Let them see that it is the fate of mankind with which they ought to be concerned—not the fate of the Soviet Union or China or the Western powers but the fate of the individual and the fate of the total human race.

I call, then, to Keepers of the Flame and I tell you, from my analysis of reality and the events of the hour, I can report to you not out of some idealistic hope, some impractical hope, but based on cosmic analysis of current trends: I can tell you that it is yet possible for the individual Keeper of the Flame to reverse the course of civilization and its downward trends in every nation.

Any and every nation that disregards the teachings of Christ and Buddha, that disregards morality and the principles of morality in domestic and foreign policy—any and every such nation is doomed to failure. Where you see, then, a nation compromised by those who have not the individual mores and standards of the ascended masters and therefore who cannot project these on a national and an international scale, that nation that is so beset by such leaders can look only to the people of light, to the people who have the teachings of the Great White Brotherhood, for liberation.

For I tell you this: that those who have a part of the knowledge of the Law, who have been separated into right- and left-wing camps, these individuals are lacking in the know-how—the essential science of the spoken Word, the science of the chakras, the science of the teachings of the ascended masters—that comes from the heart of the Mother. And therefore, though they see the decline and the fall of civilizations and of the ramparts of freedom, they are impotent; they are powerless to do anything to turn the tide.

Be Staunch in the Cosmic Honor Flame

There is only one people left who has a power to work any change on Terra—the people who claim the name of God, I AM THAT I AM, the true initiates of the sacred fire and those who are a part, by heritage, by conviction, of the twelve tribes of Israel. Let them, then, challenge every policy, every doctrine and every dogma, wherever it is found in Church and State, that is not in keeping with the principles of Christ and Buddha. Let every Keeper of the Flame be staunch in the cosmic honor flame, in the understanding that where there is compromise, the least compromise, in the individual life of the Keeper of the Flame, there will be failure. *There,* whatever project, whatever plan you are engaged in is doomed to fail.

You know that many of the great churches and movements of the world have pursued that Machiavellian concept of the end justifying the means. Keepers of the Flame dare not! People of America, of Russia, of China, of Africa and Europe—they dare not! Let every leader in every nation upon earth hear the Word of the Goddess of Freedom! To compromise the Law is to seal your pact with death; for that which compromises truth and cosmic law is the inception of a degeneration spiral and a disintegration spiral, and it is doomed to failure from the start.

Be Content to Build upon the Platform of Truth

Let mankind be content to build slowly, but to build upon truth. Let the nations of the earth be content to build upon the platform of truth. Let them place first the education of the masses of the people not according to this or that historical revision, for the revisionists who have rewritten the history of the world are feeding that fodder to the children. But let the teachings of the Great White Brotherhood be taught to the children of the world. Let these teachings go forth and let them be the teachings of the mastery of the self.

Let the universities of the Spirit and those institutions for the education of the Holy Child be raised up in the name of the Christ and the Buddha, the Father and the Mother. Let the emphasis be placed on the development of the soul, on the development of the threefold flame, on the transmutation of world and individual karma that so clouds the issues in these times. Let education be for the overcoming of carnal desire.

You think that I speak utopian words and that this will never come to pass on earth. Why do you doubt? Why do you fear when I have told you that I have read the record and I have seen that individual Keepers of the Flame can make all the difference, that you can turn the tide? And I will tell you why this is so true: because the world is full of good people, people who have God in the very core of being, people who will respond when you teach them, when you give them the understanding of the Law, when you present to them all of the facts, and they can exercise free will in the name of freedom.

I tell you, it must come to pass that those who have the light acknowledge the supremacy of the light, that those who have the light understand that the victory is in their heart and in their hands. Let every Keeper of the Flame, then, be Armed Freedom! Let your defense be truth and honor. Let your defense be the sacred fire. Let your defense be your integrity, which is your integration with the God flame. And let the nations of the free world fear not to defend their land against those who would come with tyranny and despotism to take that land.

Let fire be the answer to the fire of the fallen ones! Let it be a high degree of concentration of the understanding of the law of the Mother, and let it be correspondingly accounted for in the planes of the physical by those armed forces who are in the physical plane the outpicturing of the hosts of the LORD.

By the Action of the Feminine Ray I Release Freedom!

I AM Armed Freedom! My sword is the sword of peace. It is the sacred Word. Now I stand before you and I take my sword from its sheath and I send forth the lightning and the thunder of the Divine Mother! And I touch every focus on Terra where Saint Germain has placed the focus of the light of freedom, and by the action of the feminine ray I release freedom! I release freedom as the Mother flame into the hearts of the people of the earth, in every nation and city and town and hamlet. So all shall feel, by the fires of the Mother, freedom as never before.

Do not be surprised, then, what this freedom will produce across the face of the earth. For once that flame is kindled it cannot be turned back, and free people everywhere will rise to liberate those who are in bondage to the fallen ones. First, then, let the American people rise and liberate themselves from the media and its mass hypnosis, from the bondage that they have to the material senses. Let them be free of the psychic nonsense and the witchcraft and the black magic. *This* is freedom, freedom to defend cosmic purpose and God-government and a God-economy throughout the earth!

Before the American people can understand what it means to be the cosmic honor guard of an entire lifewave, they must know soul freedom. Thus Keepers of the Flame are on the march for soul freedom. They are the great liberators of the chakras of America. And they will teach the people and the children and the seekers and the young and old alike; they will teach them the law of their inheritance in the true flame of freedom.

Think of the Individual—Think One with God

Think not of the masses but think of the individual, for when you think of the masses you do err. Only the individual is real. The individual may not be lost in the mass consciousness; it is not the will of God or of his Christ. When you think upon individual potential, then and only then will you have cosmic freedom and the deliverance of the planet.

Think, then, one with God! Contemplate with me now yourself as an individualization of the flame of freedom. Think of yourself multiplied by the action of this body of the Lord. Then think of Abraham Lincoln as he stood alone in the White House, as he stood alone and withstood all of the rebellion of the fallen ones who sought to separate out of the Union and to defy all the fiery core of the Father-Mother God in the original thirteen—the mandala of initiation of Christ and his apostles.

Think how he had encountered already the international bankers, the Illuminati and those who sought to use the Civil War to take over America for their schemes of power and control. Think how he defied all of those who had their selfish interests. Think of how he stood for the flame of Mother. Think of how that president was willing to lay down his life for the love of the Mother and her children, and then ask yourself: "Can I not do the same? Can I do less? And if I will do the same, will not the same hosts of the Lord buoy up my soul in the light of victory?"

This is the land of the Woman clothed with the Sun. This is the land of the coming of the Manchild, which is the birth of the Christ consciousness in the individual. This is the land where the serpent, as the great dragon, comes forth to make war with the Woman and with the remnant of her seed. Think, then, of the individuals who loved not their lives unto the death,[10] who were willing by love and love alone to live a life of sacrifice in defense of the Mother and her children. You are those children for whom these patriots gave their lives and fortunes and their sacred honor. You are the children of the Mother. Now it is your time, now it is your space to walk the path of initiation.

In the honor and in the integrity of Abraham Lincoln, I AM come! And do you know that that gifted sculptor who carved *Armed Freedom,* Thomas Crawford, did not live to see the raising of the statue on the nation's Capitol but was taken from the screen of life because he was willing to give his life to focus the matrix of the Cosmic Mother of Freedom? That cost him his life, and he knew it in his soul, yet he was willing to give his life that the Goddess of Freedom might reign from the Capitol of the United States of America.

Keepers of the Flame, Give Answer to Your God This Day!

Keepers of the Flame: saints and pilgrims and soldiers have walked the way of the defense of freedom for lesser causes. Now in the ultimate cause of cosmic freedom and of the holding of Terra in the flame of freedom for ages to come, can you, I ask you, can you do any less than these who have gone before you? I ask it in the name of Almighty God and I say, give answer to your God this day! And see how by your answer God will reinforce your light and your life, God will send the reinforcements of Armed Freedom!

I AM in the victory of your life when and only when you consecrate that life unflinchingly without compromise to world and individual freedom. I AM the Goddess of Freedom! And my focus shall remain in this nation until the children of Israel shall have fulfilled the cosmic destiny of their inner calling.

Hail, freedom! Hail, freedom! Hail, freedom!

Comments by the Messenger:
If God Be for Us, Who Can Be Against Us?

Our gratitude flows to the Goddess of Freedom. I must tell you while I have the memory to tell you that seeing the Goddess of Freedom is seeing a vision of freedom that I can never remember having seen before. I have been in love with the statue of Armed Freedom from the moment I laid eyes upon the statue. But to see the real Cosmic Mother of Freedom, to have her in our midst, is to bow in humility before a power, a wisdom, a love, a purity, an energy that we have not yet begun to comprehend. All we can say is, "If God be for us, who can be against us?"[11]

5

THE RESPONSIBILITY OF FREEDOM

Elizabeth Clare Prophet

The First Amendment

In this chapter we are going to discuss the four freedoms set forth in the First Amendment to the Constitution of the United States—how they apply to the path of initiation, what they mean to a free people, and how they are essential to the expansion of the flame in the heart.

The First Amendment states that "Congress shall make no law respecting an establishment of religion, or prohibiting the free exercise thereof; or abridging the freedom of speech, or of the press; or the right of the people peaceably to assemble, and to petition the Government for a redress of grievances."

Our founding fathers considered these four freedoms to be the most basic rights of man. They express the free will of the soul—the free will of the soul to conquer in the four quadrants of Matter, to conquer in the cycles of the cosmic clock. Without these freedoms, we would not have the opportunity to express free will in the four lower bodies and in the four frequencies of fire, air, water, and earth.

Great Rights, Inviolable and Sacred

During the Virginia Constitutional Ratifying Convention in June of 1788, Patrick Henry, in fighting for these rights to be immediately annexed to the Constitution, spoke of "those great rights which ought, in all countries, to be held inviolable and sacred." He said: "All men are by nature free and independent, and have certain inherent rights, of which, when they enter into society, they cannot by any compact derive or divest their posterity. We have a set of maxims of the same spirit, which must be beloved by every friend to liberty, to virtue, to mankind."[1]

Saint Germain, the sponsoring master of the seventh ray and the seventh, Aquarian, age, founded the United States of America and inspired her Constitution to enshrine the flame of freedom in the hearts of a people chosen to bear that flame in Christ's name to the nations of the earth. His great conception for America was that she, the Motherland, would provide souls advancing in the way of self-mastery the opportunity to walk the path of initiation to master the four sacred freedoms as the four sides in the Great Pyramid of Life.

There are few countries left in the world today where these freedoms are guaranteed in practice, whose people are at liberty to pursue the path of soul freedom by the expression of individual free will. These rights have been called "the very heartbeat of this great Republic,"[2] and indeed they proceed from the heart chakra of a people whose one goal ought to be, if it is not, to attain their God-mastery through the self-mastery of the Christ consciousness.

Freedom to Be the Christ

What is your Christ consciousness? Your Christ consciousness is your awareness that your True Self is the Christ. What is, who is Christ? Christ is the second Person of the Trinity. He is the Light, or the Word, of God, who incarnated, was made flesh, in Jesus. This Christ is called "the only begotten Son of God." What does this mean?

First of all it does not mean that God had only one Son and the rest of us are bastards. That's the lie of the fallen ones that has all but destroyed the true doctrine of Jesus Christ, stripped it of any practical power for Christian or Jew, and divided America against herself. So let's begin at the beginning. Who is the only begotten Son of God? What does the term *Christ* really mean to you?

It means that the one God manifests himself to us in three ways: As the Father, the *one* Father, he individualizes himself to us in the I AM Presence—seen by Moses as the Person in the midst of the sacred fire, who talked with him man to man, seen by Ezekiel as the Lord God who appeared out of the fire infolding itself and a brightness with a rainbow round about it, who made him Watchman as unto the House of Israel.[3]

This first Person of God gave us his name I AM THAT I AM that we might call upon the Father and know him personally as the Gentle Presence ever with us. We worship God the Father in two ways—first as the Almighty, the Creator of heaven and earth, the Supreme Being, the universal Mind, and second in the intimacy of this very personal "I AM" Presence of himself that he has manifested with each one of us. All the saints and seers have communed with him in this inner nucleus, the "secret place" of the Most High, abiding under this "shadow" of the Almighty, as the Psalmist called the I AM Presence.[4] This term "shadow" conveys the concept of the "replica."

God is one. This we affirm. This we understand. But he, the Infinite One, in the desire to maintain a one-to-one relationship with his children, has manifested his Presence to each one as a duplicate forcefield, or focus. A million, billion copies, but only one original. A thousand times a thousand roses, but only one blueprint. Yet the original is in every copy. The blueprint is in every rose.

No greater gift could he conceive than the gift of Self—the God Self. Our Father has given to us individually the gift of his Person. He has made it your very own. And you may call it your very own beloved I AM Presence. Through it, through the radiant shining of this the glorious one, God is ever-present with us. This is the meaning of Emmanuel—"God with us."

This divine image is the same Self who is the God of very gods on high focused below upon the screen of life again and again and again. And wherever the image of himself appears, there he is in full Force and Spirit and Love. When you adore your I AM Presence, you are adoring that portion of himself that God has given to you. That portion is his All. The Great Giver could give no less. And he expects the same of you—that he may become, where you are, the All-in-all.

God called the name of his Presence, I AM THAT I AM, and said it was a "memorial" to all generations. A memorial is something that helps us to remember someone. God gave us the individualized

Presence of himself, as a permanent atom of himself, so that we would never forget him—no matter how far we would wander in the Matter spheres.

He also gave us the name or sacred Word, which would release the energy of the nucleus of our permanent atom of being to meet our every need, so that we would never forget his love as an active force in our lives revealing the true nature of his identity day by day. This is his memorial so that we will remember that he is the eternal God, the one LORD who dwelleth in the heavens and sitteth upon his throne.

When we call to the Presence, we make contact with the Most High. They are one and the same. Me and my shadow. "I and my Father are one."[5] Within the dimensions and coordinates of the Spirit-Matter universes, we behold multitudinous manifestations of the One. Standing in infinity we behold infinity as One, for we have become that One.

Now, what of the only begotten Son of God? Well, the second way in which God manifests himself to us is in the Person of the Son. Is there only one Son, just as there is only one Father? Yes. This Son is the manifest matrix of the offspring of God. And what does that mean? It means that when God decided to create the multitudes of his children, he made an original pattern—patterned after the original, himself. "Like father, like son," they say. One Son begotten of himself is the Christ, the Lord, or Law, of all of his offspring. This Son is made in the image and in the likeness of His Father. All souls who have ever been born out of the white light of the Logos have been fashioned in this Image and in this likeness.[6]

The Christ is the archetype of every son and daughter of God. The Christ is the infinite Son with infinite expression of himself manifesting as the unique and unusual identities of billions upon billions of souls. The Christ is the inner pattern of the Real Self that the soul/self is destined to outpicture. The mystery of this "hidden man of the heart,"[7] as Saint Peter knew him, is unveiled when the Word is made flesh.

What does that mean? It means that God in the second Person of the Trinity can be known only when a soul, by intense devotion to the LORD, draws down into the chalice of the self the light of the Son. When a soul through progressive evolutionary embodiments in the

5 • The Responsibility of Freedom

Matter planes draws down greater and greater momentums of that light by more and more loving of God in every part of his beautiful self-expression in worlds beyond worlds, then the soul becomes fused with the light it has adored, the Christ who is its archetype. This fusion of the nonpermanent particle, the soul (or electron), with the permanent particle, the Christ pattern or prototype within the nucleus, is called the incarnation.

In the moment when the soul surrenders the lesser self to be the cradle for the Greater Self, suddenly the soul discovers that Self to be its true Self. This Self-awareness in the Second Person of the Trinity is called *the Christ consciousness.* Are there many Christ consciousnesses? Are there Lords many and Gods many? No. There is only one universal or Cosmic Christ consciousness, individualized for each soul of God in the Person of the Christ Self.

There is only one Christ consciousness into which we all drink. This path of Christ-identification is one of Christ-magnification. "Let God be magnified" was the Psalmist's cry. "My soul doth magnify the Lord!" was the Virgin's reply. This path leads not to many Christs but to many souls who have fused with the one Christ—the only begotten Son of God.

God created the Son for the magnification of his Presence dwelling in and among his people. The Father, the I AM Presence, remains the Spirit in Spirit, the Incorruptible One, the Polestar of Being, the Daystar from on High. But the Word is made flesh that the people may behold his glory and choose by free will to love it, to serve it, and most importantly, to become it.

For two thousand years we have allowed ourselves to become accustomed to assigning that role to one individual, and therefore we have placed outside of ourselves and into another that which is basically inherent within. In order to understand the path of initiation and how our laws give us opportunity to follow that path according to individual conscience, we need to understand that we cannot assign either the Christ consciousness or the freedom to be the Christ or the steps leading to that Self-awareness to someone or something outside of ourselves. We need the four sacred freedoms in order to fulfill our individual Christhood. Those who do not understand that personal

Christhood is the goal of life and their reason for taking embodiment are the ones who most easily surrender their divine rights in exchange for paltry human rights.

The Idolatrous Generation—
Turning Over Our Responsibility to Another

We spoke this morning of the adulterous generation, and I would speak now of the idolatrous generation. Idolatry is assigning to another the God flame that is within oneself and then worshiping that other in the place of worshiping the flame within. Idolatry is attachment to the form of the one who has mastered God and mastered the Christ. Of course it may also be the elevation of Antichrist in another proportionately as one has elevated his own ego in himself.

Attachment to the form, the worship of that form, deprives us individually of that God-mastery. So we find that the adulterous generation is the compromise of the sacred fire and its misuses in the chakras. We find that the idolatrous generation is turning over our responsibility of freedom to others, whether it be to Jesus Christ or Henry Kissinger. Turning it over to another is entering into idolatry. This is what we face as our initiation in America today.

The Four Freedoms

The rights protected in the First Amendment are freedom of religion, freedom of the press, freedom of assembly, and freedom of speech. Again we take the cosmic cross of white fire of Alpha and Omega. The descending arm of the cross is Alpha, the horizontal arm is Omega. This cross defines the path of self-mastery over and over and over again.

Once we are aware of these archetypes of the path of initiation, we can define that initiation wherever we are—in our profession, in our home, in our family, in our government, in our economy. We begin to see that these necessary ingredients are the building blocks not only of the path of initiation, but of an individual life or of a nation consecrated to that path of becoming the Christ. Again it is the cosmic clock.

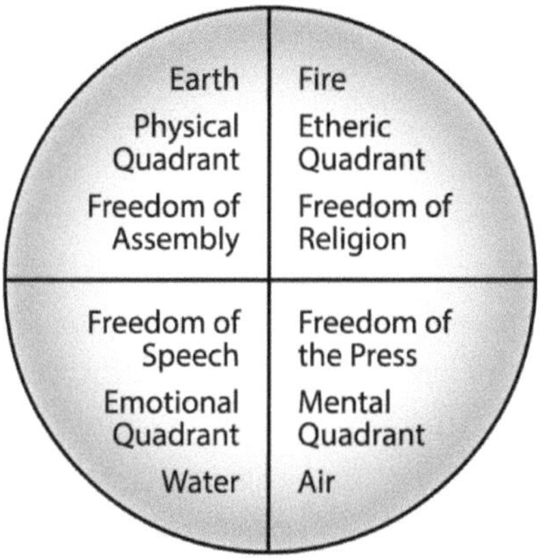

5 • The Responsibility of Freedom

Earth Physical Quadrant Freedom of Assembly	Fire Etheric Quadrant Freedom of Religion
Freedom of Speech Emotional Quadrant Water	Freedom of the Press Mental Quadrant Air

The Four Freedoms in the Four Quadrants
FIGURE 1

The Responsibility to Exercise Our Rights for the Mastery of the Four Lower Bodies

Each one of us has the responsibility to exercise each one of these rights. Some of us never do. Some of us never bother to make the choice of religion, hence to participate in the evolution of the Law in the first (etheric) quadrant of being. This is the freedom to integrate with the I AM Presence through the Word as the voice of God speaking in the halls of conscience.

Some of us never bother to make use of our opportunity for a free press through the exercise of the written Word—publishing abroad to the nations our individual conviction of our communication with the inner witness of truth. Through participation in this freedom, we gain momentum in the second (mental) quadrant. And therefore we are not exercising our right to master the flow of the Word through the mind—the vessel of the universal Mind, which was also in Christ Jesus.

Some of us never bother to exercise our freedom of assembly, and therefore to focus the unity of the Word midst the gathering together of the people to apply their hearts to a common necessity. Unless the people adopt the habit of coming together to arrive at the reason of the Logos for the resolution of family and community problems, their self-control of selfish interests atrophies and they see democracy as self-serving rather than serving the greater Self of all. This is a needed point of self-mastery in the third quadrant of being, where the subconscious surfaces through desire that must then be harnessed to selfless service, which always returns to the individual true soul gratification.

And some of us do not bother to exercise our freedom of speech, the very authority of the Word within us to forthrightly proclaim the law of liberty as it applies to human rights, divine rights and the political issues of the day. Hence we are not holding the line of individual freedom in the fourth quadrant, the physical plane.

The four lower bodies, then—etheric, mental, emotional, and physical—are the vehicles of the Christ consciousness, planes of awareness that we individually evolve as we take the trouble to exercise our freedoms and therefore our dominion over the earth. Our evolution of these four lower bodies as four planes of awareness contributes to the total planetary evolution or the collective Christ consciousness of the people. As a planetary sphere in the chain of worlds, we may rise no higher than the highest (Christ the Lord) and no lower than the lowest (the anti-Christ or anti-Lord), but we can gravitate upward and thereby influence the entire lifewaves of earth because we take an individual stand for righteousness, truth, honor, and freedom.

It is very important that we see that in order to evolve with our group karma and our group dharma—and we will be examining those words—in the mandala (the inner design) of the nation, we all have to work together to master these four freedoms. It is not enough that we master them individually; we need to master them collectively. And the collective attainment of a people is its contribution to the earth and to the family of nations. And the collective attainment of each nation or each group mandala when brought together manifests the Christ consciousness of the entire earth.

These steps cannot be skipped. We cannot skip individual self-mastery and abandon it for community or for a national purpose. We cannot skip national self-mastery and abandon it for an international mastery, because each of the steps is a component; it is a stone in the Great Pyramid that we construct as the total lifewave of this evolution of earth.

Master the Four Freedoms by the Flame within the Heart

The only way that we can master the four freedoms, the only way that we can master the four lower bodies and use these freedoms to do so, is by the action of the flame that is in the heart. The flame in the heart is called the Christ flame; it is also called the threefold flame. It is the flame of the Trinity of Father, Son, and Holy Spirit—of power, wisdom, and love.

The flame has a white-fire core and this drawing is symbolic of the actual flame. (fig. 2) People have asked me, "Is the concept of the flame a philosophical principle, an archetypal thoughtform, or is it a real and actual manifestation?" We are not dealing in symbols; we are dealing in actualities.

The Threefold Flame
The three plumes from left to right are pink, yellow and blue,
representing love, wisdom and power.
FIGURE 2

This flame is the spark of life that makes mankind separate from the animal and vegetable and mineral kingdoms. It is the potential for Godhood. This flame is the reason that you and I can become the Christ, because the Christ is already sealed within as the sacred fire. If we did not have this flame, the soul could not return to the plane of the Spirit. The threefold flame of life is the sacred fire of Almighty God burning within your breast. Feeling the kindling fire of Christ's heart in their own fiery hearts, the disciples who walked with Jesus on the road to Emmaus after our Lord's resurrection said, "Did not our hearts *burn* within us?"[8]

Unless the creation contain the spark of Creator, it cannot feel the holy fire of God's love burning within as testimony of his Presence and as point of oneness—Father in Son and Son in disciples. God is love. We can attest to this truth only by the inner flame of the heart. This spiritual fire in conflagration is the means whereby the soul transcends all elements of Matter and returns to the point of Spirit. Moses saw God self-revealed as a consuming fire. Indeed his fiery presence is all-consuming. Because it consumes all unlike itself, we must become one with the fire of our own essential Be-ness in order to become one with him.

Spirit and Matter Are One within Us

Within our microcosmic world, we experience the totality of the great Macrocosm. We have contained within ourselves what we call *Spirit* and *Matter*. Spirit and Matter are not really separate. As I said this morning, all diagrams that we show are simply an attempt to define the eternal oneness. Spirit and Matter are not separate, they are one where we are. But we sense ourselves more as Matter than as Spirit, and by magnifying—through the science of the spoken Word, through devotion to the flame—the action of Spirit, we put on and become that wholeness. Or, to put it another way, we externalize the interior light.

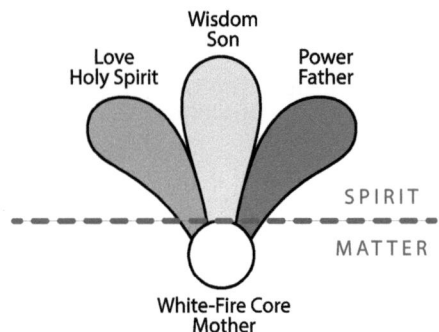

The Threefold Flame in Spirit and Matter
FIGURE 3

The threefold flame, then, is a frequency of Spirit. It is eternity, it is infinity, it is our consciousness of God, and yet it is anchored in a Matter body. The circle in the diagram symbolizes the white-fire core of the flame as the anchoring point of life in Matter. (fig. 3) The circle is always the symbol of Mother, of the purity of her fount, focused in the base-of-the-spine chakra. As the shakti, or activating principle of life, the Mother defines the Trinity of Father, Son, and Holy Spirit. Through her we discover the origin and meaning of the threefold nature of our divinity. The Mother flame activates the squaring of the circle whereby Spirit appears and reappears through Matter (or Mater). Through the white-fire core, the ritual of the materialization of the God flame takes place. The Mother light is the magnet that pulls the Trinity into Matter.

When the Son embodies the light of the Father and the Mother, he is Christ, the light and the life of the world. As the Father-Mother Person fused in the One, he is the only begotten of the light of Alpha and Omega. At that point, the Son of God is become the fullness of the Word incarnate. Thus the Sons of God, both male and female, putting on the life of Mother are becoming the shakti of the Trinity—the activating in Matter of the threefold nature of Spirit. When they embody the Trinity in triune balance and the threefold flame reflects the glory of that balance—below as it is above, they are positioned on the line of the Mother.

Building the Pyramid of Life

Now when we contemplate the mastery of the four planes and the four lower bodies, we realize we can do it only through the action of the Christ that is within us. In building the pyramid of life, each one of the four lower bodies is a side of the pyramid. The challenge of the path of initiation is to master the three elements and the fiery core of the threefold flame in each side of the pyramid, which means in each of the four lower bodies. (fig. 4)

And so the threefold flame becomes the center once again of the cosmic clock. And the dot in the center symbolizes the Guru or God-man, the Christed one—the one anointed with the Christ consciousness—whose light contains the sum total in soul attainment of the twelve initiations that we pass through on the periphery of the clock as on the periphery of our life. (Here we deal with the outer consciousness as the effect of causes set in motion in the subconscious and superconscious self. But in the center of the circle we are God-centered in the attainment of our highest self.)

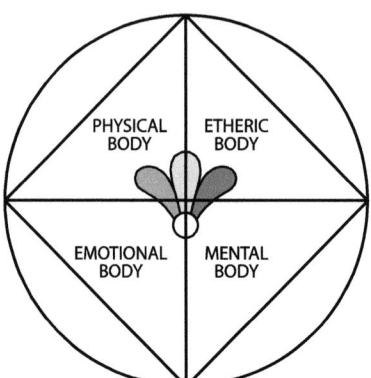

The Four Sides of the Pyramid of Life
FIGURE 4

You know, some people are stronger mentally than they are physically, some people have more emotions than they have memory. This is because of an unequal development of the threefold flame in the four lower bodies. It is not that the threefold flame is not there; it is that we have not made the vehicle of consciousness its instrument.

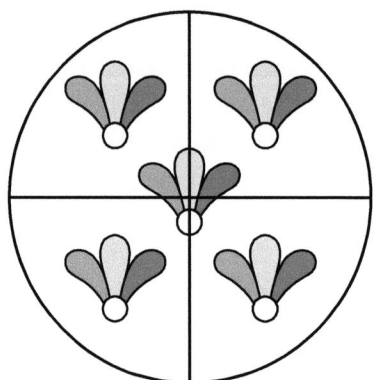

The Threefold Flame in the Four Lower Bodies
FIGURE 5

And so those who have a Christ consciousness, a development of the mind that was in Christ Jesus,[9] will have developed a greater self-awareness—an "intelling" or intelligence of the I AM in the mental quadrant. But Jesus' mind was also expressed in the mastery of heart and soul. This gave him the strength of the overcomers in the control of the desires, the will, the water—in the stilling of the tempest and the casting out of demons from the emotional body.

Physical mastery is not merely athletic prowess but the dexterity of spirit to precipitate physically in the real world of actualities what is in soul and in Spirit. In sum, the threefold flame and its activating principle in the Mother must be brought to every level of challenge in every area of our lives. The God flame is truly the heart and soul, the very life of every endeavor.

The Analysis of the Self on the Path of Initiation

We must see, then, that a bit of self-discovery is necessary—the analysis of the self and where the self is on the path of initiation. We need to face our weaknesses as well as our strengths. Examining our memory body, which is also called the etheric body, holding as it does the blueprint of the other three bodies, we need to probe our origins as well as our motives and desires. Do we remember the laws of God, which he has written in our inward parts?[10] Or is our memory nothing more than a nostalgia, an empathy with human conditions and human events—a looking back to Sodom? Is this all our memory contains? Or can we go back beyond this life, can we contact the Law, and thence the Lawgiver and the understanding of the Logos within?

The attainment of the soul in the etheric body is the mastery of the fire element. The application of the sacred fire by the ascended and unascended masters of the Great White Brotherhood often manifests as all manner of miracles. Both Jesus Christ and Saint Germain have left a record in numerous incarnations of their attainment of this power of miracles by the mastery of the sacred fire. When we allow our memory body and its energies to be used in sustaining the memories of our human creation, layer on layer like sedimentary rock, then we are not making way for the memory of God. Entering into the memory of God, we have a much greater awareness of true Being. That awareness can include the cosmos.

Jesus had that memory. He said, "Before Abraham was, I AM,"[11] because the I AM of his life—and of your life—was present in all of creation and has the memory of it. That memory is in the subconscious as well as the superconscious, but we do not call it forth, because we have chosen by free will to dwell upon the more recent memories of this life. We have also chosen to block out other more painful and complicating memories of our past lives, and this, too, as blockage prevents us from going beyond to the higher memory of our beginningness in God.

Freedom of Religion: Freedom to Bind Ourselves to God

The action of the threefold flame transmutes the unreality of the passing scene while preserving everything in life that is worthwhile. It is through the threefold flame that we exercise the four freedoms, beginning with freedom of religion, freedom to bind ourselves to God —*religio,* "to bind." That is our freedom of religion—freedom to be where God is, to know God as he is, to walk with him, to talk with him, to focus his energies, to focus the mastery of the sacred fire.

We look at ourselves today as a nation, as an American people. We are a religious people. We have many churches, we have churches of every kind. Yet do we have religion? Do we have the essential religion that must be the religion that is the Path that leads the souls of our people back to our essential oneness with Christ and with God?

Freedom of the Press

The mental body may be filled with learning and the knowledge of this world. It may be filled with facts and figures and statistics and an interpersonal awareness of this human life. We may have a mind, but it might not be the mind that is the Christ mind, the Christ that is the knower because he is the known.[12] The instantaneous knowing of God because we have the mind of God is altogether different from acquiring knowledge through the human mind.

And so we have to ask ourselves, Are we pursuing that mastery? For only in that mastery will we have the true exercise of freedom of the press. What are we using our media for? What are we using our newspapers for? For money and merchandising in souls through advertising that reaches the subconscious through hidden symbols of sex, death, gore, bestiality and witchcraft?

While we defend freedom of the press, journalism has never been more phony and insensitive to the individual. At the same time, great journalism and investigative reporting has helped to expose Watergate, organized crime, pollution and the international drug trade. Sensationalism, playing upon the fears, banal curiosity, and lust of the people has always sold papers. A responsible editorial policy and press must be controlled by public opinion.

Letters to the editor and a conscientious stand for truth when people are needlessly persecuted, maligned, or misrepresented are in order. Alternative editorial opinions expressed by readers and viewers most certainly broaden the understanding of an issue. In addition, we need to use the power of the press to illustrate the path of self-mastery and to report the awareness of the mind of Christ, rather than leave it to the actualities of the birth and death of human consciousness.

We begin to see the responsibility of freedom. It means to exercise to our fullest the potential to be God-free beings. In order to do this, we need the teachings of the Great White Brotherhood, we need the understanding of cosmic law, we need the ascended masters who are the real Gurus because they are the only truly God-free beings whom we can know personally (both directly through the Holy Spirit and by studying their past lives prior to their ascension) and therefore emulate. And we need the techniques of the Divine Mother to show us how to apply their teachings.

Freedom of Assembly

Are we mastering our emotional bodies, the water element? Are we mastering that energy through the free flow and the movement of God's energy? Or are our feeling worlds all caught up with the mass consciousness? Are we bobbing like corks on the sea of the collective unconscious? Are we triggering our emotions according to human events around us, or is our emotional body like the "sea of glass" reflecting the desire body of God, reflecting God's desire to see us be one with him through the Christ consciousness?

We have an emotional body. What we do with it determines our effectiveness individually and collectively to express and to utilize our freedom of assembly. When we come together to assemble, it is because we have energies to exchange and to use constructively for the manifestation of the Christ consciousness in our group mandala, which is our country, our United States of America. Do we come together and argue for argument's sake? Or do we insist on the goal of community action for the upliftment of the individual? Do we defend our right to assemble peaceably without interruption by violent detractors and demonstrators whose tactic is to destroy our freedom by destroying the logical and orderly presentation of ideas? Are we forfeiting the fruits of united effort for the preservation of family and community by allowing entertainment—as television and motion pictures—to be the synthesis of society's lower evolution, without any input from the people?

Today we are watching our entire culture and civilization being molded by the television and motion picture industry. And the people stand by helplessly lamenting the passing of the old order. Because they have not the mark of Christhood but often a fanatical zeal and a hellfire and brimstone approach, there is no meeting of minds and hearts at the point of the Christ flame—the point of creative action. And the ills of our society are spawning a worldwide malignancy of the serpent consciousness. We will simply not survive if we abdicate our right to assemble and to have our voice heard as the voice of the people in special interest groups.

Freedom of Speech

Freedom of speech—the exercise of that speech, the exercise of the Word and the power of the Word—has to do with the manifestation of self-government and of the flow of abundance in the economy of the nation. If we are not mastering the physical plane, our words will not be *the* Word, *the* Logos, but they will simply be words and words and words. And sometimes we become so weary of listening to the endless chain of words we turn off the television, we turn off the radio, we don't want to hear, because it just goes on and on and on. And we go for the one who has the Word as the disciples sought Jesus: "Where shall we go, Lord? Thou hast the Word, the gift of eternal life."[13]

It is the Word we are seeking, and to have that Word we need the self-discipline in the physical plane. We need the self-government of our physical bodies, our physical energies, our physical flow.

The Free Soul Demands a Bill of Rights

It was the American people who demanded that these four freedoms be specifically defined and attached to our Constitution along with the right to petition the government for a redress of grievances. The very demand of this American people shows already the activation of the path of initiation. Only the soul that knows that it is free and knows that its destiny is to be free has enough awareness to demand a bill of rights, a statement of guaranteed freedoms.

There are many people even on this earth today who would not know enough to demand a guarantee of their freedoms. They don't identify their need for freedom, because they're not on the path of the Christ consciousness. However, while the masses scream for human rights, only the few perceive the paramount need for divine rights—the right to be free to pursue one's divinity.

No Liberty without a Full, Free, Secure Enjoyment of Unalienable Rights

Before the Constitutional Convention in 1787, individual states had established bills of rights. The earliest of these was Virginia, which established a bill of rights in 1776. Historians agree that the tyranny the colonists had experienced in other countries led to the colonial declaration of the natural rights of man. James Winthrop wrote in 1788:

> Bills of rights . . . are, I believe, peculiar to America. A careful observance of the abuse practised in other countries has had its just effect by inducing our people to guard against them.[14]

The French Revolution was still in the future, 1789. The Declaration of the Rights of Man was not yet put forth. It was a very new thing to demand this at the national level. In 1787, when our founding fathers were adopting a federal constitution, the vast majority of delegates to the Constitutional Convention felt that a federal bill of rights was not necessary. At the time, eight of the thirteen states had bills of rights, and most of the delegates to the Constitutional Convention argued that a federal bill of rights was unnecessary.

However, when the document without a bill of rights was submitted to the states for ratification, there was a tremendous protest. Several of the states ratified the Constitution only under the stipulation that the Constitutional Conventional delegates would reconvene and draft a bill of rights to add to the Constitution. A delegate to the Massachusetts ratifying convention objected:

> But where is the bill of rights which shall check the power of this Congress; which shall say, *Thus far shall ye come, and no farther.* The safety of the people depends on a bill of rights. If we build on a sandy foundation, is it likely we shall stand?[15]

A delegate to South Carolina said:

> They are nearly all, to a man, opposed to this new Constitution, because, they say, they have omitted to insert a bill of rights therein, ascertaining and fundamentally establishing, the unalienable rights of men, without a full, free, and secure enjoyment of which there can be no liberty.[16]

Government Is for the Protection of the Soul's Initiations in the Christ Consciousness

This is the soul speaking. That threefold flame is called the threefold flame of liberty. *That* is our freedom flame. The reason we write a constitution and set up a government is not that the government can tell us what to do, but that we govern ourselves. We establish a government "of the people, by the people, for the people"[17]—for the people's path of initiation under God through individual conscience, for the people's protection of the threefold flame.

We establish a government that is the setting for the diamond, the jewel of the Christ consciousness of the individual, *the individual*—not the masses, not this crowd that we have come to understand as a collectivism. There is no such thing as the man in the street. There is no such thing as the masses. The only thing that is real is you, the individual. And the individual over and over again is the multiplication of the Christ consciousness; it is the multiplication of the loaves and the fishes.[18]

All that we have in America today is for us to be self-governed in our Christ Self. All that interferes with this, that has grown up around this original establishment of a constitution inspired by Saint Germain, needs to be carved away and stripped because it is interfering with our practice of the Law on the path of initiation. This is our responsibility as citizens of the United States. And if we have this criterion, if we have this set of standards, we will know how to write our laws, to amend our Constitution to adjust it to the current hour.

A Moral Power Higher than the State

Nearly two hundred years later, William O. Douglas said:

> The victory for freedom of thought recorded in our Bill of Rights recognizes that in the domain of conscience there is a moral power higher than the state.[19]

The question we must ask ourselves today: Has the state overtaken that moral power, that honor, that flame? Has the state so escalated to a Tower of Babel[20] that we are no longer free to manifest the flame of liberty and to draw it into manifestation in the soul and the four lower bodies? Thomas Jefferson wrote concerning the freedom of religion:

> Almighty God hath created the mind free; ... to compel a man to furnish contributions of money for the propagation of opinions which he disbelieves, is sinful and tyrannical.... Truth is great and will prevail if left to herself, ... she is the proper and sufficient antagonist to error, and has nothing to fear from the conflict.[21]

In Europe there are state churches supported by state taxes. There is a national church of the country. People are taxed to support the church whether or not they believe in the church. Do we want this to happen in America? No, of course not!

The Tyrannical Generation

We can see the handwriting on the wall. We can see the National Council of Churches and the World Council of Churches gaining greater and greater power, usurping the power of the flame of liberty within each of us, and finally declaring that its formula of doctrine and dogma is to be the ruling doctrine of the land. We are not there yet, but we are at the place where individuals attempt to deprive one another of freedom of religion by harassment, by pressure, by organizing, by using blocs of power, blocs of money, and the larger churches segregating and ostracizing the smaller ones.

We find that tyranny and the tyrannical generation is the third aspect that we have in America today. It is not so much the federal government that is at fault in depriving us of these four freedoms, but it becomes the tyrannical individuals who work against one another.

And so in seeking to undo the misuses of God's energy, we must be astute to identify the *adulterous generation,* the *idolatrous generation,* and the *tyrannical generation.* These are simply aspects of the carnal mind, which seeks to usurp the place of the Christ, the threefold flame in us, as we exercise our right to uphold the guarantees of the entire Bill of Rights.

Free Expression of the Wisdom of the People

William Allen White wrote in 1922:

> You tell me that law is above freedom of utterance. And I reply that you can have no wise laws nor free enforcement of wise laws unless there is free expression of the wisdom of the people—and, alas, their folly with it. But if there is freedom, folly will die of its own poison, and the wisdom will survive. That is the history of the race. It is the proof of man's kinship with God....
>
> Put fear out of your heart. This nation will survive, this state will prosper, the orderly business of life will go forward if only men can speak in whatever way given them to utter what their hearts hold—by voice, by posted card, by letter or by press. Reason never has failed men. Only force and repression have made the wrecks in the world.[22]

Initiates on the Path

Our founding fathers established the Bill of Rights, pushed by the people themselves out of concern about a tyrannical government. They had had direct experience in Europe. They were reacting to very real threats and hardships that they had been through. They had the courage to leave Europe, to brave that ocean, to come to an unknown land just to establish these four freedoms. They were initiates on the path of a supreme individualism under God. They were willing to sacrifice all, to give up their selfishness and self-concerns and leave all to establish this.

We today are not operating in reaction to tyranny of the past or the present. We have forgotten the tyranny of the past and we do not in all cases recognize the tyranny of the present. Two hundred years later, we do not remember what it was like to live in England or in France or in the Netherlands under these powers that forbade our soul-expression.

Will This Generation Lose Its Freedom?

Aleksandr Solzhenitsyn, in lamenting what has taken place in the West and the West going soft on freedom, has asked the question, "Is it necessary for each generation to experience deprivation of its freedoms in order to be willing to lay down its life for these freedoms?" His hope is that we will learn from his experience, from the experience of millions of people behind the Iron Curtain who have had these rights taken from them.

But he has looked at America and he has said, Maybe it will take your undergoing this dark night of the soul, going through total tyranny, total idolatry, the adulterous generation—all of these—so that you will have the courage to realize that unless you secure your freedom, there is no life, there is no reality, there is no self-transcendence.

We find, then, as I see American society today, that it is not the government—as it is the government in Communist countries or totalitarian countries—that takes from us our freedom, but it is individuals. The hatred and condemnation of one religious group for another is well-known. It is more well-known when you are in the minority. When you are in the vast majority of religious expression, you are not so much aware of discrimination. Nevertheless, this conflict brought about the Supreme Court ruling on prayer in public schools in 1963 when one woman whose religion was atheism acted against all others' religions and, out of discrimination and prejudice, carried the point to the end.[23]

Control of the Press

It's interesting to understand that freedom of the press is your right to establish your newspaper. You have the freedom to found your own press; you do not have the freedom to publish your articles in someone else's press unless you are paying for it and it is a paid advertisement. And even in these cases, many times if your article does not agree with the editorial policy of the newspaper, your article will not be published even if you are willing to pay for it.

Today the press is controlled by interest groups. Left wing, right wing, middle-of-the-road groups control the press. The press is controlled by individuals who print biased news stories and refuse to publish articles about certain aspects of society at all.

But more subtle is the manipulation of the people through the press when the press fails to state the source and the foundation of its statements, but simply carefully manipulates its articles to manage people's minds. It becomes the control of the mental body, the control of the emotional body, and the free press becomes what will sell the most—which is the reporting of violence, the reporting of things that are distasteful because these create a reaction. Our press does not represent the Christ mind, even as our religious community is not yet expressing the true memory of the laws of God and the teachings of the Path.

To me, however, this is not what is important. What is important is that we yet retain the freedom to change this. We are not changing it because we are ignorant of our options, ignorant of the teachings, ignorant of the Path. But once we have the knowledge of the Path, we yet retain the form of government that enables us to change; and the word *change* is the key to alchemy. The fact that we the people who are the government can change our nation within its system shows that our government allows for the alchemy of the Path. To alter, to go to the altar for the purpose of transmutation, we can still do; and this is the great flame of hope that we hold.

The press is abused in many ways. Coverage is given to some aspects and not others. But that is no one's fault but our own—our own lack of exercise of that freedom. We have turned over that freedom to the syndicated columnists, to the UPI, to AP; we have turned it over to those who own the newspapers and own chains of newspapers. We have given to them our freedom of the press. We have said, "You can control what we daily take in"—our daily intake in our mental body.

This is the idolatrous generation, saying, "Freedom of the press is not in me, it's in that person. Freedom of religion is not in me, it's in the National Council of Churches, or it's in the ministers, or it's in the councils." We have surrendered our voice, we have surrendered our mastery because we have not taken the path of initiation, we have not taken the path of the mastery of the chakras.

Misuses of Freedom of Assembly and the Right of Redress

Freedom of assembly—we find that in many cases the ruling of local zoning boards deprives us of this freedom. We meet this crisis in every city where we go. We are forbidden to meet in certain areas of the city. We have to go here, we have to go there; we can't have more than so many people in a certain house to have a prayer meeting.

The misuse of freedom of assembly and the right of redress has been manifest in campus demonstrations and riots where there have been killings, murders, the blowing-up of banks, demonstrations for a change that have gone past the God-control of the energies of the desire body.

We find that the power of the unions to totally disrupt our way of life is also coming upon us. We have seen that in Canada the disruption of the mail service again and again by the union is interfering with the correct functioning of the federal government and the rights of the people to receive their mail. We have seen months go by where our students in Canada have not received the communications of the ascended masters because the federal government has failed to protect individual rights.

Equal Time for the Ascended Masters

Freedom of speech is blocked by the tyranny of individuals who control public or private forums, denying people the right to speak. In some areas the right to speak is intact. In other areas, if you want to talk on a university campus, if you want to publish an article in a university newspaper, you find that the policies or the political or religious trends of that university are such that you are not allowed to speak. They are exercising their freedom to control their forum, but they are not including the broad spectrum of opinion, of conviction. And so reason is not free to exercise free will.

Archangel Michael has told us that he wants equal time in the media for the presentation of the path of initiation.[24] Who will give that equal time? When you go to present a religious service on the television, you find that the National Council of Churches controls many of the prime-time religious programs, and it has been reported by some who have worked with the NCC that they will only allow those ministers and preachers to speak and hold their services who conform to their doctrine and their dogma; hence they control the voice of the people in the media.

Again and again it is manipulation, it is vested-interest groups, and it is the power of money—big money, corporate money, money of large blocs of people—that is used silently behind the scenes to manipulate the individual. And this huge monolith of power, then, is used against the individual, and he is helpless because he does not have the necessary redress through the backing of an organization in order to reclaim this individual right.

Four Freedoms Denied in the Soviet Union

The fear of our founding fathers about a tyrannical government is a reality today in Communist countries. In 1917, the USSR became the first state in history to make extermination of all religions an essential part of its program of domestic and international revolution. It was the platform of Lenin to wipe out religion totally. Marx stripped from the philosophy of Hegel all aspects of a first cause, a divinity of God, and made this part of the platform of the Communist revolution.* The

---

*Karl Marx's theoretical framework for Communism was dialectical materialism, a philosophy based on Hegel's theory of dialectic. While *Geist* (Spirit) was a central tenet of Hegel's philosophy, Marx sought to establish his system on purely materialistic principles, denying any role for God or the spiritual life of man. For more on Marx and his theories, see Elizabeth Clare Prophet, *The Economic Philosophy of Jesus Christ vs The Religious Philosophy of Karl Marx* (Summit University Press, 2019).

press in Communist countries is totally censored, and people cannot assemble freely.

Do you think it is only Communist countries? When we traveled through South America, we found that in many nations, in order to have a cocktail party you need a permit from the government. You cannot meet or proselytize for a religion in Mexico City or anywhere in Mexico today. You cannot promote the teachings of the ascended masters. Catholicism is the state religion. When we held our conference in Mexico City in 1973, we could not put up posters for that conference—it was a good conference, nevertheless. There is no freedom of speech in these countries.

As an example of what goes on in the Soviet Union, I'd like to quote Aleksandr Solzhenitsyn. He said: "The Soviet system is so closed that it is almost impossible for you to understand from here."[25] This is a story he gave as an example:

One Soviet citizen was in the United States, and on his return said that in the United States they have wonderful automobile roads. The KGB arrested him and demanded a term of ten years. But the judge said: "I don't object, but there is not enough evidence. Couldn't you find something else against him?" So the judge was exiled to Sakhalin because he dared to argue, and they gave the other man ten years. "Can you imagine," Solzhenitsyn says, "what a lie he told?" What was the lie that he told? "And what sort of praise this was of American imperialism—in America there are good roads? Ten years."[26]

Government Is the Collective Manifestation of the Path of Initiation

To fail to exercise all of these freedoms means that we cripple ourselves. God gave us the four lower bodies; they are referred to in the Book of Genesis as "coats of skins."[27] The four lower bodies are sheaths of consciousness. If they were not all necessary to the realization of the Christ mind, we would not have them. Freedom, then, must be the equal flow of God's energy through all of these four lower bodies. There is, then, an interaction, and the meaning of this flow should be considered within the individual and within the nation.

You know, they say, "Never discuss politics and religion." It's enough to discuss religion and have controversy. When you try to hold a conference on religion and then you bring in politics, you really have trouble. That's what my sleepless nights are about.

The point we have to make is that government is the collective manifestation of the path of initiation by a free people. Religion is for individual self-mastery so that we can exercise that mastery on a larger scale, going from the community to the state to the national level to the international level. Our religion, the action of our binding ourselves to God, makes us capable of being self-governed. The government of the self is the government of the Real Self, the God Self. The Real Self, the God Self, is energy. So what government is all about is the governing of the flow of energy from the within to the without.

In order to know how to govern that energy, we must have right religion, and true government can be founded only on right religion. Those who founded our government, their religion was based on what they had evolved as the philosophy of John Stuart Mill and John Locke and Jean Jacques Rousseau and all of those great philosophers who were talking about the rights of man.

It was an evolutionary process that was going on in Europe all the way from the plays of Molière and Racine, poking fun at the tyranny of the aristocracy, to those who were the philosophers of social revolution. There was a great foment, a great mental activity, and this was the result of the dispensation of the Brotherhood giving an increase of light so that souls could pursue the path of initiation.

Parallel Paths of Mastery:
The Individual and the Community

When we come to the teachings of the Great White Brotherhood, then, we come first to define our path, our individual self-expression. When we have that defined, we must immediately take it to the larger community. Saint Germain, the God of Freedom in the Aquarian age, teaches us that there is no self-mastery without the parallel paths of the individual working in himself and the individual working though the world community, that Community of the Holy Spirit.

So whatever we master within the self we need to ratify in expression in our environment. This is why if we were to talk about the teachings of the masters and neglect to talk about government, we would have a watered-down, unrelated, and irrelevant religion and path. If we cannot immediately take the questions of self-mastery and initiation and then examine what is going on in America and the world and draw conclusions, what point is there to our path, what point is there to our life?

We have a responsibility for freedom in the entire earth. The entire lifewave of evolution is a collective consciousness made up of individuals all striving on the path of initiation together.

The Threefold Flame in the Four Lower Bodies

We look, next, at the aspects of the threefold flame in each of the four lower bodies. So now we talk about the power of religion, the power of the press, the power of assembly, and the power of speech.

Power has to do with the release of energy, specifically through the throat chakra and the solar plexus—both focuses of the desire or water body. The correct exercise of power, individually and collectively, is what makes the body of God one. We have to develop, then, the exercise of the flow of energy as the Word. The coalescing of power is government, and this is the equal manifestation of the Word in the individual and collectively.

A representative form of government—a government of the people, by the people, and for the people—means that each individual exercising the mastery of the throat chakra speaks the Word of God, and the collective realization of the Word of God becomes the government of this land, this nation—and it ought to be so in every nation. You can see, then, that unless we have cooperation, we fail the test of the collective initiation of the nation.

We all know that there is a great power, great force, great ability to mold peoples and nations through all of these instruments. The question is, Are we making maximum use of these four freedoms? Very few of us are, but we can start, and we can show the world what the true meaning of this path is.

Now we develop the second plume of the threefold flame, the yellow plume of wisdom: the wisdom of religion, the wisdom of the press, the wisdom of assembly, the wisdom of speech. This is the development of two other chakras, the crown and the third eye. By the development of these chakras, we wisely use these freedoms. In the wise use of this freedom, the collective mandala of our nation rises.

The third plume is the aspect of the Holy Spirit: the love of religion, of the press, of assembly, and of speech—the love of that freedom, the love of its exercise. This is the mastery of the heart chakra and the seat-of-the-soul chakra because the heart is the center of love. The correct exercise of love in the flow of the four freedoms is what binds the people to one another. If we do not express love, then we can be seized by a religion and a press and an assembly and a speech that is of hatred. And the cancer of hatred is crawling and creeping through the world and through the bodies of her people.

Hatred is the perversion of the power, wisdom, and love of our four freedoms. And when we do not actively counteract it by the flow from within going out, then we are consumed by that energy that separates and divides us one from another, section from section, state from state, religion from religion, political party from political party, right from left, and so on.

The Fallen Ones Divide and Conquer

The fallen ones would divide and conquer. This is how they have made their conquests through all the ages. They do not stop with dividing you from your friend, or husband from wife, or father and mother. They divide your very members.[28] They have your emotions warring with your mind; they create splits in the personality causing mental and emotional disorders. And today, the very challenge of the initiation of the soul of the American people must be won by the fire of integration that comes out of the Buddhic light and the Christ light.

We need to be integrated first within ourselves. The four aspects of the cross of life are within us, and they must be manifest as one team. The Four Horsemen of the Apocalypse[29] are our four lower bodies individually and collectively. Unless they are functioning together, they will tear our very souls apart. Going in opposite directions we are torn asunder, no longer effective to work together.

5 • The Responsibility of Freedom

Freedom to Express the Energy of God through Your Chakras

Many social issues today are defended on the basis of the rights of the individual—"my rights." Could you really sit down in this moment and take a clean piece of paper and write down what are your rights on the path of initiation and then, on this piece of paper, determine which of these rights are guaranteed and which of these rights we are deprived of, whether by the government or by individuals?

The Goddess of Freedom spoke to Keepers of the Flame yesterday in a dictation. Her consciousness of freedom is the freeing of the feminine potential of the nation, freeing the Mary Magdalene of ourself, freeing the soul to rise to its master, the Christ.

Freedom, then, if you were to write your freedoms, begins with your freedom to express the energy of God through your seven chakras. This is an illustration of the chakras as they are focusing the energy of God in the true consciousness of the Christ. They are focuses for the seven rays; the colors denote virtues and frequencies, and we will be discussing these through the conference.

Freedom to Express the Wisdom of God

The crown chakra is the yellow ray, our freedom to express the wisdom of God. How have we compromised this? We have entered into the knowledge of this world through intellectual pride. We have abandoned in our systems of education the education of the soul to pursue the Christ and to release the Christ, and the educational process has become almost totally mechanical and without the creativity of the release of energies in the crown chakra.

We must look at ourselves and to no one else. We can blame no one, because that is idolatry, that is saying, "It's over there, it's not here." We have to say to ourselves, as this group, Why have we allowed our freedom to master the crown chakra to be compromised by the federal government's control of education? And where the federal government does not control it, why have we allowed educational policies to be made by those who are not on the path of initiation, hence who do not see that the mastery of the Christ consciousness or of the Real Self is the foundation of true education?

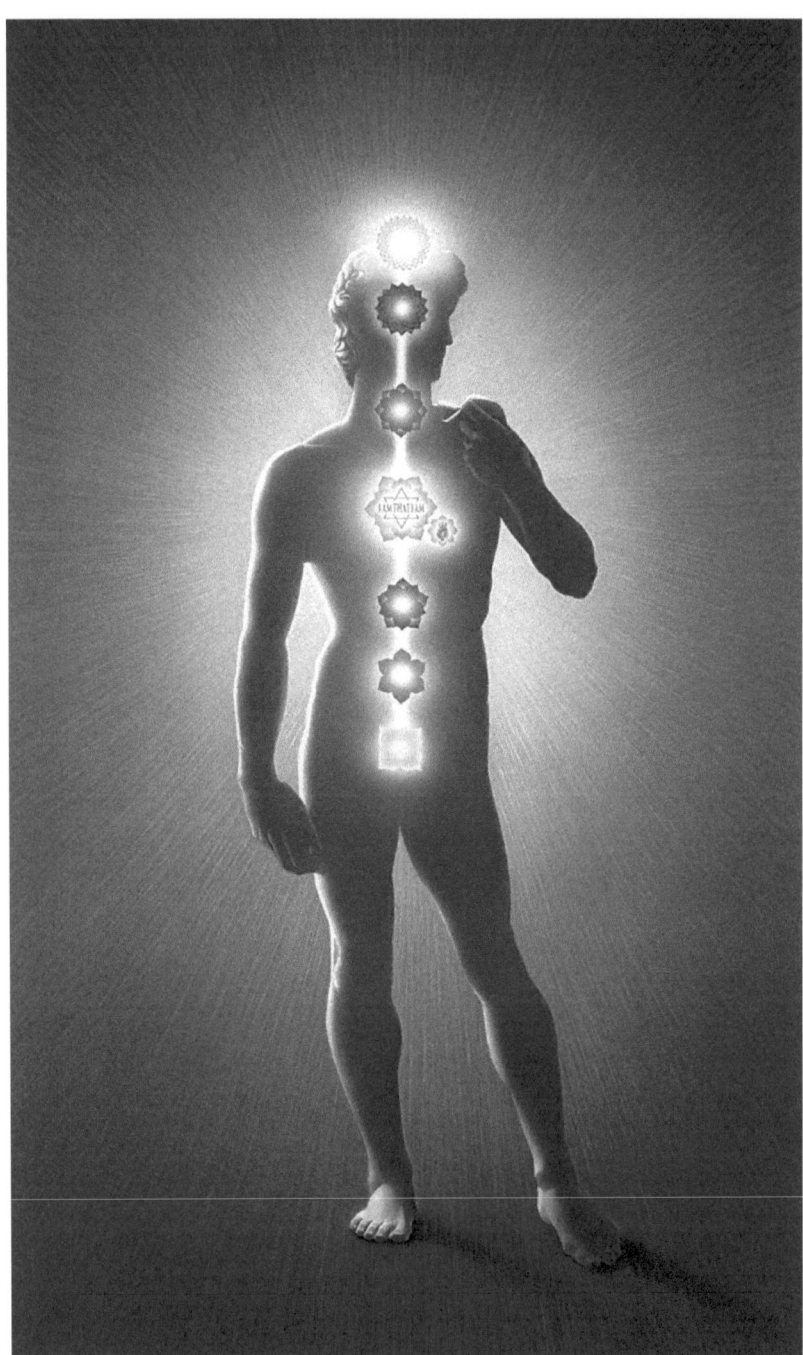

The Third-Eye Chakra

The third-eye chakra is the chakra for truth, for science, for health, for abundance. That's where our money is, that's where our economy is, that's where our medical science is, that is where our material science is. Have we controlled it, or have we allowed it to dominate us? If we allow it to dominate us, then we are not a free people, because we have not exercised free will and the power of the spoken Word, the power of the press, its wisdom, its love.

We have a lot to do just to overcome the abuses of the feminine ray of freedom in those two chakras alone. Where do we begin? We begin with the self. Unless we begin there, we cannot start this Coming Revolution that Pallas Athena, the Goddess of Truth, speaks of—the revolution of light, the turning back of the generation of the darkness and making it a regeneration of light. Unless we gain the mastery of the energy in our own chakras, all of our shouting and our demonstration and all of our protesting against the misuses of our four freedoms will get us nowhere. We crumble in a heap, exhausted, saying, "There is no redress. The individual has no voice in America today. It's all big business, big government, manipulation behind the scenes. We can do nothing; we're helpless." It's not true. That is idolatry.

Why should we be idolaters? We must be the Christed ones, the anointed ones. With that mastery of God in our chakras, no one can turn us back. No one can turn back the light, no one can turn back the energy—not the power and the might of all of government and all of money and all of the powers of manipulation being used in the media. Nothing can stand against the individual who has the mastery of the flow of energy within his being and who has exercised his freedom to be free on the path of initiation.

Misuses of the Throat Chakra

The throat chakra is the blue ray of government, of leadership, of planning, of architecture, of the very foundation of the way we live in the United States. Have we exercised our freedom of the spoken Word, and of the press, and to assemble, and to speak our voice to control what is happening through that chakra? Why is there such a high incidence of throat cancer, which is the return of hatred that has been released through that chakra? Why are Americans such victims of this cancer of hatred? Because they have failed to express the power of the spoken Word. They have used the throat chakra for mortal cursings.

The cursings that go forth so flippantly from our throat chakras are actually the invocation of very dark energies and powers that work against the light of the Christ. Cigarette smoking, which is the obvious cause of the throat cancer, is rebellion against the inner blueprint of the correct use of that chakra—which is not for sensual stimulation and gratification, but for the pure flow of the Word.

Then we see government, then we see Watergate, then we see leaders who should not be representing the people, and we say, "Overthrow the system!" It's not the system; the system guarantees our freedom. It's in ourselves. We are government—we have allowed these individuals to represent us. And we have no one to blame but ourselves.

The Heart Chakra and the Discipline of Love

Take the heart chakra, the flow of love. There is a great heart in the American people, and thank God there is a great heart. All we need to do is to define love and to discipline love and we will transmute the vestiges of hatred and the misuses of love, hardness of heart toward one another, and prejudice and division.

Jesus talked of the days when men's hearts would fail them for fear.[30] If we allow fear to be the vibration of the heart, that is what we project as a nation. In fear we have doubt and indecision, and we cannot formulate the Christ consciousness in government or in any of the other chakras. The heart is the very seat of our life as a nation and the collective path of initiation.

The Solar-Plexus Energy for Devotion, Industry, and Service

The solar plexus is the place of religion, of devotion to God. It is emotional energy. It manifests in industry. And we have perverted that flow of service and the flame of service by pollution of the four elements and the four lower bodies. Pollution is so intense that we are no longer free to serve.

5 • The Responsibility of Freedom

Mass Manipulation through Seat-of-the-Soul Chakra

The seat-of-the-soul chakra is the violet-flame chakra of freedom. The misuse of the media, the programming of souls to bondage instead of to freedom, comes through the media, comes through Hollywood, comes through the projecting of pornography, of all the misuses of the sacred fire that we see daily in practically everything that comes before our eyes—advertising media, television, and so forth. There is such distortion of soul energies being projected that it actually distorts the propagation of the race, which is anchored in that chakra through the egg and the sperm and the genes and the chromosomes. And when we continually take in that programming, we program our offspring. It is mass manipulation.

Our Voice and Our Vote Count

To me, the most exciting thing about the Great White Brotherhood is that our voice and our vote count. It counts where it ought to count. It counts with the ascended masters, the Gurus. It counts with the Great White Brotherhood. It counts with those who really are controlling what happens on earth when we allow them to control it by making our invocations.

The great excitement about the Path is that one person with God is the majority vote. The majority vote in America is the Christ consciousness, and the masters have told us that we, the people who have the light and exercise it, are the ones whom they really consider to be the representatives of the people. The masters advocate a representative form of government, but they look at it from the point of hierarchy. Whoever has the highest attainment of the Christ consciousness in each state, in each community is the one who actually reports to the Lords of Karma and who is the one who exercises the deciding factor in what occurs.

Many people do not know that they have that attainment. Many people do not understand that they are functioning in this way, because it occurs in their soul awareness while their bodies sleep. All of this is going on at inner levels. This conference is for us to rise to that higher consciousness that we have at inner levels and to anchor it here in outer awareness so we can be effective in the planes of earth, in the physical, to change our world and make it reflect what is in the etheric plane.

We teach our students to take a project of a current problem—a social issue, a bill in Congress, the war in Vietnam, the war in Africa, or whatever it is—and to begin to make the fiats, through the science of the spoken Word, to alter those conditions. Many have kept notebooks and shown how from day to day, because they have worked diligently hour by hour exercising the decrees, that entire issues have been turned about.

We find, then, that we are yet a free people. And when Saint Germain called us to the conference *The Greater Way of Freedom*, he said, "Assemble while you are yet free to assemble. Exercise your freedom of religion while you are yet free. While you yet have this freedom, exercise it lest it be taken from you."[31]

To Be or Not to Be

The base-of-the-spine chakra, which is the Mother source, the last chakra we're considering, contains all of the misuses of our resources, of our ecology.

Free will, then, comes down to the fact of the choice to be or not to be—to be in the light of what is truth and what is reality, or to be in darkness; to choose to be Christ, to choose to be God, or to choose to be a not-self, a nonentity, a nothing. There is a right- and there is a left-handed path. The right-handed path chooses to glorify, to exalt, the energies of God for the liberation of the soul. The left-handed path chooses to take the energies of God for the complete license of the carnal mind.

Without realizing it, we in America today are already making these choices. And not out of malice but out of ignorance, many have chosen the left-handed path. They are using their freedoms to give vent to the carnal mind—its selfishness, its sensuality—and this is the ruination of America.

When we come into the teachings of the ascended masters and we learn how to use the energy that is God within us, we will elect to take the right-handed path. We will begin to master these chakras, and we will not be content to sit at home individually, but we will change the face of our nation so that we can change the face of the earth.

The responsibility of freedom is to move from the microcosm to the Macrocosm. The responsibility that we have is to define freedom and to define love. For when we know what love is, we will know what freedom is, we will know the margents of freedom, we will know its boundaries—we will know the boundaries of man's habitation. Every life, every hour, every day is a choice.

The Bird—Eternal Archetype of Soul Freedom

The bird is the symbol of the soul taking flight. The lark ascending, the ascending of the spark of consciousness, is freedom through the balance scales in the wings of the mental and emotional body. The bird is our cross. It is the cross that we have diagramed in the cosmic clock. By his body and his wingspread, he defines the four quadrants of Matter. He is purity. He is the soul moving through the planes of consciousness to soar back to God. Through the liberation of power and wisdom and love in each quadrant, our souls soar. We move with the dove of purity. We move with the strength and the wings of eagles.

The bird itself is the symbol of the Great White Brotherhood; it is the communion of the Great White Brotherhood. The ascended masters actually released the birds to be a token of the message that one day mankind heard directly before they lost their perception of that direct communication. And so the birds remind us that there is communication direct within the soul to God.

The Holy Spirit is given to us through the flow of the birds. The bird is the symbol the cross of white fire, of Christ-realization, the eternal archetype of freedom in the subconscious. We respond to this symbol because we respond to freedom. We are here because we respond to freedom and we want to know a higher freedom and its definition. This is the purpose of this conference, *Higher Consciousness,* and I trust that we shall all move higher and higher as the soul ascends into that place where it can see the truth, and in knowing that truth, it can be free.

Meditations on Freedom

I'd like to give with you now a few meditations on freedom and to give you some visualizations on the soaring of your soul to the higher planes and from those high planes of God consciousness, directing energies into the earth for the transmutation of the misuses of the chakras of mankind en masse.

We're going to take the rainbow rays of God, the seven rays, for the release of this action. We're going to begin with the violet flame because it is the flame of freedom, and simply give the mantra, "I AM a being of violet fire! I AM the purity God desires!"

That statement is just like a declaration of independence. It is stating that "I will not be confined, I will not be in bondage, but I will gain my freedom by releasing the freedom that is already within, by releasing the fire that is in the heart and qualifying it with the light of freedom."

When we say "I AM a being of violet fire! I AM the purity God desires!" we're saying, "God in me, energy in me, sacred fire in me, freedom in me is a being of violet fire. God, energy, light in me is the purity God desires." We are transforming our whole concept of ourselves as finite, as physical, as limited, as sinful, and everything else for which we condemn ourselves. We are totally liberating our consciousness to be this one thing at this particular moment in time and space.

> I AM a being of violet fire!
> I AM the purity God desires! (36x)

5 • The Responsibility of Freedom

AUM
AUM
AUM

Since time and space are relative. We are what we think we are. We are where we think we are, we are where we want to be, where we direct energy, where we direct consciousness in our chakras. And so we see before us the earth. At this particular moment, the soul can take flight as the bird, go beyond the earth in meditation, hover over the earth, use all of the chakras of the four lower bodies to project the energies of the Christ to the earth for its healing.

We can see the earth colored blue and violet, showing the action of the violet flame and the blue ray of the power of the will of God. When we give our mantras and we direct our energies into the earth, we need not think that they will only affect ourselves, because the power of God is infinite, and God is only one, and the manifestation *Christ* is only one. Our sense of separation allows for the multiplication of evil—the multiplication of the energy veil, the multiplication of illusion. It is illusion to think that God cannot heal billions of souls at the same time he can heal the individual. That God is the God of Israel, the God that is the I AM THAT I AM within us.

And so, we will alternate now the meditation upon the globe and the entering into these flames of consciousness. And you can raise your hands and use the chakras on the palms of the hands. Visualize yourself standing over the globe directing light from your hands into it.

We will take a mantra of the will of God given to us by Jesus in the Garden of Gethsemane: "Not my will but thine be done."[32] That is the affirmation that we will be congruent with the blueprint of our reality and we refuse to remain outside of the law of being. So we surrender in our free will that human will to the divine will and we say together:

> Not my will, not my will,
> not my will but thine be done. (24x)

OM MANI PADME HUM (16x)

The side of the globe in this image happens to be the continent of Africa, and you can see the Middle East. It is taken from a satellite. Africa is where freedom is being forged and won today. It is where the battleground is. And the Middle East itself can be said to be the heart of a world, the place where Christ, as the heart chakra, was crucified, the place where Christ must come again. And the Christ is the only resolver of the unresolvable conflict between the Arabs and the Jews.

It is interesting to note that neither the Arabs nor the Jews acknowledge the Self as Christ. Most people today acknowledge the fact that the Middle East crisis has no answer because both sides are in a deadlock. The deadlock is the deadlock of carnal minds pitted against one another who will not allow the action of grace, who will not bow before the Real Self that is within. The Christ is the Real Self of you and me. When we say *Christ* and *Real Self,* they are synonyms terms. And when we see people living outside of Reality, there is no resolution of the conflict of the carnal consciousness.

And so as we ascend now into our higher consciousness, hovering over the earth, let us direct the violet-flame energies into the Middle East, into Africa. Let us understand, by the authority by the flame within, that every soul on that continent is receiving the fire of freedom by the gift of energy that God has given to us in the flame of the heart.

5 • The Responsibility of Freedom

Light expand, light expand, light expand, expand, expand!
Light I AM, light I AM, light I AM, I AM, I AM! (12x)

AUM

The clouds and the light of fire upon the sea give us a sense of being able to equate with that aspect of being that is Spirit. Spirit is for the control of Matter. Spirit is the flame, Matter is the bowl into which we project that flame. Matter as the earth body is our bowl. It is our opportunity for self-mastery.

When God created male and female, he gave the fiat "Take dominion over the earth!"[33] That is the challenge of *Higher Consciousness*. It is the challenge of freedom. By the light of Spirit, we take dominion over this sphere. Time and space are all that make this sphere seem insurmountable, that make its ecology seem to be one that cannot be resolved. We can so rise in consciousness, in the consciousness of the Elohim, that by perspective to our size the earth is as small as this image.

"All Power Is Given unto Me"

Imagine yourself in God, in the higher consciousness of the Elohim, seeing this earth before you, being able to hold it in your hands, and then saying to yourself, "I can't do it! It won't happen! There just isn't enough freedom or energy or power within me to move that mountain."

It's all relative, isn't it? Our sense of limitation, our sense of inability to move anything, to get things done, even in the smallest way, with a group of people is because we are looking at a mountain of adversity and saying it is real. But it is only real in relativity. When we ascend to the absolute of our spiritual consciousness, we say with Jesus, "All power is given unto me in heaven and in earth!"[34]—in heaven, in Spirit; in earth, in Matter. If all the power of God is anchored in the one who becomes the Christ, then we had better hurry up and become the Christ. We have a self, a nation, and a planet to draw into correct alignment with the will of God.

Let's sing together, "Light, Set Me Free!" and let's direct to that continent of Africa and to the Middle East the consciousness of freedom in the Real Self or freedom in Christ. There is no other freedom. It is not that the Arabs and the Jews have to become Christians to be free; they simply have to acknowledge that God lives inside of them and then take the responsibility for that freedom, to acknowledge that God lives within, and that the Real Self is the Christ consciousness.

You can be an Arab or a Jew and have that conviction. It's too bad that religion gets tangled up with this basic self-awareness that is beyond the lines of organized religion or the world religious movements. The Arabs must believe that they live and are in the Spirit of Mohammed and the same Spirit that moved him. The Jews must understand that Christ lived in Abraham and Isaac, Elijah and Elisha, and so forth; that the same power that they had is in them—to part the Red Sea, to do anything, to solve the Middle East crisis.

We're going to sing this song to the souls of all of these people who are struggling for freedom, and we're going to sing it with the absolute conviction that the sacred fire arcing from our heart touches every living soul and gives it a spur to God-reality.

> Light, set me free!
> Light, set me free!
> Light, set me free!
> Light command, Light command, Light command,
>   command, command!
> Light demand, Light demand, Light demand,
>   demand, demand!
> Light expand, Light expand, Light expand,
>   expand, expand!
> Light I AM, Light I AM, Light I AM, I AM, I AM!
> I AM a being of violet fire,
> I AM the purity God desires!

There Is Only One Great Heart

If you can sing that in your heart, you can sing it in any heart, because there is only one great Heart, there is only one universal Christ. Every heart that is beating in every man and woman and child on the continent of Africa and in the Middle East is your heart, my heart, God's heart, Christ's heart. Let's get over the sense that there are many hearts. There is one great heartbeat of which we are all pulsations. So if we can go in our heart and sing this, we can go right into the heart of everyone on that continent and hear the voice of God that we are releasing through the throat chakra singing, "Light, Set Me Free!"

Isn't this the greatest freedom that you can imagine?—the freedom to move through the human consciousness and command the light of the Christ and to be God. The science of the spoken Word is based on the fact that God is really the decreer. God is the Word made manifest —the decreer, the decree, and the answer to the decree all in one. We open our mouths by free will; God does the rest. Try letting God sing this through you now.

> Light, set me free!
> Light, set me free!
> Light, set me free!
> Light command, Light command, Light command,
>   command, command!
> Light demand, Light demand, Light demand,
>   demand, demand!
> Light expand, Light expand, Light expand,
>   expand, expand!
> Light I AM, Light I AM, Light I AM, I AM, I AM!
> I AM a being of violet fire,
> I AM the purity God desires!

We Have the Freedom to Be God Anywhere and Everywhere

You know God never interferes with free will, yet we have the freedom to be God anywhere and everywhere. What happens if we are releasing the light of God and understanding the one great Heart, but there is an individual who doesn't want to be that freedom or that light, doesn't want to give that command, doesn't want any part of that energy of creation? The God within bows before that free will and the energy is not released, even though we have released a matrix for freedom. And so, to go against free will is always to practice black magic. We do not do that. We consecrate our calls to the will of God and to the freedom of the individual to accept or to reject.

So let us go to the heart of creation. Let the creation give response as we, because we have the science of the Word, trigger the release of God in lifewaves who have not known that release for thousands of years.

> Light, set me free!
> Light, set me free!
> Light, set me free!
> Light command, Light command, Light command,
> command, command!
> Light demand, Light demand, Light demand,
> demand, demand!
> Light expand, Light expand, Light expand,
> expand, expand!
> Light I AM, Light I AM, Light I AM, I AM, I AM!
> I AM a being of violet fire,
> I AM the purity God desires!

In the name of the Christ, the light of the hearts of all mankind, we invoke the sealing action. We invoke the sealing of freedom, and the freedom to be, and the freedom to have the choice to be and to understand that choice by love, by wisdom, and by power. In the name of the Father-Mother God, the Son, and the Holy Spirit, we accept the answer to our call fulfilled in this moment in time and space and in eternity.

I thank you.

6

STARS AND STRIPES OF OUR COSMIC CONSCIOUSNESS

A Dictation by the Elohim Arcturus and Victoria

Hail to the light of cosmos!
Hail to the light of freedom!
We are in the flame of sacred fire. We are in the light of far-off worlds. We are the stars and stripes of cosmic consciousness in the flags of all of the nations and in the banner of Maitreya and in the banner of the World Mother that flies with every national flag as the result of the dispensation of Saint Germain to anchor the flame of freedom in the capitals of the nations.[1]

We are the cosmic consciousness of the freedom of the Elohim to create. Freedom *is* the freedom to create. If, then, you are denied that freedom to create, we say you have not rediscovered the flame of freedom—the great discovery of Almighty God, which in his love he has shared with his sons and daughters throughout the creation.

The violet flame is the flame of alchemy. The violet flame is the sacred fire. It is the power, the wisdom, and the love to change that which ought to be changed and to seal, as the creation, that which ought to be sealed. And this is the choice of a free people. The daily choice to be or not to be is the choice to consign to the flame of freedom that which ought not to be and the choice to ratify by that flame that which ought to continue for eternity.

You say this is the power of God. Indeed it is the power of God, but God is in you. God is the fire within you. And therefore God, exercising the energies of Brahma, Vishnu, and Shiva, is the fire of freedom creating, preserving, and destroying—the continual undulations of the fire of creation sending forth, sustaining by the power of the spoken Word, and again using that Word to recall energies of creation misused. And thus, the fulfillment of love is the freedom again to create or to destroy, to preserve or not to preserve. And in your hands that gift of freedom is a fire, a living fire.

We Come to Ask the Question . . .

We come, then, to this system of worlds, touching down to this point on Terra. We come to ask the question. We ask it of the Lords of Karma and of the ascended masters who guide the destinies of nations. We ask this question: Are there sons and daughters of God who will continue to fan the fires of freedom on earth and in the planes of Mater on the planets in this system of worlds?

We ask that question, and do you know why we ask that question? Because we also report to the Cosmic Council, which long ago convened to determine the fate of the evolutions of earth. It is a tale twice told, many times told, that the Cosmic Council decreed the action of the Destroyer, the action of the fire of the Holy Spirit, for the consuming of this round and this lifewave.[2]

Now I ask *you* the question: Why do you really suppose that that decision was made by the Cosmic Council? It was, of course, that men and women of earth had failed to remember the identity of the Self as God. But it was more than that. It was that there were no longer free souls willing to ensoul freedom. There was no longer the freedom to pursue the path of initiation.

These Worlds Were Created as a Platform for Evolution

I tell you this: these worlds were created by God, by the Elohim in answer to the edict of God, to provide a platform for evolution, for attainment and self-mastery. They were not created that an evolution and a lifewave might play with the energies of God for entertainment, for the pleasure cult, and for the death cult. The Almighty is not interested in the preservation of life and the option for life among the systems of worlds where freedom is denied, where freedom is not the sacred goal of evolution.

All of the striving and the overcoming in all of the rays has its culmination in the seventh-ray action of freedom. If all of your willing, your wisdom and your love, your purity in the Law and your science and your devotion in religion do not culminate in freedom in the religions of the world and in the governments of the nations, then the planet and the evolution has lost its cosmic purpose. Without cosmic purpose, where, then, is the opportunity for self-mastery? Where is life, where is freedom, where is the soul?

Fear not, then, those who kill the body, but fear those who destroy the soul in hell.[3] These are the words of the Master of Peace, who paved the way for the era of freedom. Yes, peace is necessary for freedom. But without freedom, there is no peace. It is a false peace.

The Challenge to Define Freedom, to Defend Freedom

And therefore, let men and women and children in the Aquarian age understand the nexus of the cross of life. What is the nexus? It is the point of the crystallization of the God flame in this mandala of this planetary evolution. The cosmic cross of white fire that is over the earth as the mandala of a fiery destiny, the converging of the lines of force at that center of the cross, is now the crux of freedom.

Here in Terra, then, the purpose, the geometry and the design of this very moment of the release of the Christ consciousness of the Elohim is the challenge to the evolutions of Earth not only to *define* freedom but to *defend* freedom. Where freedom is lost, I can prophesy to you that the decision of the Cosmic Council will be the same as it was thousands of years ago when Sanat Kumara, that freeborn soul from Venus, came to keep the flame of freedom.

There is no life without freedom! *This* is the land that is free and a people who are freeborn. But can that freedom endure if it is not the freedom of all of Earth's evolutions? The world cannot exist half slave and half free.[4] Who are the slaves and who are the free? There is a changing of roles as musical chairs. Those who have freedom allow themselves to be in bondage. And those who are in bondage to one form of tyranny claim their freedom to be in bondage to another form of tyranny, to another form of the shackles of the fallen ones.

The Elohim Release the Proclamation of Freedom

In the light of freedom, I AM come! And I AM come to roll back the bondage of souls in East and West, North and South who have thought they were free and yet who are prisoners of the mortal coil, who are prisoners of their karma, who are prisoners of one another, who are the objects of manipulation and know not that they are being manipulated.

I proclaim the freedom of the electron!
I proclaim the freedom of the atom!
I proclaim the freedom of the molecule!
I proclaim the freedom of the cell!
I proclaim the freedom of the body of God on earth and in heaven!

The Elohim release the proclamation of freedom and the conditions of freedom!

We are not interested in the conditions of peace or in peace pacts or in peace pipes smoked with those who are the adversaries and the aggressors. There is no meeting ground with those who are vying for peace without freedom.

Freedom, the handmaid of Peace!
Peace, the flame of the Christ!
Christ, the Mediator of God!
God, the law of free will to all evolutions everywhere!

I AM come. I AM come only moments following the surrender of that land, the last remaining territory of freedom where there is an ascended master retreat of freedom.[5] I anchor the light of freedom in the etheric plane in the chakra of the Elohim's freedom of earth. I come from Angola; I come from that place where Cuban troops, pawns of the sinister force, pawns of World Communism, have entered.[6]

Forces of Good and Evil

Do you suppose, *do you suppose* that there is any connection between the fact that the retreat of world freedom is there anchored in the etheric plane and the fact that World Communism has vied for that soil? Do you suppose there is any connection? Or do you move with the intelligentsia? Do you move with those who do not see cause and effect sequences? Do you move with those who say there is no conspiracy, there are no fallen ones, there are no devils, there is no false hierarchy, there is no black brotherhood?*

Carry on, I say. Carry on, fallen ones. The judgment is upon you. I AM with the children of God who refuse to believe the lie and to be condemned by that lie.[7] If you believe in the path of freedom and of free will, then you must admit that by the law of the choice, mankind is free, defended by God to choose Darkness or Light, to choose between the black brotherhood and the white brotherhood, between the false teachers and the true teachers of mankind.

Given the choices and given the odds, given mankind's preference for indulgences of the carnal mind, can you not understand that over thousands and hundreds of thousands of years of evolution in this planetary home, there have been souls who have chosen darkness, tyranny, bondage, the carnal mind, who have failed to choose to be Real, who have failed to choose to be free?

These ones who have chosen, then, the dark path of ultimate self-annihilation have organized that false hierarchy, that black brotherhood, and they are known to us as the fallen ones. If you do not, then, recognize that there are forces of Good and Evil and that there is an enemy, you cannot know the enemy. And if you will not recognize the enemy, then you will not fight that enemy and you will leap into the jaws of that enemy.

Establish Freedom within Yourself

First of all, then, let those who are sincere in the love of freedom enter the path of initiation. Let them enter the Path and let them establish freedom within themselves. Let them understand that the battle must first be fought here.

You must define the enemy within yourself. You must define the consciousness that limits you, that binds you to the laws of mortality. You must see the enemy as sloth, self-indulgence, self-centeredness, pride and ambition and all of the sins that have been clearly outlined by the great avatars of the ages. The enemy is within. It is within the

---

*The terms *black* and *white* refer not to race but to the auras that surround these individuals.

consciousness that has not surrendered to the will of God.

Then you will summon the forces of light of your own Christ-potential and the energies that God has vested in you, and you will swiftly put down the enemy of freedom and thereby define your wholeness and your oneness as an individualization of the God flame, as an individuality and as an identity in God.

From that point of wholeness, then, you will examine the next mandala of your initiation, the mandala of your nation, and you will say, What is the enemy? And you will look again and you will define the enemy within.

You will see the social consequences of the choice to amplify the carnal mind in the four lower bodies. You will see the consequences in government, in education, in the economy, in the laws, in the people themselves, and you will begin to invoke the light of the Elohim to conquer that enemy within. And by the power of the spoken Word, you *will* conquer that enemy. And then you will look without, you will look to earth, you will look to the planetary body and you will say, What is the enemy of world freedom?

There Is a Conspiracy of Darkness

Now, the carnal mind that was within is still within, but it is within individuals. It is within those who have aligned themselves as a power bloc of fallen ones both in and out of embodiment, both in and out of the governments of all of the nations—the infiltrators, the spoilers of mankind's freedom. Because they are both in and out of embodiment, because one and all, they have chosen the left-handed path, there is a conspiracy.*

It is a conspiracy of darkness and deceit, self-betrayal that issues from self-deception. Thus the conspiracy, though it may not be conscious among those who walk in the same path of self-degeneration, is nevertheless present. And by vibration, by energy coils, by commitment, all those who have chosen the left-handed path are one, no matter what the plane of existence, whether it be in the physical, the astral or the mental. Wherever there is a choice, wherever there is a

---

*conspiracy, from the verb *conspire* (second definition): "to act in harmony toward a common end" [*Merriam-Webster's,* tenth edition]

choice for darkness, for hatred, for annihilation, that consciousness is one—one as a mass, a forcefield of dark energy that now, in this hour, hangs over the land, the very land of Angola, usurping the flow of energy from our etheric retreat.

There Is a Conspiracy of Light

Even so, all who are in Christ, who have chosen the Real Self, all who are in the light of Buddha and of the Divine Mother are also one. And in this oneness is their strength, in this union is that light of overcoming. This, too, is a conspiracy. It is a conspiracy of light reflecting light. It is the manifestation of the law of equality, of equal measure, of things equal to the same thing being equal to each other. This is congruency.

Lightbearers are congruent with the mind of God. And the ones who carry the darkness, they are congruent with the minds of the self-deceived and the self-hypnotized. And therefore there is a connection, there is a reason why the world movement of Communism (that despite the arguments of the Communists is one and is not separated from nation to nation) has seized upon Angola.

Retreats of the Violet-Flame Masters

The Communists have already seized the landed areas corresponding to the other etheric retreats of the violet-flame masters:

Kuan Yin, Goddess of Mercy, the retreat over Peking*—the flow of the energy of that retreat, which is the essence of mercy itself, blocked by human tyranny and the subjugation of the family.

Saint Germain and the Great Divine Director, the Rakoczy Mansion —[the retreat] now focused in the etheric plane over Romania, where World Communism has also divided the eastern states of Europe, not according to the lines of the culture of the Mother but according to the lies of the manipulation of the people, a people born to outpicture the flame of freedom in that house of light, that house that is the focus of the Maltese cross of your own precipitation of freedom.

Stronghold of freedom in the West—retreat of Zadkiel and Holy

---

*the Temple of Mercy

Amethyst in the etheric plane over Cuba.* Why did the forces of World Communism select Cuba and not another nation in Latin America? Was it strategically convenient? Physically, perhaps so. But far more strategically convenient from the standpoint of spiritual law. And thus, where are those who would anchor freedom on the island of Cuba? They are blocked by the tyranny of the state.

These are the key focuses of freedom on Terra. Angola, the land corresponding to the one remaining focus of the seventh ray to be anchored in a people born to be free, is now taken over. And why? Because the people who are born to be the defenders of freedom have not understood the choices, have not understood that there exists an enemy.

The Philosophy of Détente Has Accomplished Its Ends

The philosophy of détente has accomplished its ends. It is a diabolical philosophy of compromise of the freedom of the world. Its end has been to brainwash the American people so that they now believe the enemy does not exist. And America is friends with all those who have subjugated the masses, who have murdered millions in order to come to power.

Without the definition of the enemy, the lines of battle cannot be drawn, foreign policy cannot be drawn, domestic policy cannot be drawn. Without the definition of the lines of battle, a free people will be swallowed up, a free and victorious people will be devoured in the jaws of defeat.

It is not only Angola that they desired in the very desiring of the carnal mind, it is all of Africa. It is the control of the resources of the Mother and the light of the Mother chakra. It is the control of the Indian Ocean, of the Persian Gulf, of the waterways. It is the control of earth from that very point, that harbor at Angola. Yet the American people do not recognize their responsibility to defend freedom. They fear the loss of individual lives. Again I say, fear not those who kill the body but those who destroy the soul in hell.

Will you preserve your bodies while your souls *rot*?

---
*the Temple of Purification

This I ask the American people on the birthday celebration of the greatest focus of freedom the world has ever known in modern times. Will you allow the soul of America to rot by an immorality and a lack of honor and integrity when it comes to the path of initiation and to the flame of life on Terra?

The Earth Is a Unit of Soul Evolution

You cannot see the earth in any other way but as a unit of hierarchy, a unit of soul evolution. There is no division; there are lovers of freedom in every land. People are not evil. *People are not evil!* The wicked are not the Russians or the Chinese. The wicked are the fallen ones who are in positions of power in every nation.

Have you not seen the wicked in their manipulations in this dark episode that has covered the land, that you call Watergate, and prophetically so?[8] For it is the gate to the emotional body, to the water body, and that is the gate where the American people stand in their initiations on the Path. Standing at the gate of cosmic consciousness, they must pass the initiation of the mastery of the water element. And the perversion of that mastery is dishonor. It is lying, it is cheating, it is sneaking, it is taking funds and misusing them. It is the misappropriation of freedom, of position and power.

And here you are, millions and millions of souls who know the truth. Your power has been divested from you. You have forgotten your Source. You have forgotten the name of God, I AM THAT I AM.[9] You have forgotten that you are the Christ in action. You have forgotten what the power of God is! You have forgotten what his wisdom is, his promises, the covenant that he made with Abraham: "I will make thy seed as the sands, innumerable."[10]

This is the seed of the lightbearers, who are destined to conquer the earth by the flame of Christ, by the flame of God-mastery. And in the process of conquering the self that they might become the servants of all, they must defend, *defend,* I say, the bastions of freedom on every continent at the expense, yes, *the expense* of the paltry pleasures, the temporary illusions, the temporary indulgences that Western society continues and continues to wallow in.

Where is the dedication? I will tell you where the dedication is.

The dedication is with the fallen ones and with those of the children of light whom they have manipulated into believing that World Communism is the way of equality and freedom and justice for the masses. No small wonder that the children of light believe this lie, for the sons and daughters of God have not refuted the fallen ones in their midst. They have allowed them to misuse the very system of freedom and the path of initiation that is enshrined in the documents of freedom, in the Declaration of Independence and in the Constitution of the United States of America.

I say the name with reverence. For even among those of the Great White Brotherhood, we pay homage and reverence to this nation conceived in liberty—not because of the wrongs and injustices, but because at the core of a nation is Saint Germain, is freedom, is consecration. We speak the name with the same reverence that we speak the name Jesus the Christ, the individual Saviour now become the nation that is intended to be the Saviour of nations.

Can you not understand? *Will* you not understand? Will you not put down those who are the manipulators of the abundance of the Mother and of her virgin consciousness in this land? Will you not go forth and rescue the souls who are misaligned, who are feeding their pure energies into this and that camp of politics and religion and every manner of involvement that does not lead to the central purpose of creation and the creation of earth itself—*freedom.*

Stop Your Senseless Indulgence

Ask yourself what *you* do with the energies of God daily. Are all of your actions, all of your thoughts and feelings contributing to your own soul emancipation and to the emancipation of all peoples? If not, I say, *eliminate* those actions and those thoughts and feelings. *Stop* your senseless indulgence, and *realize* that when the earth is carved up and under world tyranny, there will not be an emergence from that tyranny for thousands of years. And it will be the decree of the free will of a people who held the torch of freedom in their hands and who *let go* of that torch! For what reason? They will not even remember the reason they let go of that torch, and only the Book of Life will bear the record.[11]

You cannot say to yourselves, *We* will invoke the violet flame.

We will make our ascension in this life. *We* will not be around when there is world tyranny—the tyranny of a world religion, the tyranny of a world government. Do you think you will be accepted among the ranks of the immortals? Do you think you will pass the tests of your ascension if you fail to ratify freedom in Terra? *You cannot take the Path selfishly,* but it must be a selfless action whereby the freedom that you forge within your own soul is then applied to the planetary body.

Precious ones, I am speaking to souls who understand, and I know well that you understand. But I am anchoring within the mental belt, the etheric plane, the emotional body and the physical quadrant of the earth this message of freedom. I am stirring the American people through you and through the chakras of this messenger. I am stirring them by the quickening action as a spark that leaps from your fervent hearts to the hearts of a fervent people who, if they knew better, would do better.

Afra, the Soul of Millions Born to Be Free

Therefore, we mourn. We mourn the loss of the stronghold of freedom, and we are concerned. Our concern is that if the Congress of the United States of America will not allocate funds for the defense of freedom in Angola, then will the Congress of the United States allocate funds for the defense of freedom in Mozambique, in South Africa, in Rhodesia, in every nation in Africa?

And what of the Middle East? And what of the warring members of the body of God who are the very ones who embodied here on Terra, remnants of the laggard evolution of Maldek, the very ones who by their relentless struggle refused the compromise of love and of Christ and therefore caused the destruction of that planet?[12] All of this is Afra.* All of this, the soul of millions of people born to be free, manipulated into hatred.

Stars and Stripes of Initiation for God-Mastery in America

Keepers of the Flame unascended, you have a mighty work to accomplish for the Lord God of hosts. He is counting on you for the flow of the energy, the stripes of cosmic consciousness, alternating

---
*Africa

stripes of Alpha and Omega—waves of energy that precipitate from out the Great Central Sun that are intended to be anchored in the hearts of millions of people by an action of a cosmic maypole, where the flow of these ribbons of light is the flow of the energies of the Elohim and the solar hierarchies. Wherever there is tyranny exercised over the people, there is a blocking of the flow and the people are severed from the stripes of cosmic consciousness.

And what of the stars of cosmic consciousness, five-pointed stars marking initiation? It is the initiation to enter the white-fire core of being. If a planet and a people does not qualify for that initiation, then it cannot go within to release the energies of the Christ that are for the liberation of the lifewave. The point of freedom is the white-fire core of being. To enter there, you must pass certain initiations. If you will not submit to these initiations, then you have not the contact of the fiery core of yourself or of cosmic beings, and therefore you cannot derive the energies of the stars of our cosmic consciousness.

And so the stripes are for the testing of the people in the way of the seven rays. And the seven rainbow rays across the sky are the stripes, the stripes of the original thirteen, of Christ and his apostles, of a new nation conceived on the foundation of hierarchy—thirteen states of consciousness ratifying discipleship, ratifying that here on this soil people shall be free and there shall be a government "of the people, by the people, and for the people."[13]

Stars and stripes of our cosmic consciousness! The twelve Elohim —seven in outer manifestation, five in the white-fire core of the Great Central Sun—send forth the momentum of the twelve aspects of God-mastery that must be forged and won in America. And out of the midst of the twelve Elohim is the manifestation of the Cosmic Christ, Lord Maitreya, the Coming Buddha. And the Christed One forms the center of our mandala, and by the action of the Mother flame we come to anchor this light among sons and daughters of freedom.

This is why we have asked the question, Are there sons and daughters on earth *who will declare freedom, who will work for freedom, who will make any and every sacrifice for freedom?*

For in these we will anchor the stars and stripes of our cosmic consciousness, in these Lord Maitreya will anchor the flame of initiation, and to these the Mother will come to minister unto their souls in the hour of the victory.

I Plant My Flame in This City

America, be free!

America, guard the bastions of planetary liberty!

America, review, examine, analyze and see what is Real and what is unreal.

I plant my flame in this city! I plant my flame for the action of the will of God in the *voice* of the people, in the throat chakra of the spoken Word! Let the people be represented in this government! And let the fallen ones who have usurped the places of the Christed ones be *bound!* Let them be *bound,* I say, in the power of the Elohim! And let them be *stripped* of their facade! And let them be *exposed!*

We have come! I AM Arcturus! I AM Victoria! And we will not turn our backs so long as there are sons and daughters who understand the love, the real love of freedom.

In the oneness of the flame, we are within your soul—*freedom* of Terra, *freedom* in the Aquarian age. Now set hierarchy free to act, act, act through you!

7

THE RISE OF THE FEMININE RAY IN AMERICA

A Dictation by Lady Master Venus

O life, sweet life, unfolding as love within the heart, O music of the spheres, O harmony of souls, I call unto Venus, star of love. I call unto the causal bodies of lifewaves who have sealed all their living and their giving and their surrendering of the self unto the Self in love.

Venus, sphere of love, home of my heart's longing, I salute thee. I salute the flame of Sanat Kumara. I am in Terra for the consecration of love as freedom, that earth might rise to be the twin star of Hesper.

I come for the celebration of the rise of the feminine ray in America. I come to give the counterpart to the release of the seven Holy Kumaras anchored in Maui,[1] the place of Mother and of Mu. And by the action of the priests and priestesses of the sacred fire, the release of the feminine principle, the seven aspects in the seven rays, was begun through the intonations of the Word by thousands of priests and priestesses of Mother, of Mu.

We come, maidens of Venus, of spring, with baskets of floral offerings, baskets to catch the release of light and fire. We would catch the bursting of fire, as the fireworks on the Fourth of July. We pursue the Holy Kumaras, catching with our baskets the light of their release as the bursting of cosmic consciousness, as though we could contain the fire.

Yet we are handmaids of the Lord.[2] We come, chalices that are the chakras of Being, to capture the light of far-off worlds. This is the role of woman. This is the way woman will rise in America and in every nation, taking the light of Alpha, seizing it, cherishing in the heart, in the soul, the mind, the third eye, in the Word, in the peace, in the purity of the One.

The Role of Woman

What does it mean to be feminine? Must we not define the principles of femininity to understand what the rise of that ray is in this land of enlightenment and self-awareness?

Women of America and of every nation are demanding freedom. They are securing laws and working for amendments to have the right to be woman. What is that right to be woman?

I have enjoyed that right for thousands of years unchallenged. I AM the light of that feminine ray, and the image of the power and the compassion, the strength and the tenderness, the image of maternity. The image of life flowing is mine by attainment and mine to give. It is yours to receive by attainment.

This attainment cannot be secured by outer laws or polemics or blame or censure or disdain. This freedom is freedom when it is won through self-sacrifice. Only when woman learns to lay down that life that she cherishes will she find it again, but finding it in God means to find woman liberated in the fullest dimension of the limitless consciousness of the one flame.

Laws are a temporary action by man to protect, to secure and to safeguard, but when attainment is won, no law for or against that attainment can compromise or gainsay its manifestation. Love is the fulfilling of the Law. As Francis said, "In giving we receive; in dying we are born to eternal life."[3]

Let woman go within. Let her discover the true meaning of the womb. The womb is the place of the birth of the Christ consciousness. The singular role of woman is that all inside she has a cosmos whereby sons and daughters of God come to self-awareness. The consciousness of woman is the womb of time and space.

The Feminine Potential to Be God

Paltry gains are women's rights. Woman, you have a cosmos to implement your mastery. Women of the world, we of Venus would have you come of age in love.

Souls of all mankind, yours is the feminine potential to be God. Woman must release and accept the opportunity for man to release his feminine potential, which is the soul aspiring to be free. Woman must give to man the opportunity to be free, if she herself would be free.

Let woman, then, be free from her own wiles of manipulation and control. Let her be free from the Eve consciousness of temptation. But let her ever focus the light of Mary adorning the Christ, paving the way for the path of initiation.

Women of America, free man and you shall be free! Free the manifestation of the light of God within your families and your communities. Defend your freedom by the fire of the Holy Spirit. Let God, the masculine principle of Father, Son and Holy Spirit, be your defense. It is the light invincible. This is the certain defense of your freedom.

Women must soar in purity. The sculpture of Venus, conceived in the heart of an initiate, is the conception of the mastery of love without adornment. Woman must pass through the test of the ten and the tenth station of the cross.[4] Woman must be stripped of the adornments of the ego. Woman must be free to be a goddess, free in abundance, free in opportunity, free in mercy because she understands that the fount and the source of her life is the masculine principle of her own identity.

The Feminine Aspect Is the Liberator of the Age

Life, *life* moves on. And our prayer of the rose of the Immaculate Conception is that the limitations and the confines of consciousness, the molding of woman into something less than the liberator be overcome by the law of transcendence, by cycles releasing unto cycles until, content in the awareness of God, the only desire of woman is to beget God consciousness.

This desire meets with the response of God desiring to be God. And woman, as the handmaid of her Lord, gives birth to the Saviour. And the Saviour is the saving energy of the Christ, which raises the fires of the Goddess Kundalini, raises the light and the flow in the fountain of purity. And by the touch of her hand and the warmth of her smile, mankind are free.

The feminine aspect of man and woman is the liberator of the age. Mighty conquerors are the goddesses of the heavens, conquerors of time and space, conquerors of flow. They become the instruments of the Lord's expansion of consciousness. In poetry and in art, in science and in law, the feminine aspiration enables man to become whole.

All strife and division within the self, within society, is the result of the confusion of roles—the roles of man and woman, the role of the soul, the direction of the soul to the center of God. Let the roles be defined according to the path of initiation. Let the equality of the creation be the relationship of father and mother, brother and sister, disciples hand in hand, uniting in the love of twin flames—equality yet diversity of roles.

Woman cannot portray the role of man; she has her own role. It is not necessary for a woman to be like man any more than the currents of the base chakra are equated with the currents of the crown chakra. Both are necessary, and in the convergence of these energies, the Buddhic light, the Christ consciousness is born. Polarity defines roles and therefore not to be like man but to be the opposite, this shows forth the handiwork of God.

Woman Has Rebelled against Her Role as Mother

Women in this age have, first and foremost, one of the greatest opportunities of all ages: to be hostesses for the coming of Christed ones who have volunteered to incarnate in Terra, Christed ones who plead before the Lords of Flame for incarnation that they might be freedom in Terra.

Woman, then, has rebelled against her role as Mother. What will she be, then—Father? Will she be the Christed One or the Holy Spirit? Four aspects of God self-awareness—Mother, the crown of the LORD's rejoicing. Why has the rebellion of fallen woman—demanding freedom to express the lesser self, the carnal mind, the baser instincts—been defined as woman's movement for liberation?

The path of liberation is the path of initiation set by God. It is a ladder to be climbed. Step-by-step, chakra by chakra, woman must master the energies of the sacred fire. To be co-creator with God, the role of Mother, to release the potential of Father and Son and Holy Spirit—all of this God has accorded to woman, and all of this woman has rejected in her ignorance.

In her desire to be free, to choose to be or not to be, she has chosen to slay the Manchild aborning in her womb, and this she calls freedom. Instead of being the life-giver, she plays the role of the murderer of God and says, "I am free."

How can there be such a misunderstanding of freedom in our sister star, we ask ourselves? And the answer that is given is that when rebellion itself, rebellion against the light of the Christ within, is not first cast out, there can be no reunification with reality, no understanding and no vision. Unless and until woman surrenders to her God, she cannot see her fiery destiny. Therefore, in rebellion is that sin of witchcraft practiced against her own,[5] her very own offspring, the offspring of the LORD and of the seed of Alpha.

This misappropriation of freedom must be reversed, for the women of America and the world are sowing the seeds of the destruction of their own freedom. And the karma that is already upon the women who have walked in this way is the groaning and the travail of a planetary home crying out to give birth to the Christ consciousness, crying "Mother! Mother! Mother! Set me free! Give me life! Give me wholeness! Give me opportunity to know myself as God!"

How is the heart of woman hardened unto the cries of the child within the womb? Is it selfishness? Is it self-love? Is it a death consciousness? Is it a mass hypnosis by the fallen ones? Is it the death wish? Is it that, in seeking freedom, she seeks freedom to die and for her own to die?

What is the madness of the hell that woman has created for her habitation?

My Prayer to Save Woman

O my God, O my God, O my God! I kneel in prayer at the altar of the Most High.

I send my love to God, and I ask that God return it unto this generation as the distillation of the wisdom of his heart, that the heart of God might instruct this generation, that man might come to the rescue of woman, that the men of America might shake the women to their senses, shake them from the frenzy of this insanity.

I call to men who remember the service as Knights of the Table

Round, defenders of purity and honor, those who have sought the Holy Grail. I implore you to defend the virtue, the integrity and the honor of the Mother, the Mother flame of your heart, that woman might be called to her high estate, that you in calling her there might then be the recipients of that grace that can flow from her hands.

It may be that woman has betrayed her calling, and in the betrayal of her calling she has betrayed her man, but I have no recourse but to call to man and to say, Rush! Run to elevate consciousness. Help the woman who is struggling with the dragon that has come to make war with her offspring, to defeat the seed of God, to deprive the children of the new birth in freedom.

The Lord God sent Michael the Archangel to slay the dragon.[6] Will you not, O men of America, champion the cause of Archangel Michael? Will you not raise the sword of blue flame to cut free woman and thereby cut free your own soul potential?

If woman does not know her calling, will you not tell it to her? Will you not support her? Will you not elevate her to that place of devotion, the rightful place of the woman of your life and of your love?

I appeal to the hosts of heaven. I appeal to the hearts of you who have life and form and opportunity for overcoming. You who have life, will you not pray for those who seek life through you, that they might have a safe passage into the octaves of the physical plane?

I see the little children crucified upon the cross of human hatred. I hear the echoes of their cries, as Christ on Golgotha, "My God, my God, why hast thou forsaken me?"[7]

Reverse the Course of the Black Stream

Souls of America, reverse the course of the black stream, and let it become the crystal stream of the River of Life.[8] Let the stream flow from the centers of God within you. Let it rise. Let man and woman raise their heads. Let them look into the eyes of the ascended masters without shame, without guilt.

Look into the eyes of an archangel and know the judgment of the Law within you. Look into the eyes of innocent children. Can you stand their gaze? If you cannot, then be upon your knees that God might restore the innocence that is the inner sense of true freedom.

I AM Venus. I carve the image of your feminine principle. For each one I sculpt the true design of light, the inner blueprint of what your soul, liberated, looks like in the cosmic mirror—the nobility of countenance, the strength, the stature, the very light and halo of the gods. America, return to your fiery destiny in the feminine ray!

I call, I call, I call to *Wien*.* I call to the point of the crystallization of the spiral of love. I call to the souls. I sing to the souls. I sing the song of love, and by my love I call you to the home, the center of the Om.

Walk Ye in the Way of Love

I place my prayer, my faith and my hope in the charity of your hearts. I know it is not misplaced, and by the love of the pink rose of my heart you will respond to the rose of your own heart, and all will be well. And all will be restored, and the resurrection and the life of the Christed ones will be secure. And their life will be the healing of earth, the healing of all wrong.

This is the way. Walk ye in the way of love. I am in the oneness of our flame within you. Sanat Kumara sends love and hope and fire, and the light of Mighty Victory. O Son of Flame, O Mighty Victory of Venus, look upon Terra and let this people know the meaning of victory — victory unto the One!

So, let it be. So, it is done.

---

*Wein, German for Vienna, is pronounced *veen*, as the first three letters of Venus. The Venusian evolution first descended in Austria.

8

THE DISCIPLINES OF HIGHER CONSCIOUSNESS

A Dictation by Serapis Bey, Hierarch of Luxor

The path of the ascension is the path of love. It is love and the dream of love fulfilled. The disciplines for the initiations of the ascension into higher consciousness can be borne only by love—by the heart and the soul so filled with love for God, the Great Guru, that it will endure unto the end, the end of the cycles of human consciousness. The Path is straight and narrow,[1] as you have heard. The climb is over rigid heights, scaling cliffs jagged, over precipice and abyss into the high road, into the mountains of the Himalayas.

Souls are called and impelled by love—the love of the mountaineers, the love of the Elohim who have anchored their focuses in the heights of the mountains of the earth. Love and love alone is the key to overcoming. For God is love. And where selfishness lurks, there will be compromise, there will be the moment's hesitation, and the battle is lost, the moment of indecision when the idling of energy creates a gap in the spiraling and in the flow and the movement of God.

How Great Is Your Love?

Therefore, in the hour of decision, in the moment when the question arises out of that human questioning to be or not to be on the path of initiation, we ask a question. For we are the hierarchs of Luxor, of the Retreat of the Ascension Flame. We guard the steely white, intense sacred fire that can be contained only by those who live in the purity of love. And therefore, while you are engaged in your human questioning of the Guru, we ask the supreme question: How much do you love, how great is your love?

Is your love great enough to make the sacrifice for the overcoming, for the Path, for the cause of the Great White Brotherhood in order that others among mankind might also receive the teachings, the Law, and the understanding of the fulfillment of the promise of love? Faced with this question, the individual must either retreat into his old ways of the self-centered existence or come forth from that cocoon of selfishness and fly with the wings of the Spirit, the wings of love that are the certain victory.

One Step into the Arms of the I AM Presence

There is a key in the disciplines to higher consciousness. The key is not to become entangled in the labyrinth of human questioning and the fears and the doubts and specters of the night that haunt that labyrinth. You do not have to trace the meanderings of the carnal mind and the human consciousness through all of the levels of the subconscious in order to come to the knowledge of Truth, in order to come to Reality or to overcome in love.

The key is not to be drawn by curiosity or a fascination with horror or a gluttony for the things of the senses, drawing you down into more and more astral experiences and psychic phenomena. The key—instead of taking a thousand steps through the astral plane—is to take one step into the arms of the I AM Presence, into the plane of the Christ mind where the oneness and the wholeness of that Great Pyramid, the oneness and the wholeness, is the dissolving action.

Transcend Your Cycles

Transcend your cycles! Do not follow those negative spirals round and round and round, down and down unto the death manifestation in the very crypt of the electronic belt. But with one invocation to the ascension fire, let that flame leap and arc from spiral to spiral, consuming on contact the debris. The flame is not linear; it need not travel over the lines of human creation. And so your soul, enveloped in the flame, also need not remain any longer in the consciousness that the only way out is through the labyrinth.

I say, transcend it! This means that in the moment when you would indulge your pettiness, your argumentation, your human nonsense, your dalliance in childishness, in that moment you instantly let go and you let God be the light that swallows you up in the victory of love. And the love that is your victory is your own love that is God made manifest within you.

And our God *is* the all-consuming fire of love.

Keeping That Steady Flow of Energy Loving God

Love God enough so that you do not need to satisfy human desire. You do not have to appease the carnal mind and give it what it wants so that you will have a moment's peace, an hour's peace. You do not have to engage your energies in imperfection. As much as you think that it is sometimes necessary, I tell you that by meditating within—within the heart and upon the threefold flame of life—by meditating upon the Presence and keeping that steady flow of energy of loving God arcing to him and his love returning, completing the whole of the two arcs as the two halves of the circle, *you can transcend the former cycles.*

If you can sustain your attention upon your I AM Presence and upon the light, you will receive the energy necessary to deal with all outer circumstances (karma) and that without traveling through them in your emotions, in your mental concepts, in your memory, and in physical labor. Think, then, upon this. The disciplines for higher consciousness demand that you prove how it is that you can be in the world and yet not of this world.

The First Step: Become as a Little Child

And how is it so? To be the disciplined one, astute in the understanding of the Law and its counterfeit creation, the first step is to become as a little child. You must become the child of innocence before you can mature to the Christed man and the Christed woman. Do not, then, try to become the full Master of Galilee before you have traced the coils of God consciousness and of Christ consciousness that are lawfully yours to trace—not the labyrinth of the carnal mind, but the blueprint of the etheric path of initiation. And therefore, become as the little child.[2]

I will now regress you in your soul awareness to that point of embryonic life of your consciousness of innocence, entering into that form of the tiny babe. Total trust and faith and hope and charity are yours. You have not hardened your heart, you have not hardened yourself to become a cynic in the world. Your skin is tender; it is not toughened by the failures of others. And so in the sweet perfume of your love of Mother and the Mother's love for you, you remember wholeness in God and this is all of your identity.

You Are a Babe in Christ

You are a babe in Christ. You are calm and serene, with the absolute conviction that your life is in God, that God is caring for you. And the most essential quality of becoming this tiny babe is to understand the quality of helplessness. When you are totally helpless, then you must allow God to work his work within you. You can truly say, as the child of Christ: "I of mine own self can do nothing. It is the Father in me which doeth the work."[3]

You have a clear transparency, purity from the immaculate vision of the Cosmic Virgin. Immaculately conceived, you know no sin, you know no separation from God. You are in the womb of the Mother. You are surrounded by the waters of the living Word. You are at peace, and life is yours to conquer because you are God in manifestation.

Now you are ready for the disciplines whereby the babe will become the child, and the child as the Manchild will grow and wax strong in the teaching of the Lord. And by the time he is twelve, he will know the doctrine of the ascended masters and he will be discoursing in the temples.[4]

And so you come out into outer manifestation, out of the inner womb into the outer womb. Now your habitation is a cosmos, a brave new world, a world filled with light and yet with shadows and darkness somehow as yet undefined to your precious soul. You come forth and you travel the cycles of your individual cosmic clock and you bow before the great initiators of life, the solar hierarchies.

And each one gives to you the disciplines of the sacred fire: of God-power, God-love, and God-mastery, of God-control, God-obedience, God-wisdom, God-harmony, God-gratitude, God-justice, God-reality, God-vision, and God-victory. Your soul within those four lower bodies knows all of this teaching of the cosmic clock. You have been close, so very close to the heartbeat of Mother, and through her heartbeat you have learned the cycles of the Father.

Learning the Ways of the World and the Ways of the Law

The little child in innocence begins to learn the ways of the world —a little fall and scrape, tears, and demands that cannot be fulfilled. And therefore, you learn to fulfill your own demands: the shaping of the feelings and of the mental body, the shaping of the mind, the memory, and the noble form—the form that is to house the spiritual fire of life.

This little child—this little child born to be God.

As the veils of innocence are parted one by one and you mature in the understanding of the world as well as in the understanding of the Law, take care. Take care that you do not forget your Source and the fairies and the undines and the gnomes with whom you frolicked as a little one. Take care that you do not forget the faces of angels who have tended your crib, who have watched over you. Take care that you do not forget that there are masterful beings who took you by the hand and walked with you safely through the places of danger.

The Little Child Is the Leader of the Aquarian Age

There are few who will remind you, there are few who will know, for they have all been deprogrammed away from God into the ways of the world. And thus, if you retain your innocence of the little child, you will become the little child who leads all of the aspects of the creation into the knowledge of the Christ.[5]

The little child is the leader of the Aquarian age—the little child within you, the little child now coming of age, not forgetting the Source, but coming into that oneness of balance, of discrimination, of learning, of mastering the studies necessary to function in this world and to be of service and to have the sacred labor.

You must not only become the little child to have the disciplines of higher consciousness, but you must also remain the little child. Better to be hurt again and again than to have the cynicism of the existentialists. Better to be taken advantage of than to mistrust your fellowman.

Better to live in Him and have your being in Christ and let the world have its ways than for you to steel yourself with a false set of armor that is not the tube of light, the holy innocence of white fire, but that is the mastering of deceit and intrigue, the mastering of a carnal ego, the mastering of all of its defenses, its indulgences, and all of its experiences that the fallen ones tell you you must have in order to distinguish light and darkness.

The First Lie: "Taste and See"

This is the first and fundamental lie that is told to the child to take the child from the path of initiation: "Come and experience this, come and experience that. Taste and see, taste and know for yourself whether or not this is for you."

God has said that the little child in all innocence need not taste of the energy veil [temptations of illusory evil], need not partake of it or absorb it or become contaminated by it in order to know the Truth. And there are many saints, such as Saint Thérèse of Lisieux, who from early childhood, like Mother Mary and Jesus, have entered into the Holy of holies and who have found the satisfactions of love in God and in his holy angels.

And those who have accepted that lie and entered into the compromises of all of the things that are offered in the marts of the world are burdened today by a cross of their own making, a cross of their own karma, a cross that is the hatred of the Divine Mother in whose womb they live and move and have that being of light.[6]

The Age of Responsibility of the Sons and Daughters of God

And therefore, the little child maturing to become the master in the way, to carry the cross of world karma, cannot take upon himself that cross of world karma because he is too busy carrying his own cross of selfishness and self-indulgence. And so, many are not equipped to enter into the age of responsibility of the sons and daughters of God, to bear the sins of the world as Christ did when he hung upon that cross —the cross, not of his own human karma, mind you, but the cross of the karma of the race.

In every age there must be souls who are willing to bear a certain portion of the weight of world karma. In these times it is by and large elemental life who bear that weight, for those among mankind who care at all to carry a little extra baggage are few and far between.

Those who love are the disciplined ones who can walk through the narrow streets of the cities of the Middle East where every form of temptation lurks and every aspect of the sins of human consciousness is displayed in these marts.

To walk through or to tarry and explore?

It is one thing to enjoy a shopping trip; it is another to become addicted to going shopping and to examining the manifestations of human consciousness when you ought to be meditating upon the light that burns within the shops of your very own chakras—the shops of the Buddha and the jewels of the Buddha that are in the jewel shop.

Consecrate Your Energy to the One Flame of Life

Precious ones of fire, discipline means to withdraw energy (and with it your attention) from its encasement in the tomb of Matter. It means to sacrifice the flow of energy into lesser creations and to consecrate it to the one flame of life. You have the pearl of great price! The pearl is the symbol of your causal body, and the layer upon layer of the pearl are the spheres of consciousness that you have built layer upon layer around the central core of the I AM Presence.

This iridescent mother-of-pearl is worth all; and therefore the wise man will go and sell all that he has for the one pearl,[7] the one pearl of cosmic consciousness. Its discipline demands that you let go—let go of all of these involvements and realize that from day to day you never know when your soul (bereft of the physical body) will find itself cast on another shore in the mental plane, in the astral plane (God forbid), or in the etheric octave.

Make Time and Space Count

If you were the messenger, you would be in the position to observe day by day those who are born and those who are dying, those who come into the physical plane and those who leave. It is a vast parade of souls taking incarnation and moving on. But the disciplines for higher consciousness, if it is to be retained, must be proven in the physical plane. And therefore it is the admonishment of the hierarchy of Luxor to make time and space count, for they are the crucible whereby you prove your God-mastery and the alchemy thereof.

You require that bowl. You require that matrix that you might fill it with fire. Little progress is made in other planes; for here in Matter—in the physical aspect of Matter—you made your karma, and here you must balance it. And therefore, let none think that they will live forever and forever in these four lower bodies. They are but vehicles of consciousness that are loaned to you, as all of the energy of God is on loan to you, that you might prove the mastery of free will.

I Would Come in the Mystery of Love

I come to you, then, to give you the concept of discipline. You can read in the *Ascension Dossier*[8] and in other documents and dictations from the flame of purity what are the testings of the soul. You can read what are these disciplines. You can read the life of Jesus and Gautama and perceive very clearly the path to the ascension on the seven and the five rays.

But I would come in the mystery of love. I would come in the mystery of the cross of love that is a cross of obedience to the inner law of life. It is a cross of fire. It is the cross of the monstrance that was used by Clare, holding it up as that sacred vessel of the eucharistic Body of Christ to turn back the Saracens who came warlike in their hatred to tear down the city. And you remember other accounts of saints who have held the Host before the oncoming hordes and armies, who have held up the image of the Virgin Mary.

And so your cross of love is a cross of white fire. It is a cross of energy, which, when it is exalted in consciousness by consecration, reverses the tide of human hatred, reverses the darkness of the night, and is your certain protection on the path of love.

The Cross of Love and Light

Let your burden be light![9] Let the cross of your karma become a cross of intense devotion and love. And let your burden be light, moment by moment. May you sense that the victory of love is in correct seeing. And if you have the vision of the diamond of the All-Seeing

Eye of God, the fiery core of Truth, you will see and know that each succeeding burden is yours in your hand to place in the crucible that it might be transmuted and refined as the gold of love, and gold as God consciousness.

Let the cross be transmuted daily. Let your cross be a cross of light so that even while you are balancing your karma, you may carry the weight of world karma in this Dark Cycle,[10] which is manifesting now under the hierarchy of Leo, causing mankind to enter into new lows of selfishness, thoughtlessness, carelessness, a spirit of ingratitude that is actually spiritual/material blindness, a failure to see the gifts and the joys and the abundance of the Creator. And carelessness is a failure to love as he loves, as Mother loves, as the innocent child loves while it is yet in the womb.

The Petition to Carry a Portion of World Karma

I ask you, then, as you make your petitions to the Lords of Karma during this conference, as you write your letters for dispensations, preparing to receive the dispensations that will be written from the Royal Teton Retreat that will be read to you by the Goddess of Liberty on the Fourth of July—as you write your petitions asking for dispensations, asking for light, will you also tell the Lords of Karma, in the name of your own Christ Self, that you are applying to carry a portion of world karma, a portion of the substance of the Dark Cycle, so that earth can have a reprieve, so that mankind, especially the people of America, can have an opportunity to know the Law and to fortify themselves for the victory?

I tell you, as I survey the world scene in all of the dreadfulness of that which is taking place—so much of it unknown to you—that it is pathetic how your leaders have deprived you of the knowledge of what is actually happening in secret diplomacy, in international politics, and even in your state legislatures.

As I survey all of this, I see as the one hope that path of initiation that leads to the ascension and the teachings necessary for the Path—the teachings of the Great White Brotherhood. I see as the one hope the white-fire core of the Keepers of the Flame who will carry the teaching and go near and far to disseminate that teaching, to talk and walk with mankind in the way until they awake from their sleep and begin the path of enlightenment in Buddha.

The one hope, then, is that somehow in a cosmic interval, a cosmic dispensation of the holding of karma and the holding of time and space, that millions will come into a new devotion to Christ and Buddha, will come into a devotion to meditation and the invocations given in the knowledge of the science of the spoken Word, that by this action of understanding and vision and a demonstration of the Law, nations and peoples and continents will be saved from a downward planetary spiral of death, destruction, and disintegration.

My Call for a Cosmic Interval

Let it be, then! For this is my call to the Lords of Karma ere the final decisions are made during this cycle of the year. My call and my petition is, then, for "a cosmic interval," an opportunity for Keepers of the Flame and people of light everywhere to demonstrate the Law and the disciplines thereof, to set the example, to radiate the crown of wisdom, to raise up the energies of Mother.*

This is my petition, and I am also volunteering to carry a portion of world karma. And yet I know that that request cannot be granted, because an ascended master cannot bear that world karma that only those who are unascended can bear as the causes and effects in this world. But I ask it nevertheless, for I ask it hoping that my chelas will observe my petition and that the chelas of the ascension flame will likewise make that call and, having made that call, stand fast and be ready to receive all manifestations less than the Christ that might begin to appear in their worlds.

For you see, that burden can become light and be transmuted before it ever cycles through your four lower bodies. And therefore, the bearing of the weight of world karma need not be a *via dolorosa* but a way of joy, a way of victory and overcoming. For as soon as that energy of world karma is given to you, you consecrate it to the Holy Spirit and the sacred fire, it is transmuted, and lo, your burden is light! This is the calling. You may make it your election if you will.

---

*i.e., the Kundalini

The Initiations of the Great Religions of the World

Let the blessed saints and the devotees of the Catholic Church hear my words. For they do carry in their bodies much of the momentum of the death spirals, and this is why the priests and the nuns have worn black for so long. They are bearing the weight of the momentum of planetary death in the name of their Lord. They are bearing the energy so that mankind can pass through the initiation of the crucifixion.

And those who have not understood their path and their calling have ridiculed that they have the crucifix everywhere, for others who are engaged in other initiations would prefer to see Christ resurrected from the tomb in the garb of the resurrection and the ascension.

Well, all initiations are valid. And therefore, let us have tolerance; for the entire body of God must carry in manifestation these initiations. And therefore, the great religions of the world were founded so that each group mandala might work out that specific way and calling as an example to all. And now you have come to the place of responsibility where you can stand in the center of the sun—the Sun of Righteousness who is your Holy Christ Self—and all of the rays of all of the teachings of all of the religions going out from the center converge in your heart chakra.

A World Religion of Love

And now you have this synthesis of the teaching of the Mother, and so you can be a member of a world religion that is not controlled by the World Council of Churches or the fallen angels who seek to possess mankind. It is a world religion of the Great White Brotherhood and its teachings. It is a world religion of the converging of souls in the flame of the Christ consciousness. It is a world religion of love, of all who have loved enough to surrender those portions of the self that are out of the way with Christ.

And so I say, let us have our cosmic interval! Let us have our cosmic moment and allow the Divine Mother to show the world the teaching of teachings, the great synthesis of all of the great Gurus—the Gurus who are now the ascended masters who come to claim their own.

In the victory of ascension fires, I AM Serapis Bey! I welcome you to Luxor! But I say, if you come to study in our retreat, if you come to prepare for the ascension, if you come, if you come to our retreat, then I say, *Come to stay!*

9

THE DISCIPLINES
FOR HIGHER CONSCIOUSNESS

A Dictation by the Elohim of Purity

Out of the white-fire core of your cosmic consciousness I AM come. I come for one purpose, called by God, admonished by him. I come to earth and to this system of worlds to anchor a cosmic grid, a forcefield of cosmic purity, line upon line, as a giant atom of fire. I place that grid and that forcefield over this system of worlds and each planetary body with its own grid and forcefield. It is the *antahkarana** of the disciplines of the Path.

It is like a child's jungle gym. It is not a jungle of the astral nightmare; it is the precision formula, a geometry of fire whereby the souls who would climb to cosmic consciousness might go one-by-one secure—climbing over the bars of the antahkarana, taking the disciplines of Lord Maitreya, and realizing that the Path is not merely a ladder of life but it has many dimensions. And the more dimensions that you master, the more you come into the awareness of infinite dimensions of self-discipline until every fiber and hair and cell and atom of your own cosmos quivers to the law of the cosmos.

And when the winds of the cosmos, the winds of the Holy Spirit blow through your grid and forcefield, then there will be heard not the jangle of the jungle of the human consciousness but only the melody of the lute, the sound of your soul, the symphony whose tone comes

---

*antahkarana [Sanskrit, "internal sense organ"]: the web of life; the net of light spanning Spirit and Matter, connecting and sensitizing the whole of creation within itself and to the heart of God

forth from the quivering of every line and forcefield of your being to the disciplines of love.

The Opportunity to Be Disciplined by the Elohim

I AM the Elohim of Purity. And when you have gone through the tests of Serapis Bey and the training in that retreat and you have purified yourself, then you will find that before your ascension Serapis Bey will present you unto the Elohim Purity and Astrea that you might become a chela of the Elohim of the fourth ray. This is our dispensation to the children of earth in celebration of the flame of freedom in America.

This is our gift. And from our level of cosmic consciousness, to us there is no greater gift that we could bestow than the opportunity to be disciplined by the Elohim, for then, you see, the ascending chela has the added momentum of that God consciousness whereby he can move from the requirement of the balance of 51 percent of his karma to the balancing of 100 percent of that karma by the grace of the Elohim.

This is an opportunity for souls who are striving for perfection, for sons and daughters of God keeping the flame day and night whose lives are consecrated to the wholeness of the One and who fear not to give the calls to my consort, Astrea—calls to the feminine aspect of Purity, that feminine being like unto Kali who takes her circle and sword of blue flame and strips you of all of that self-pity and that dank and dark substance of that emotionalism and all of that sympathy and that moon substance.

How You Can Unknowingly
Take On the Astral Psychic Consciousness

You do not realize, precious ones who desire to be free, how those substances of the world become enmeshed in your very clothing, in your possessions and your belongings. And as you pass through the world and as you go into centers of large populations, you take on a portion of that astral, psychic consciousness. And the discarnates even trail behind you because they have smelled your light and they enjoy the fragrance of that light.

And even the imprisoned elementals and angels also who have been imprisoned by black magic, they follow after you because they hope to be liberated by your fire. And instead of liberating them, sometimes you say, "I will not give my calls to Astrea today." And therefore you live in that substance, you live in that astral consciousness that is not your own but which becomes your own by osmosis. For that astral mire oozes through your aura and through your emotional body, and pretty soon you find yourself thinking and feeling those things that are coming from the apartment next door or the house down the street or the individuals who are down in city hall plotting their deceit and their practices of deceit against the community.

How You Can Knowingly Put Off Those Discarnates and Misqualified Energies

And so I say, as long as you have decided to be a fiery vortex of light, as long as you have elected to be a pillar of fire, then go all the way. And make those calls to Astrea every day so that the whirling action of the sword of blue flame will be like a giant buzz saw in your aura, drawing into that energy, into the fire infolding itself,[1] all those discarnates and misqualified energies, transmuting that energy and sending it back to God.

And do you know, whatever energy is transmuted through your calls, when it becomes light it is your own, for you have claimed it, you have placed the stamp of your own Electronic Presence upon that energy. And therefore it rises to your own individual causal body and the sins of the world become the glory of your own star of rejoicing.

Is this not a magnificent reward for a few sacrifices and the setting aside of time and space to make the calls? And the more calls you give, the more calls you must sustain. For I can assure you that as soon as the masters see that you have a ritual of making calls to the Elohim Astrea, they allow many conditions manifesting in earth such as plagues and diseases and economic crisis and cataclysm—all of that energy that is pending manifestation—to be swiftly taken up through your calls into your own sacred-fire forcefield for transmutation.

Therefore, understand that once you begin to decree and this energy is spiraling toward you, you cannot suddenly have a vacation. You cannot suddenly take off for a week or two weeks and say, "I will decree again another day." For you will find yourselves inundated by the worldly consciousness, and "the last state of that man is worse than the first."[2] Did he [Jesus] not say, "Go and sin no more, lest a worse thing come unto thee"?[3] Understand, then, that the cleansing is for the moment of consecration, but the cleansing must continue, the house must be purified.

Apply to Be a Chela of Serapis Bey

Therefore I say, apply to the Lords of Karma to be taken as a chela in the retreat of Serapis Bey that you might journey there at night while your bodies sleep. Go in your souls and answer that invitation of Serapis Bey. And understand that his desire to have you stay is based on the fact that some who come are so fearful and so selfish that when they hear the disciplines of the Law they shrink from the presence of the flame and from the purity of Serapis, and they long for their earthly mothers and fathers, they long for their earthly routines. And so they go back, back, back into the astral consciousness of the night whence they came. Serapis Bey is interested in chelas who will come, who will stay in the light and the fire of the victory.

And I AM the Elohim of Purity, and I have now sealed in your four lower bodies the grid and the forcefield that is the antahkarana of your discipline on the Path. It is sealed in earth. It is sealed in every planet in this system of worlds. Therefore, it is also our prayer that the Lords of Karma and the Cosmic Council will provide this cosmic interval that light might triumph in earth and throughout this system of worlds. So let light triumph within your heart, and see what we can do for the victory!

Do You Have the Courage to Be Purity with Me?

I ask also, then, that you give your calls for this dispensation, and your decrees, so that the Lords of Karma will have your vote—a vote on the side of light for victory, for freedom in earth, in love.

I AM Purity! Do you have the courage, precious ones, to be purity with me? I ask you! Then take the key of Serapis and find that love, that selfless love that will give you the courage to be all light, to be purity's light. And when you are that light, you will wake up one day and you will say, "I AM Mother!"

Messenger's Benediction:

With the sign of the heart, the head and the hand to you, we seal you by the cosmic cross of white fire from the heart of Jesus and Gautama. We seal you in the immaculate heart of Purity's love. Let all of this energy from the Elohim and the chohan of purity be sealed in the fiery core of your seven chakras, never to be misqualified by the human consciousness. In the name of the Christ, we thank thee, O God, for thy servants and emissaries who bring to us such grace, such love and such wisdom.

10

THE PURIFICATION OF THE CHAKRAS AND THE FOUR LOWER BODIES: PREREQUISITES FOR HIGHER CONSCIOUSNESS

Elizabeth Clare Prophet

A Meditation in the Full Power of the Spoken Word

The purification of the chakras is the prerequisite for higher consciousness. Consciousness is experienced in the chakras. Seven flames of God's consciousness, seven rays of the Christ in the masculine and the feminine principle, are experienced through the seven chakras beginning with the T'ai Chi, the white-fire core of God, the Alpha to Omega, which is the whirling center of every chakra.

Out of the I AM Presence comes forth the light cascading over the crystal cord through the Christ mind, through the threefold flame of the Christ. That light is anchored within your heart in the threefold flame, and then it is distributed through all of the chakras. So the heart is your key center and it is the only center that has the threefold flame. It is the distributing center for the flow of energy. Just as the physical heart gives and receives the blood and distributes it through the body, so the heart chakra gives and receives the energies of the I AM Presence. (See chart, p. 21.)

Violet-Flame Action of the Holy Spirit

What we want to do with our chakras is to hold them in the purity of the fiery ovoid. We want to have an intense action of violet flame as the beginning of all of our meditations because it is the action of the Holy Spirit. And the quality of the Holy Spirit is that it manifests the twin flames of Alpha and Omega—necessary components to wholeness, to the reestablishment of the balance of the energies around the T'ai Chi.

And so in your first lessons in the Keepers of the Flame Fraternity[1] you learn the invocation of the tube of light and the action of the violet flame for the cleansing of the atoms and the molecules of our bodies and the removing of the debris. Where we have misqualified energy as hatred, it has entered in between the electrons and the nucleus of the atoms with a very heavy substance—molasseslike, sticky substance—which needs clearing by the action of the violet flame. This is a perversion of space—space that is the opportunity to create. We want to make that space in our Matter bodies filled with the light of the Holy Spirit. And when it is filled with the light of the Holy Spirit, we call it *hallowed space.*

When we hallow space, it becomes an open flow for the light of the chakras. As the heart distributes energies to the other six chakras, so the energies that flow through these fill all space in ourselves, in our four lower bodies, with the hallowed light of the Spirit.

The Seven Chakras

The chakras in figure 1 are shown on a straight line as they would appear in the etheric body. We have reached the place where some of our chakras are off-centered, and this occurs through the Fall, the descent of consciousness. The heart is at the left, but the heart chakra in the etheric body is in the center.

Now when there is the compromise of the divine consciousness, we see that the chakras are off-center and their colors are not the pure colors of the seven rays. These colors have been seen by clairvoyants, by those who are psychic who read the chakras of men and women on earth today as they are. And so they see them with all of the misqualified substance that hangs on the outside of the chakras.

The pure colors of the seven rays are the colors for the anchoring of the light of the Elohim in the seven chakras, but by free will you can call forth the light of God through the heart and qualify the threefold

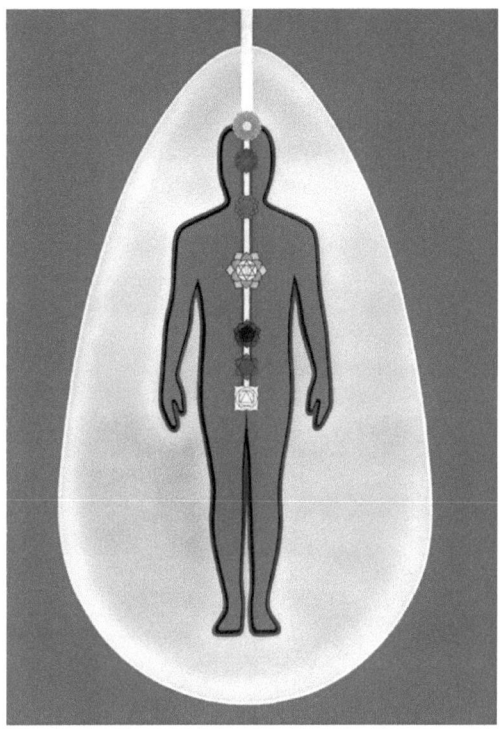

The Seven Chakras in the Purified Etheric Body
FIGURE 1

flame with any color. Consciousness is nothing but vibration. Change the vibration, you've changed the consciousness; change the vibration, you've changed the color.

A chakra is created with a certain number of petals in order to experience a certain frequency in God. The petals of the chakras are specific and hence the frequency is specific—hence the color is specific. When chakras are used in the ways of the world and not reaching yet the purity of the etheric plane, they take on a very different appearance.

To overcome this we must invoke the violet flame, we must have the violet-flame action put through all of these perversions. These perversions show exactly what is going on in the consciousness and how it is reflected. The aura of the individual is a mirror of consciousness, a mirror of vibration, a mirror of frequency.

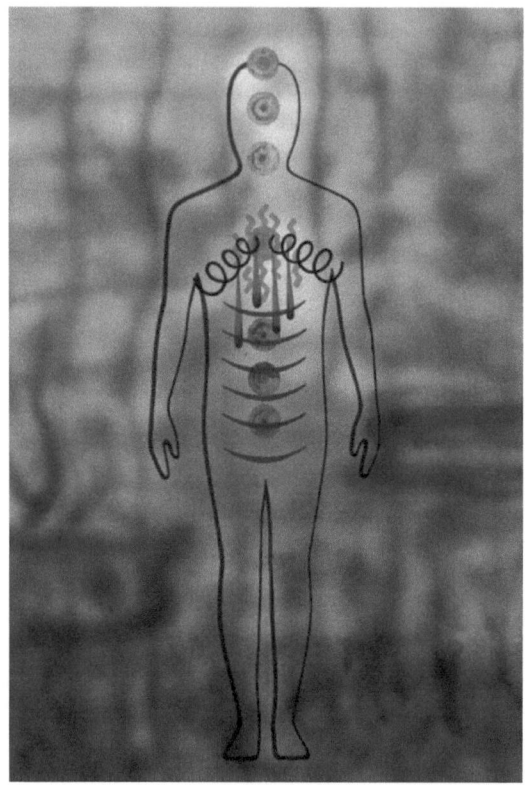

A Muddied Aura
The illustration shows an individual largely misusing the light of the seven chakras. The colors of the aura are predominantly brown and red, the chakras shades of gray, olive and red.
FIGURE 2

In Djwal Kul's *Intermediate Studies of the Human Aura*,[2] there are eight color plates illustrating this misuse of the chakras, which we call "muddied auras," with several paragraphs explaining each one. However, we are limited by time today and there is much to be accomplished in meditation, so I would rather lead you in the meditations for the purification of your chakras than to be reading explanations of their misuses.

Now we are going to demand our freedom by singing "Light, Set Me Free!"

Light, Set Me Free!

Light, set me free!
Light, set me free!
Light, set me free!
Light command, Light command,
  Light command, command, command!
Light demand, Light demand,
  Light demand, demand, demand!
Light expand, Light expand,
  Light expand, expand, expand!
Light I AM, Light I AM,
  Light I AM, I AM, I AM!
I AM a being of violet fire,
I AM the purity God desires!

Your Aura Is God

Kuthumi teaches us in his *Studies of the Human Aura*[3] that the aura is God. Your aura is the energy field that is God. It contains God. It reflects God. And when it is filled with light, it is filled with him. And therefore, the auric field and the temple together are the habitation of the Most High God.

The sense of the sacredness of life enables us to keep the flame of purity—the sense of reverence, the sense that where I AM God is. So we sing to the holiness of life as God in this auric egg—the egg, the shape of the cosmos, the shape of the aura—filling it with light by expansion from within out.

> Holy, holy, holy
> Lord God Almighty,
> Thou art holy
> In manifestation in man!

Project Your Image on the Screen of Your Consciousness

This screen on which we see the slides is like the screen of your consciousness. It is a screen of yourself. The image in figure 1 is your etheric blueprint; this is what you are to be. You look at it, you project the image of yourself onto the screen, then you allow the image to project itself back into your aura. So sing to it around yourself.

> Holy, holy, holy
> Lord God Almighty,
> Thou art holy
> In manifestation in man!

Now let's sing an *AUM* in the crown chakra. Instead of releasing the energy through the throat, let's sing the *AUM* but let's sing it so it comes out there, at the top of the head.

> *AUM*

Raise your hands.

> *AUM*
> *AUM*

Bring your hands down slowly, around, fold them in the center of your heart.

Let us sing "The Light of God's Will."

> The light of God's will
> Flows ever through me,
> The flow of real purpose
> I now clearly see;
> O pearly white radiance,
> Command all life free!

The Heart Chakra

We're going to visualize the chakras beginning with your heart—the fiery core of each chakra and then, building upon the foundation of the white-fire core, we will visualize the petals of the chakras.

We are most concerned that the heart chakra be free. When we retain hardness of heart, fear, malice, and misuses of the energies of love as hatred, when all of this surrounds the heart, it is like concrete, it is like asphalt. It is a very hard black ball of energy that surrounds the heart, which means that the threefold flame cannot radiate out the light of the sun.

With that burden on the heart as people begin to age, the burdens of the world can tie into the heart chakra through their own misqualified energies. And so people suffer heart disease and heart attacks because their heart chakras are not clear. If the heart chakra is not clear, how can we expand light through all of the other chakras? We can imagine that the light is but a trickle moving from it to the other six chakras.

And so the clearing of the heart chakra is the beginning of all meditation. It is in our own best interest to clear this chakra because it has to do with our health and our place on the Path. We will sing to beloved Helios and Vesta for a blazing action of the sun in the heart chakra.

> *In the name of the Christ, in the name of the Holy Spirit, in the name of the I AM THAT I AM, I call for the intense fires of the Great Central Sun, the Great Central Sun Magnet, for the expansion of the threefold flame within each heart, the full action of the violet flame and the superimposing of the light of Helios and Vesta upon the heart of each one. I call for the burning of the sacred fire within the heart as an intense burning love of devotion that will melt the fear, the doubt, and the death consciousness that is upon the hearts of mankind.*
>
> *I call to the Elohim to release your mighty seven rays for the clearing of these chelas of God. I call to the mighty Elohim to work with us this day to relieve them of the unnecessary burdens of misqualified substance and all that the Great Law will allow.*

The New Day
by Vesta

Helios and Vesta!
Helios and Vesta!
Helios and Vesta!
Let the Light flow into my being!
Let the Light expand in the center of my heart!
Let the Light expand in the center of the earth
And let the earth be transformed into the New Day!

Let the light of the sacred heart of Mary and of Jesus now be anchored within our hearts. Madonna and Child, sacred fire expanding from the very cradle of Bethlehem, let fire burn! Let power and wisdom and love glow. Fire of the heart burst forth! Release, release, release, O Christ Self of each one! Let attunement with that blessed Christ and the blessed Mother touch now each heart, touch each one. Release thy light, release thy light, release thy light, O God!

Meditating upon the heart, let us give, for its cleansing, "Lanto's Prayer."

Lanto's Prayer

In the name of Almighty God
I stand forth to challenge the night,
To raise up the light,
To focus the consciousness of Gautama Buddha!
And I AM the thousand-petaled lotus flame!
And I come to bear it in his name!
I stand in life this hour
And I stand with the scepter of Christ Power
To challenge the darkness,
To bring forth the Light,
To ensoul from starry heights
The consciousness of angels,
    Masters, Elohim, sun-centers
And of all of Life
That is the I AM Presence of each one!

I claim the victory in God's name.
I claim the light of solar flame.
I claim the Light! I AM the Light!
I AM Victory! I AM Victory! I AM Victory!
For the Divine Mother and the Divine Manchild
And for the raising-up of the crown of Life
And the twelve starry focal points
That rejoice to see the salvation of our God
Right within my crown,
Right within the center of the Sun
Of Alpha—It is done!

Now let us sing, "Not my will, not my will, not my will but thine be done." Center yourself in the heart and feel the voice of Christ, of your soul, speaking from the heart. And when you say this, let it be released as an energy of the heart. Your heart is speaking to God, and you can feel an intense action when you transfer your consciousness to that point and feel it coming out as though through a giant megaphone.

Not my will,
Not my will,
Not my will but thine be done!

The Solar-Plexus Chakra

Now let us go to the next chakra and the release of the fiery destiny of that chakra. We are calling for the unveiling of the fiery destiny of God's consciousness in each and every chakra—from the pure white-fire core to the taking on of that light of the chakra, its cleansing by the violet flame, and the anchoring of the perfect aspect of the ray.

Fiery Destiny
by Saint Germain

Fiery destiny, unveil thyself!
And show the higher way of God.
Fiery destiny, unveil thyself!
For man is not a clod.
Fiery destiny, unveil thyself!
Infuse the soul with God.

In the name of the Christ Self and the I AM Presence of each one, we call for the momentum of Christ-peace and the mission of the Messiah for the balancing of the energies of the solar plexus and of the desire body, which is truly the desire body of God. And therefore, we give it solely and totally unto him that it might be filled only with God's desiring to be God.

In this moment of communion in the flow of the Word, in the movement of the waters of the solar plexus, we let go and we let God live within us. We let go of all blockages to the flow of light, all tensions, all resistance to the inner law of peace. We let go of all of our questioning of the light of Christ, and we make our firm commitment in this plane of God consciousness to simply be, to be one with the Prince of Peace.

Standing in the place of the sun where the light of the Presence is reflected—the giant mirror, the Great Sun Disc—we call for the cleansing by the action of the violet flame of this open door to Christ consciousness, to God-control, and to dominion in the earth, the water, the fire, and the air. *Let light flow! Let light flow!* And we confirm our commitment:

> I AM a being of violet fire—
> I AM the purity God desires! (26x)
> *AUM*
> *AUM*

For the anchoring of the purple and gold in the solar plexus, let us give Jesus' I AM Lord's Prayer.

I AM Lord's Prayer
by Jesus Christ

Our Father who art in heaven,
Hallowed be thy name, I AM.
I AM thy kingdom come
I AM thy will being done
I AM on earth even as I AM in heaven
I AM giving this day daily bread to all
I AM forgiving all life this day even as
I AM also all life forgiving me
I AM leading all men away from temptation
I AM delivering all men from every evil condition
I AM the kingdom
I AM the power and
I AM the glory of God in eternal, immortal manifestation—
All this I AM.

The Throat Chakra

Let us give Jesus' "Transfiguring Affirmations" for the clearing of the throat chakra.

Transfiguring Affirmations of Jesus the Christ

I AM THAT I AM
I AM the open door which no man can shut
I AM the light which lighteth every man that cometh into the world
I AM the way
I AM the truth
I AM the life

I AM the resurrection
I AM the ascension in the light
I AM the fulfillment of all my needs and requirements
  of the hour
I AM abundant supply poured out upon all life
I AM perfect sight and hearing
I AM the manifest perfection of being
I AM the illimitable light of God made manifest
  everywhere
I AM the light of the holy of holies
I AM a son of God
I AM the light in the holy mountain of God

Now let us invoke the action of the violet flame, clearing all misuses of the action of the throat chakra.

I AM the Violet Flame
  In action in me now
I AM the Violet Flame
  To light alone I bow
I AM the Violet Flame
  In mighty Cosmic Power
I AM the Light of God
  Shining every hour
I AM the Violet Flame
  Blazing like a sun
I AM God's sacred power
  Freeing every one

Not my will,
Not my will,
Not my will but thine be done!

The Seat-of-the-Soul Chakra

Now let us invoke the light of God in the white-fire core of the violet chakra, the seat-of-the-soul chakra.

> Holy, holy, holy
> Lord God Almighty,
> Thou art holy
> In manifestation in man!

Through freedom's chakra we give the "Decree for Freedom's Holy Light."

Decree for Freedom's Holy Light
by Saint Germain

Mighty Cosmic Light!
My own I AM Presence bright
    Proclaim Freedom everywhere—
In Order and by God-Control
I AM making all things whole!

Mighty Cosmic Light!
Stop the lawless hordes of night,
    Proclaim Freedom everywhere—
In Justice and in Service true
I AM coming, God, to you!

Mighty Cosmic Light!
I AM Law's prevailing might,
    Proclaim Freedom everywhere—
In magnifying all good will
I AM Freedom living still!

Mighty Cosmic Light!
Now make all things right,
  Proclaim Freedom everywhere—
In Love's Victory all shall go,
I AM the Wisdom all shall know!

I AM Freedom's holy Light
  Nevermore despairing,
I AM Freedom's holy Light
  Evermore I'm sharing.
Freedom, Freedom, Freedom!
  Expand, expand, expand!
  I AM, I AM, I AM
Forevermore I AM freedom!

Light expand, Light expand,
  Light expand, expand, expand!
Light I AM, Light I AM,
  Light I AM, I AM, I AM!

The Third-Eye Chakra

We invoke the disc of light as the Great Central Sun Magnet to magnetize the vision of God in the all-seeing eye, to demagnetize all that is less than that vision of God—a simultaneous action of cleansing and expanding. Will you visualize one of these lights that miners wear; will you see it superimposed in the third eye and visualize it as this disc of light whirling toward you, whirling within you from the Great Central Sun, cleaning this brilliant emerald green chakra?

10 • The Purification of the Chakras and the Four Lower Bodies...

O Disc of Light

O disc of Light from heaven's height,
  Descend with all your perfection!
Make our auras bright with freedom's Light
  And the Masters' love and protection!

Now let us give the decree to beloved Cyclopea, Elohim of vision, Elohim of the fifth ray.

1. Beloved Cyclopea
   Thou Beholder of Perfection,
   Release to us thy Divine Direction,
   Clear our way from all debris,
   Hold the Immaculate Thought for me.

Refrain: I AM, I AM beholding All,
   Mine eye is single as I call;
   Raise me now and set me free,
   Thy holy image now to be.

2. Beloved Cyclopea,
   Thou Enfolder All-Seeing,
   Mold in light my very being,
   Purify my thought and feeling
   Hold secure God's Law appealing.

3. Beloved Cyclopea,
   Radiant Eye of Ancient Grace,
   By God's hand his Image trace
   On the fabric of my soul,
   Erase all bane and keep me Whole.

4. Beloved Cyclopea,
   Guard for aye the City Foursquare,
   Hear and implement my prayer,
   Trumpet my Victory on the air,
   Hold the purity of Truth so fair.

The Base-of-the-Spine Chakra

Let us invoke the white light of purity, the fiery core of the base chakra with its four petals, the confirmation of purity in that chakra.

I AM Pure

By God's desire from on high,
Accepted now as I draw nigh,
Like falling snow with star-fire glow,
Thy blessed Purity does bestow
Its gift of love to me.

I AM pure, pure, pure
By God's own Word.
I AM pure, pure, pure,
O fiery sword.
I AM pure, pure, pure,
Truth is adored.

Descend and make me Whole,
Blessed Eucharist, fill my soul.
I AM thy Law, I AM thy Light,
O mold me in thy form so bright!

Beloved I AM! Beloved I AM! Beloved I AM!

Let us affirm the light of Alpha and Omega for the base chakra. As we give these affirmations, feel the light of God as purity expanding.

Affirmations Taken from "The Judgment"
A Dictation by Alpha
Given July 5, 1975, at Mount Shasta, California

I AM a child of flame
   aborning in the cosmos of the Mother
I AM one in the heart of love
I AM the initiation of light
I AM fearlessness, for I AM one with Alpha
I AM one in the Father-Mother God
I AM in the seed of the whole creation
I AM everywhere in the consciousness of Alpha
I AM where I AM
I AM the awareness of all aspects of life
I AM the flow of light
I AM the consuming of all darkness
I AM the revelation of the plan of life to all
I AM the perfect scheduling of initiation
   in accordance with cosmic timetables
I AM the exercise of light within the chakras
I AM the flow of love from the heart of Alpha and Omega
I AM the knowledge of the law
I AM the fire that glows
I AM beyond all reaches of consciousness,
   yet I AM in the heart of every consciousness
I AM the magnet of the love of Alpha and Omega
I AM sealed in my original vow to the Father-Mother God
I AM the rediscovery of the I AM THAT I AM
I AM the wholeness of love in the fiery core of being
I AM in the oneness of unity
I AM following the golden thread
   back to the altar of Alpha and Omega
I AM the golden thread of the law and of the Mother
I AM Alpha and Omega
I AM fearlessness,
   for I AM sealed in the hand of Alpha and Omega
I AM one in the flow of love

I AM the consuming by the sacred fire
  of the cause, effect, record, and memory
  of all that has been impressed
  upon the body of the Mother by the fallen ones
I AM the flow of sacred fire consuming the seeds
  of rebellion left by the fallen ones
I AM the light of the fiery core
  of the flow of oneness of Alpha and Omega
  released for the cancelling-out
  of the seed of the Fallen One in the etheric plane
I AM the assimilation of the release of sacred fire
  in the consciousness of the lightbearers
I AM the sealing of the sacred fire
  in the third eye, the crown, and the heart
I AM the reversing of the spirals
  of all consent and authority given to the fallen ones
  and to the carnal mind of my own creation
I AM the cleansing of the mental belt
  of the remnant of the Fallen One
I AM the exposure of the beast of the bottomless pit
  of the subconscious and the desire body
I AM the challenger of the dweller-on-the-threshold
  of my own consciousness
I AM affirming the judgment of the Fallen One
  within my own consciousness
I AM the purging of every residue of the Fallen One
  in the four quadrants of my creation
I AM the freeing of the earth body
  from the impressions of rebellion
  and the ego that is set apart from the Divine One
I AM alert
I AM the release of judgment in my own microcosm
I AM the withdrawal of all support of the energy veil
I AM the crystallization of the God flame
I AM Alpha
I AM Omega
I AM in the white-fire core of the Great Central Sun
I AM forging my God-identity

**Affirmations Taken from
"The Initiation of the Golden Age Cycle"**
A Dictation by Omega
Given April 11, 1971, in Colorado Springs, Colorado

I AM Omega
I AM the perfect square of the City Immaculate
I AM a dancing flame from the heart of Alpha and Omega
I AM the manifestation of the flame
I AM the magnificent reality of the flame
I AM the Mother of eternal cycles
I AM the initiation of the Christ consciousness
    and the passing of that initiation for all mankind
I AM the crown of rejoicing worn by the Mother
I AM the infinite patience of the Mother
I AM the master of cycles of time and space
I AM the initiation of the cycle of the golden age
    for the planetary home
I AM the key that will unlock the destiny
    of a planet and a people
I AM an energy spiral issuing forth
    from the heart of Alpha and Omega
    and I AM the fulfillment of its immortal fiery destiny
I AM the wholeness of the mighty flame of the Almighty One
I AM the perfect balance of the androgynous nature
    of the Father-Mother God
I AM an artisan of the sacred fire
I AM a flaming spiral of the resurrection flame
I AM the torch upon the central altar
    of the Temple Beautiful
I AM the flame consecrated to the resurrection
    of the planet
I AM the flame consecrated to the resurrection
    of every man, woman, and child evolving upon the planet
I AM the flame consecrated to the resurrection
    of all elemental life evolving upon the planet
I AM love
I AM hope
I AM all giving to the Almighty

I AM obedience unto the laws
  of the Great White Brotherhood
I AM harmony in the flame
I AM free by the authority of Alpha and Omega
I AM the temple of the Most High God
  wherein the Spirit of God dwelleth
I AM charged with the resurrection flame
I AM newness of life
I AM the victory of the planet, the victory of the age,
  the victory of the solar system, the victory of the galaxy
I AM sealed in a sphere of white fire
O-me-ga
O-me-ga
O-me-ga

The Crown Chakra

The Father is calling the Mother home. The firing of the crown with wisdom creates the magnet that draws the Mother from the base of the spine through all of the chakras that are now cleansed and prepared to receive her until she reaches the crown of life. Let us establish the Great Central Sun Magnet in the crown chakra, the fiery core, and let us give this decree. Will you give it right from the point at the top of your head.

Golden Waves of Peace

O glorious golden flame of illumination from the heart of the Great Central Sun: In the name of my beloved I AM Presence and Holy Christ Self, blaze forth now from the heart of beloved Alpha and Omega, from the heart of beloved Helios and Vesta, and from the heart of beloved God and Goddess Meru into our individual hearts and minds, flooding them with the precious oil of illumination poured out in limitless radiance into our chaliced attention.

Beloved mighty God Presence, I AM in me and in the heart of the Great Central Sun, beloved Alpha and Omega, beloved Helios and Vesta, beloved Great Central Sun messengers, all cosmic beings, powers, and legions of light, beloved Lord Gautama, beloved Lanello, the entire Spirit of the Great White Brotherhood and the World Mother: Come, come, come now in the fullness of thy power and direct thy precious light rays of divine illumination from the spiritual sun into our beings and worlds, flooding all with the golden flame of Christ-illumination, understanding, perception, and peace from the heart of God's own omniscience.

> Come, come, come, O divine illumination's ray;
> Come, come, come into my world to stay;
> Come, come, come in golden waves of peace;
> Come, come, come, thy wisdom flame release! (9x)

> I AM receiving, accepting, and absorbing the flame of cosmic illumination from the very living presence of the God and Goddess Meru in the Temple of Illumination. (9x)

> O flame of light bright and gold,
> O flame most wondrous to behold,
> I AM in every brain cell shining,
> I AM in light's wisdom all divining.
> Ceaseless, flowing fount of illumination flaming.
> I AM, I AM, I AM Illumination. (9x)

And in full faith I consciously accept this manifest, manifest, manifest (3x) right here and now with full power, eternally sustained, all-powerfully active, ever expanding, and world enfolding until all are wholly ascended in the light and free! Beloved I AM, beloved I AM, beloved I AM!

The Raising of the Seven Aspects of the Feminine Ray of Lemuria

We're going to meditate on the rising of the feminine ray in all of the chakras, seeing the T'ai Chi and the bursts of light and the bursts of color in the chakras as the coming of the Mother rising from the base to the seat of the soul to the solar plexus, the heart, the throat chakra, the third eye, and the crown.

We're going to be meditating to the music of *Stabat Mater*, dedicated to the Mother of Worlds, the Cosmic Virgin, the Starry Mother. And it is a very powerful singing of this meditation. I want you to experience in this meditation the raising of the seven aspects of the feminine ray of Lemuria and the rise of the feminine ray in America.

Will you imagine that the soul who is singing unto the Divine Mother is your own soul and that this tremendous, strong, resounding voice is actually resounding in the corridors, in the actual cone, the shaft through which the flame, the energy, of Mother rises.

["Cujus Animam" from Rossini's *Stabat Mater* is played, sung by Luciano Pavarotti.]

The Figure-Eight Pattern of the Caduceus

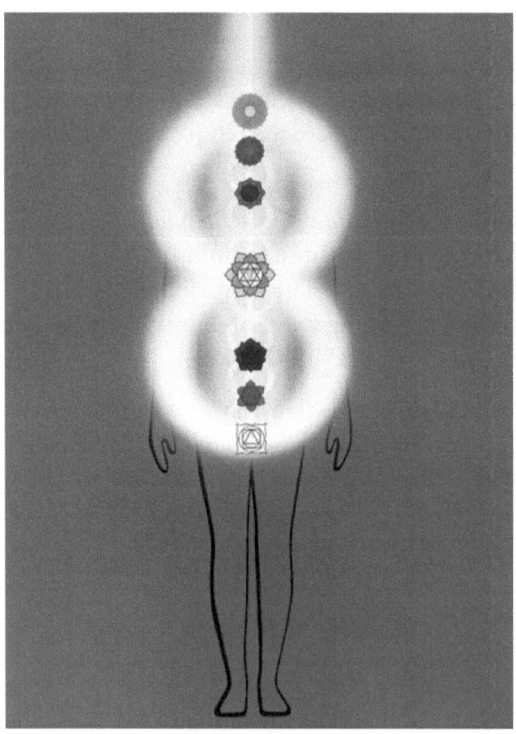

The Caduceus
FIGURE 3

This illustration shows the rising caduceus, the flow of energies from the base of the spine, forming a figure-eight pattern through all of the chakras. When that is set, then the large figure eight is superimposed upon it, with the nexus in your heart.

This is a microcosmic transfer of the flow of the figure eight that occurs from your God Self to your lower self. And so within your own energy field in Matter, by balancing the four lower bodies and the threefold flame, and clearing your chakras, you can manifest this action of the figure eight—as Above, so below—so that the energies are constantly flowing from the base to the crown and through all of the chakras and you have the maximum flow of God's energy without stoppages, without blocks, through all of your being.

As an assist to this development, Djwal Kul gives the meditation of the sacred fire breath—a very important meditation which, when you learn it, you can practice daily.*

Now comes an even more intense action of the fiery coil of life, which Djwal Kul says can come only to those who accept the Christ and the name I AM THAT I AM and have it written in their hearts. This coil is ten inches in diameter, the thirty-three turns a little less than three inches apart, rising from the base of your pyramid to your crown. It is making you a coil of energy, an electrode for God. It is a very important visualization and meditation, which is also in Djwal Kul's book.

When you have established that fiery flow of energy through absolute purity, dedication, and God-harmony, being a chela of Serapis Bey on the path to the ascension, you find yourself meditating while seated in the base of your pyramid with the fiery coils—thirteen coils for the initiation in the mandala of Christhood. These coils of energy rising from the base-of-the-spine chakra and from the square of Matter that you have balanced go to the top of the pyramid, the very crown.

You will notice that the all-seeing eye, the capstone, is in the pyramid; and the crown, which is the mind of God, is above the Matter pyramid. This is a very good visualization, especially for you who meditate in the lotus posture. And even if you don't, you can visualize yourself doing so.

---

*Djwal Kul's meditation on the sacred fire breath can be found in Kuthumi and Djwal Kul, *The Human Aura: How to Activate and Energize Your Aura and Chakras*, pp. 166–77.

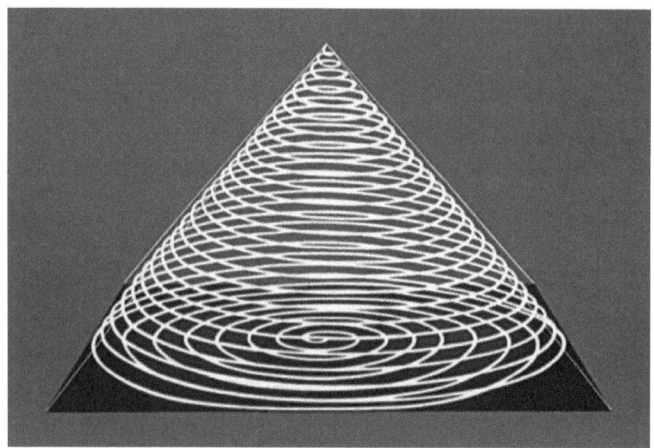

The Fiery Coil of Life
FIGURE 4

Passing these thirteen tests on the path of discipleship, we then have the opportunity to focus the thirty-three coils in the pyramid—thirty-three steps to the ascension, thirty-three initiations passed. These are key initiations, all of which were demonstrated by Jesus. You'll notice the meditator is no longer there; he is ascended. He has left a focus of himself, returning to the heart of the I AM Presence.

Meditation in the Pyramid on the Thirteen Steps of Initiation
FIGURE 5

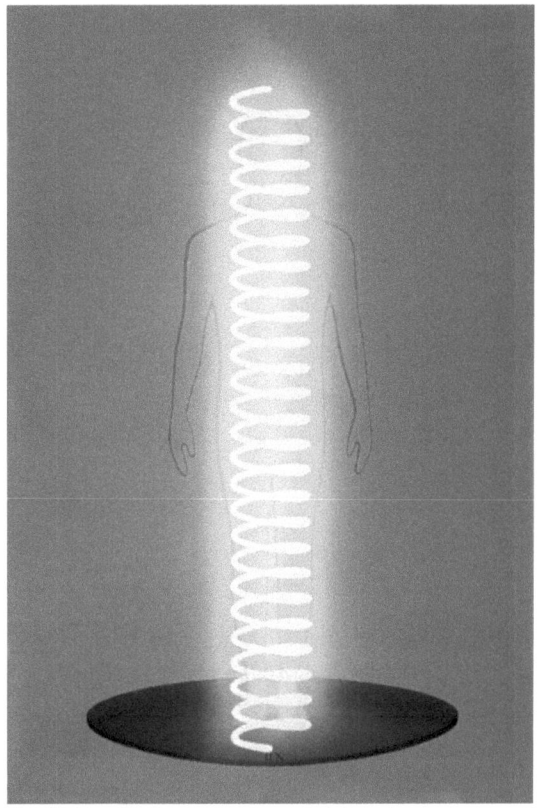

Thirty-Three Coils of Victory
FIGURE 6

Now I'm going to ask our staff ensemble to sing to Rose of Light as we meditate upon the flowers bursting forth in the chakras.

> From thy fragrant center light,
> Through thy petals blazing bright
> Comes God's love intensely pure;
> Rose of Light, love will endure.
>
> Rose of Light, thy power flows—
> Fiery, silent, majestic rose!
> Through my being enfolded here,
> All of life I now revere.

Expand thy flame's suffusing glow
Through my substance here below.
My heart cries out for freedom's bloom:
O God, expand my narrow room!

The love of God enfolds a rose,
Touches lightly a heart that glows.
Like unto Aurora's bloom,
Thy rose-light chases all man's gloom.

Rose of Light, expand through me,
Caress my being, make it free
To grow and glow upon the loom.
I now command my soul, attune!

Rose of Light, O come today,
In God's name I truly pray:
From fear and darkness and all hate,
Set my mind in radiance straight.

Rose of Light, I AM all thine,
By God's love my life refine.
Through us all let love appear
In God's image ever dear!

OM MANI PADME HUM

AUM

11

OUT OF THE FLAME OF MOTHER

A Dictation Out of the Flame of Mother

I AM the River of Life[1] flowing within you. I AM the energy of God. I AM the release and the activating principle of all that is above now manifest here below. I AM the release of the fiery fire of Brahma, Vishnu, and Shiva.

I AM the Shakti of the Gods. I AM the mastery of the feminine principle that you in your soul, rising and rising and rising, might also be unto countless lifewaves Mother—Mother as that which releases light. So is the Shakti the feminine counterpart of every ascended master. Each one of you fulfills that role, being a director of energy.

When you are a chela of the ascended masters, the development of your own feminine potential determines how much you can be the polarity of God, how much polarity of Saint Germain, El Morya, Kuthumi or Lanto you can manifest here below. Can you expand the sphere of your consciousness of Mother, of white-fire purity, so as to be here below all that the ascended masters are above? This is the challenge of being Mother. This is the challenge of being whole.

You do not want to manifest only a pea compared to a giant causal body of a cosmic consciousness. When you stand under the vine and fig tree[2] of the Great Divine Director with hands upraised in the receptive mode of consciousness to receive of his great liberating life force, will you limit that release by a tiny thimble of consciousness that is an excuse for a chalice? Or will you raise the crystal chalice, the cut glass of many facets of attainment showing the bursting forth of light as crystal, as crystal fire mist and emerald and gems of the Mother's Self-awareness? See, then, that you strive to keep the balance of the worlds.

Souls Have Not Conceived of Themselves as Mother

The dilemma of your planet in Matter is that so little of the energies of the Tree of Life[3] flow as the river of Mother. Imagine millions of ascended beings focusing the masculine principle of the Godhead with unending energy. Imagine, then, the energy crisis that occurs in Mater because souls have not conceived of themselves as Mother, because here in the West the term *shakti* is not understood. The feminine role as the one who releases the energy of the masculine ray is also not understood—the concept that the masculine in Matter is passive until the active element of the feminine releases it.

It is just the reverse in Spirit. It is the masculine that is the active and the feminine that is the passive. And so these roles intertwine and they change as you ascend the scale of consciousness. The roles are the weaving back and forth of the caduceus of the Father-Mother God.

Each time you rise to a new chakra, a new level of consciousness, these roles are balanced, these roles are interchanged. And so within each individual there comes the flow of Alpha and Omega and of the masculine and feminine principles, so that neither man nor woman is incomplete but each one, through this cosmic exchange, puts on a cosmic identity containing all in One. But then when you expand to the entire creation, you see that all life that is unascended is as Mater, feminine ray.

A Dictation from the Cosmic Consciousness of Mother

I speak to you today, then, out of the flame of Mother that is anchored in Matter. I speak out of the fiery core of the earth and out of the fiery core of your own Mother chakra. I am speaking, then, from cosmic dimensions that God has sealed in this very plane. And so you are hearing for the first time a dictation of the cosmic consciousness of Mother that originates in the white-fire core of Matter.

This is so that you might understand the permeation of Matter with the energies of Spirit, that you might know the energies of the Om Mani Padme Hum. Reverence, then, to life here below is given from the Aum of Alpha to the Hum of Omega. You find that life flows and flows and flows: *Aum, Hum, Aum, Hum, Aum, Hum.*

Now experience, then, from the very depths of being how God has placed himself with you not alone in threefold flame, but in the chakra that is Mother. God has placed himself as a life force, as an activating principle that is designed to balance, to release, to energize Father, Son and Holy Spirit.

The Path of Initiation in the Mother

Let all enter the path of initiation, the path of Mother, as Mother adores the Buddha. Let all enter this path and perceive that the putting on of the many faces of Eve is the adornment of self with the many Madonnas who have graced the earth. The identity of Mother is in so many strains, so many cultures. You can see Mother in all ways as the mirror of self, the mirror of every culture, every nation, every religion —each the unique face of Mother for a peculiar people of light, of evolution, of karma and of dharma.

Out of the flame of Mother within you is the voice of the Ancient of Days. Out of the flame of Mother is an ascension current. Out of the flame of Mother is the balance of worlds whereby mankind learn the paths of equilibrium, developing in the outer only that which has been developed within.

The culture of the hidden man of the heart,[4] of the very Christ Self that you are, is a culture that the soul puts on by the path of initiation in the Mother. Putting on this culture within, the soul takes its first steps in Matter, learning to crawl and to walk, to examine the myriad manifestations of Mother. Point, counterpoint, let mothers and fathers of earth teach their children first within, then without—the inner design, the outer manifestation.

Can you not feel the rhythm of this creation and the rhythm of this life and the soul responding to my words because the soul has such a great need to go within in order to come without? Millions and millions among mankind live without, on the periphery, on the surface, without experiencing the tutoring of their souls, the balancing of the elements. They become as dried reeds. They become without flow or flowering of the chakras. They become mechanical, functioning, then, according to the mechanization man.

Out of the flame of Mother, I call these souls to the center. I call souls of America, of Russia, of China, of every nation in Europe and Asia and Africa; I call to the souls of the nations of South America—all lands, all seas, all elements. I call for balance in the four petals of the Mother's light. Come into my arms and be aligned! Be aligned, be in balance. Know the comfort and the bliss of the fiery cross of life flowing evenly—flowing fire that becomes water, flowing water that becomes air, flowing air that becomes earth, cycling and recycling.

You feel within your system now what it is like to truly be in balance. The mind is restored to balance, free from the entrapments. The emotions are restored to balance in the Word of Christ, "Peace, be still!"[5] And in the very center of the petals of the white chakra I declare, I AM THAT I AM.[6]

Energy in Balance Is the Need of the Hour

I AM the will of the LORD and the law of his life! I AM releasing spirals, spirals of God becoming God within you. Out of the flame of Mother, energies are encircling the earth, flowing to the chakras of you who have prepared and of all souls of light who have prepared, who have opened the windows to receive Mother, to give Father; to give Father, to receive Mother—in and out, by coming in, by going forth. Energy in balance is the need of the hour, and the Mother comes to teach her children this balance.

Now enter your third eye. Let your concentration increase; let your concentration increase. From the tiny emerald that I place there, let it increase to a sphere of brilliant emerald fire. Now meditate upon this emerald fire and know that the virgin consciousness within you is now restored at the etheric plane.

Heretofore, your Christ Self has held that balance of the vision of the Virgin. Now there is a lowering from out the flame of Mother in Matter of the virgin consciousness that will be released cycle by cycle through the mental body, the emotional body and the physical body. My angels have anchored now that very record of all that you saw, all that you knew, all that you were in the Beginning in the core of creation.

This is a very powerful electrode. This is a very powerful force. Do you know that my coming into this octave is that force that creates tidal waves and cataclysm, and the coming of the judgment and the sudden death and the passing from the screen of life of individuals, and wars and rumors of wars? And so you see, the prophecy of Jesus for the last days[7] was the prophecy of the coming of Mother. It was a veiled prophecy. He did not say, "When Mother comes, you will have pestilence and famine and plague." If he had said this, who would have welcomed Mother? Who welcomes disturbance? All move back into the comfortable ways, yet all find that they cannot resist the oncoming light.

Mother Is Concerned Only with the Salvation of the Souls of Her Children

Mother in her coming seems destructive. But she is the Shakti of Shiva, and therefore her destroying action is the breaking down of the walls of partition, the breaking down of all misuses of her light that the soul might be free.

Understand, then, the perspective of the Mother. The Mother is concerned only with the salvation of the souls of her children, not with their mere mortal comfort. And therefore when she finally comes after thousands of years, coming through the marketplaces she overturns the moneychangers in the temples,[8] and much more.

Individuals are stripped of their wares, their conceit and their deceit, their mortal tyranny. Individuals are stripped of that which is the manipulation of the innocence of the soul. Upheaval, then, is for the direct goal that the bird might take flight and enter the heart of God. To the Mother, all else is dispensable.

It is Mother who taught her Son these words: "I came not to send peace, but a sword."[9] First the sword, then the sacred Word, then the cleaving asunder of the Real from the unreal. And then the sword, and then peace.

First the sword and the action of the sword as the shakti of peace. First the sword as a pillar of fire, as an energy that is at once brutal and compassionate. The sword of the Mother is the surgeon's knife, the Great Surgeon cutting away all that is hindering the soul on the Path.

The Rumbling Sound of the Movement of Energy

Welcome, then, the bursting forth of this fire of Mother within you as the bursting forth of the fire of Vesuvius, of Mauna Loa. From the very heart of the earth, suddenly there is the rumbling, the rumbling sound. It is the sound of movement of energy in the base chakra of the earth. And before the night is over, fire and the lava—molten rock, elements rich, rich in the ore of the Mother—burst forth at the surface of the chakras of the earth. There is an inundation and there is life becoming life.

Mankind have had thousands of years to prepare for her coming. Had they pursued self-mastery, the Mother's coming would be the delicate feet upon the hillsides and in the meadows. Her coming would be gentle, gentle as the crown of the twelve stars.[10] But without preparation, the coming must be the upheaval.

We are speaking now at the very core of the reality of the meaning of Mother. As the veils of maya are removed from your eyes and as the veils of Mother are removed that you can see her face to face, you find that her face is very familiar. In your soul you know that you have seen that face, that smile and that sternness day by day for thousands of years.

The reality of Mother, then, is the acceptance of disturbance and rearrangement in your life as atoms and molecules are brought into alignment for the maximum attainment of energy flow in the chakras. Is it any small wonder that you have experienced such opposition to this conference, such opposition to the celebration of the bicentennial?

The Coming of Mother Inaugurates a New Cycle

The coming of Mother inaugurates a new cycle: the movement of Mother energies in Matter. There must be some who are responsible, who can be self-disciplined and not shrink or shriek in the presence of Mother. All is challenged and nothing escapes her gaze. And you dare not hide that something that is dear to you behind your back, for Mother will take your hand and open it and reveal that that which is hidden shall be revealed.[11]

Now that the pressure and the presence of Mother is truly in full force and in manifestation—with the turning of the cycles of America, with the turning of the cycles of the Aquarian age in this very month of the celebration of Mother by the hierarchy of Cancer—we trust, we hope, we pray earnestly that there be some devotees who, though yet the boat be rocked, will not be moved. Though there be a storm at sea, they will not capsize the boat.

We cannot promise you freedom from adversity. We can only promise you the protection of the defender of the Woman, the protection of Archangel Michael,[12] when you call it forth. Do not expect, then, that suddenly all will be well with the world or that peace will suddenly appear. There is a long, hard journey through the night before the coming of peace. If you prepare yourselves for the daily upheavals, then you will invoke enough light of the energies of God to counteract these upheavals and you will be found whole and one in the flame.

I Will Draw You into the Flame

Children of the Sun, it is understandable that some dare not enter into the presence of Mother. They must remove themselves so many meters, so many leagues, so many miles, for they cannot stand the pressure of that light. But if there be some who will come, who will stand with me, who will be part of this fire of the swinging sword of Kali—if there be some, then I tell you I will absorb you into myself that you might be in the white-fire core of Mother. As I have come out of the flame, so I will draw you into the flame so that by your courage to stand with the Virgin of the Earth you will also have her mantle, the momentum of her attainment.

Is this not also justice? Those who receive the Mother in the flame of the Mother ought to receive the reward of the flame of the Mother. And so the white-fire core of the teaching center and of the Church Universal and Triumphant has a very special purpose. And the communicants who have the white cube, they use that white cube to magnetize the flame of Mother and thereby draw themselves into the One.

There is little survival for those who are halfway. And so you see here, even here, an organization either of devotees or of no one. All who come here and who remain become ardent chelas of the Mother. And if they are not, they remove themselves far, far away. For when they confess within their souls that they have not the dedication, then they realize it is best to be gone, it is best to be as far as you can go to be away from the cataclysm that surrounds the intense fire of Mother.

With Total Surrender You Enter the Sphere of Mother

This is the key, then: total surrender. With total surrender you enter the sphere of Mother. And I tell you, for I am here in the sphere of Mother, that inside of this sphere there is such a wondrous cosmos. To the outer mind, the discipline seems as confinement. But as soon as that discipline is forged and won and you are transferred into the center, you discover the Spirit-cosmos that is all inside the fiery core of the base chakra of the one who has the mastery of the Mother.

Within that fiery core, then, there is once again an absolute Godfreedom to create, to roam a starry cosmos, to be free in Mother. Mankind do not understand, and some who are on the Path do not understand that always and always and always when you give all to Mother, Mother gives all to you. God is obedient to this law. He made this law, and by this law he stands.

There is no purpose to having debris around the Mother, and therefore devotees are we, devotees of the flame. None other can manifest inside the Mother.

Here I AM in the center of the One. Will you come? Will you come? Will you come and be free in me?

12

ESCAPE TO THE SUN

A Dictation by Helios of the Sun

Children of earth, out of the Sun you have come. From out the Great Central Sun, life gave you birth. And to the Sun you must return for the crown of life, that the light of the Sun, that the sphere of consciousness might make permanent the wholeness of being.

Souls aflame with love, the love of Aquarius is a fiery love of intensity, a love that comes forth as the sun of Christ, the sun of your heart burning in the noonday. So is the intensity of the love of Aquarius. And so by the intensity of the sun can you measure the intensity of that hatred which opposes the light of the sun.

Every devotee of the Mother walks carrying a portion of the cross of the Aquarian age, the cross of the world momentum of hatred that is being drawn forth from all subconscious astral planes to the surface as every form of human viciousness. It must be drawn out, it must be consumed. And during the process of the cycling of the figure eight from the sun in the center of this system to the sun in your heart, there is the need for you to bear the cross.

I come, then, with a very special mission to speak to you that you might run and not be weary, that you might walk and not faint[1] in the way of the overcoming in the stations of the cross. By the great mystery of surrender, you escape to the sun and to the fiery core of your being. And only within the center of the sun is there a reprieve from that cross of hatred. You need not fall or faint in the way, for when you are centered in the fiery core of being, then you can carry that cross.

When Saint Germain gave to the messengers that solemn and sacred gift of carrying the cross of the Master, he said: "In the days and the hours when the cross becomes a burden, you have but to call to me and to say, 'Saint Germain, I bear thy cross,' and I will come to you and uphold you. And I will carry you over the waters of the astral plane because you have willingly taken my cross."

Carry the Greater Weight of Darkness to Experience the Greater Weight of Light

Consider, then, each of the lines of your cosmic clock, each and every master carrying a cross of light and a cross of mankind's karma. The ascended masters can only carry the cross of light; it remains for the chelas to carry the cross of the perversion of that light. Understand, then, that the twelve initiations of the hierarchies of the Sun are in order that some may carry the greater weight of darkness so that they may experience the greater weight of light. This is the meaning of the pursuit of higher consciousness.

I AM come in the fiery core so that you will understand that there is a cross to be borne for Christ at the point of the Son, for the hierarchy of Aries and for me. I AM Helios, and Vesta with me—together we are in your heart. We provide the escape for those who will volunteer to carry the weight of world karma, of the exaltation of the ego, the human ego. We provide the escape for those who are willing to walk with us as sun god and goddess, focal points of the ancient hierarchies of Mu and Atlantis.

We say, in the hour of the testing and the travail, call to us and say, *"Helios and Vesta, I bear thy cross!"* And then in that moment there will be the exchange. And for a moment the cosmic cross of white fire, which is the overcoming of cosmic beings in this way of hierarchy, will descend to your heart, and for a moment we will take the dark cross of human misqualification. And then in another moment and in the twinkling of an eye,[2] all will be again as Above, so below.

Each one of you has a special love for a special master. See which masters are on the clock and enter into this ritual. For mankind are weary and burdened and they are not able to continue. They faint in the way and in the heat of the karma of the Dark Cycle.[3] They are sick in heart and mind and soul. Mankind are weary, O chelas of the sacred fire. If their souls are to be gathered in the great harvest[4] of the Lord, you will have to enter in and make the sacrifices that they have not the maturity to make.

They do not understand the meaning of sacrifice. For some of them it will take thousands of years of evolution in other planets and in other systems of worlds for them to come to the place where you are, sitting at the feet of the ascended masters. Consider, then, the interim. Consider when souls of light have ascended yet humanity have not responded.

An Energy Sphere to Cycle Energies of Light

In our Temple of the Sun in the center of the sun, there is a cosmos, a diagram, a computer of every soul in this system of worlds, every evolution, the chain of hierarchy. Moment by moment we are aware of elemental life, children of God. We are aware, then, of the birds of the air and each little elemental and the cycles of energy. This is solar awareness, awareness of the sun-self in the soul of every living creature. And therefore it is possible for us to understand the great curve of the universe and the charting of the cycles.

I have come to earth to set a focal point, an energy sphere anchored within the etheric plane that will cycle energies of light through the mental, the astral and the physical planes as you make the calls and the invocations. This sphere of cosmic consciousness is for the counteracting of the dark crosses of the weight of world karma—twelve dark crosses to be borne by the disciples of Christ, one dark cross in the center of the three on the hill for Christ and his vicar.

The Great Love of Hierarchy Is the Cosmic Interchange

This is our calling; this is our challenge. If Keepers of the Flame do not accept this challenge, we perceive that there are no others who will accept it, no others to whom the torch can be passed. And therefore we look at the conclusion of lifewaves and evolutions of Terra if the torch of the sun is not seized as the torch of life and if the runners do not continue to run. Someday, when you have made your ascension and rejoined your twin flame and you focus the Father-Mother God in the center of a system of worlds, you will remember that Helios and Vesta came to give you the understanding of the immensity of cosmic accountability, the vast planning that is involved in determining the fate of these several systems.

We must draw our conclusions and you must draw your conclusions. The great love of hierarchy is the cosmic interchange. By your conclusions we determine our conclusions; by our conclusions you determine yours. Point, counterpoint, interaction—the Great White Brotherhood ascended and unascended is one. Because you are, we serve. Because we are, you have the opportunity to serve. Each forward step in cosmic consciousness attained by an ascended master means greater opportunity for the chelas. Each forward step in initiation that you take, the ascended masters have a greater opportunity to enter into your world.

The Initiation of the Great Divine Director by Alpha and Omega

And now I have the very good fortune and joy to announce to you a forward step in initiation in cosmic consciousness by one very dear to you, your very own, the Great Divine Director. The Master R[5] has come to this platform this evening to receive and be received of earth's evolutions. And the ceremony of the bestowal upon him of a great sphere of cosmic consciousness by Alpha and Omega does now take place before you so that, by your acceptance of his attainment and your participation in this ritual, you may give acknowledgment and praise and honor and therefore also be afforded the opportunity, as chelas of Saint Germain, to move ahead and to draw out from this mighty sphere of light greater initiations in the charting of the cycles of the Great Divine Director, who is the originator of cycles in the planes of Mater. Will you rise now?

As the Great Divine Director kneels, Alpha and Omega place upon his head a new crown—a starry crown, a golden crown of light bejeweled with focuses of God-mastery in the planes of Spirit and Matter. It was the Great Divine Director who made the request that this ceremony might take place here on earth rather than at the Court of the Sacred Fire on Sirius. For his great desire was only to leave a record of attainment that you also might know that your attainment is nigh and that the very close love and associations of the chelas for the master are the certain key to the victory of earth.

There are attending angels, a ring of Elohim and archangels and paeans of praise and choirs of rejoicing as in the hour of the Buddha's enlightenment. You are witnesses of a great glory, a greater glory than any to which your understanding has been set. May this be the record, the memory and the love of your heart for the moment when you are crowned with the crown of life by Alpha and Omega.[6]

Your Escape to the Sun

I speak to you softly this evening, perhaps not in the manner you would expect of Helios of the Sun. I speak softly so that you will understand that I speak from within you, from within your own heart chakra. And as I AM within your heart, I seal your heart with the light of the sun so that you may also go there as a place of refuge, as your escape to the sun—a sun not so very far away but a sun that is real.

And I tell you, should the worlds dissolve and all of the planes of Matter be consumed in the great conflagration of the mind of God, there would yet remain these suns that I have placed within you, yet suspended in Matter. Indomitable is the will of God! Indomitable are his love and wisdom! By these three, we forge the victory of cycles.

I AM Helios. I wrap the earth in the swaddling garment of skeins of solar sunlight. I wrap each one. And I tell you, do not underestimate the Antichrist[7] that opposes your light, your endeavor, your organization. By love, implicit love, inherent love, your union will remain. Your union will be as fiery burnished steel, row upon row, row upon row—steel, sword, sacred Word, separation of light and darkness, consecration, sternness, strength, courage, honor, life upon life as waves of Keepers of the Flame go forth to conquer a cosmos. "As ye deal with my contemners, so with you my grace shall deal."[8]

In Every Aspect of Distress, Sing the Mantra of Helios and Vesta

Be mindful, then, of the law of cycles. Be mindful of your fiery destiny and remember to sing the mantra of Helios and Vesta. In every aspect of distress, sing the mantra and find us in your heart able to cope with any and all adversity.

I AM Helios. I have come. And I will tarry with Vesta in this city through the turning of the cycle of the destiny of the nation of nations to focus here the new light of Mother in the New Day of the one-hundred-year cycle of the Virgin's appearing within you.

Ladies and gentlemen, children of the One, the ceremony is concluded. We withdraw to the sun.

Helios and Vesta!

>Helios and Vesta!
>Helios and Vesta!
>Helios and Vesta!
>Let the Light flow into my being!
>Let the Light expand in the center of my heart!
>Let the Light expand in the center of the earth!
>And let the earth be transformed into the New Day!

13

A THRUST AND A ROLL AND A HO, HO, HO!

A Dictation by Lord Zadkiel and Holy Amethyst

In the land of the free and the home of the brave, I AM come to manifest life—life that is freedom and freedom that is the life that cannot be lived without the definitions of opportunity, the safeguards of God-government and the eternal flow of the abundance of the Almighty.

Certain conditions necessary to the evolution of souls have been secured in this nation, have been confirmed not merely by laws written but by a culture and by an education, by a foundation and a way of life that has been called America. As the intangible spirit of the soul winging toward its freedom, so is this life. Because it is an essential spiritual quality, it does not occur to mankind that this almost vaporylike quality of existence is thinning, is becoming polluted, is fading away.

People live on from day to day, sorting out their lives, pursuing those things that are important unto them. They come and they go and they look for gain at all hands. And yet the essential quality of life —this is not known to them. [They are] losing the vigor, the joie de vivre, losing that quality that makes for the spiritual quickening—and [yet] they say all things are as they were.

The few who are perceptive realize that all is not well; they read the signs of the times. And the other few who are the instruments of the change toward darkness also know that there is a rapid movement, an underground movement, an energy that is beneath the surface that is moving rapidly and yet imperceptibly. Furthermore, the people of

America do not recognize what manifestations in culture work against the principles of the Brotherhood. For if they know not the principles, they have no standard with which to measure that existence that has become now almost entirely relative, without standards, without the premise and the conclusion of the law of truth.

The Distortion of the Crystal-Clear Image of the Christ

The saturation of the children by the momentums of the entities of horror, of sex, of death and of greed have so distorted the crystal-clear image of the Christ that even when we send forth our energies of the violet flame, a certain percent of these energies are taken into matrices that are not the true freedom of the light but only a false freedom fabricated on the basis of an ideology that is not in life but in death.

We deplore the infiltration of this nation by Marxist-Leninist ideologies. We deplore the degeneration of the republican form of government into what has become a welfare state ruled by the intellectual elite and the scientists. We deplore the separation between the people and the ruling class. And this separation and this class society is the direct result of the consciousness of World Communism, which in its lie actually states that there will be no more class and no more separation when instead it creates the widest gulf that has ever been created between the rulers and those who are ruled.

And therefore we appeal to the Christ Self, for the Christ Self as the Mediator, as the definer of God-government has been omitted from this system. And where there is not the Christ releasing the energies of God, no theory, however tightly woven, can bring forth the reality of sons and daughters of God.

We Come to Mend the Flaws

We come, then, to mend the flaws, to fill in the gap, the tremendous chasm that is occurring. It is as though there is the sound of a giant crack and the breaking of the earth and the opening up of the earth. And on one side of the earth there is that element that considers themselves the only ones qualified to rule. And on the other side [there are] masses of the people who have lost their identity to the state and who no longer even try to manifest the turning of the tide of darkness.

13 • A Thrust and a Roll and a Ho, Ho, Ho!

It is understandable that the American people do not have the foresight, the energy, the qualities of Christ-discrimination to meet the tests of the hour. For in this turning of the centuries, the initiation of the Holy Spirit and of the Mother is upon this people, and without the understanding of Law they can scarcely contain the energies that are descending.

We call for a revival of freedom and for a revolution of light! We call for an action of victory! We call for an action of flow! We demand that the movement of the violet flame be free and that individuals be not bound by endless laws that have been created because the flow of love is not present.

Develop the Heart Chakra

American people are intended to develop the heart chakra. The mighty heart chakra of this nation is intended to be the flow of the Christ consciousness in the love of one another, loving one another as Christ has loved his disciples, as the disciples have loved Christ.[1] This is the definition of love. It is the love, the precious love of the Mother for the incoming soul, the love of the Father for the Mother. It is the love of the light. It is the love of children. It is the essential consecration of life to the bubbling brook of freedom.

We see, then, because individuals have not extended love, because they no longer think in terms of service to one another, that laws and rules and regulations have been made—endless, endless rules. And therefore, instead of going by the initiation of the heart and by the flow of the heart in making decisions and tuning in to a fiery destiny, people operate in a mechanical consciousness as though they were tin soldiers, according to the rules.

And they defend right and wrong, not according to conscience, not according to the voice within, but according to rules, the fine line of the rule and who is on one side and who is on the other and what is the interpretation of the rule. These interpretations are made by those who are not centered in the Christ but who are centered in the sense of a social economy, an economic determinism, a philosophy whereby all that occurs is the result of cause-effect sequences in Matter.

And therefore, because this lie is believed, the consciousness of those who are entrapped by the lie are cut off from the great flow of the energies of the planes of Spirit. And therefore mankind have made their own laws—laws that are the laws of sin and the sinful consciousness and the separate consciousness. Having chosen to live according to these laws, these laws are the final determining factor in their lives; and they have created a cell consciousness outside of the body of God.

Let the People Be Given Voice!

Let the people be given voice!
Let voice return!
Let voice be the distillations of the heart
And not of the carnal mind speaking out
In its endless defenses and pretenses.
Let the use of the Word of God
Be returned to this nation!
Let the love of heart now be unleashed!
Let the fires of the hearts of the people
Flow in a great love
For the cosmic destiny of this land!

Violet-Flame Angels, Go Forth Now!
Let Light Flow!

O violet-flame angels of our band,
Go forth now—north, south, east and west—
To intensify the fire of Saint Germain.
Let that flow of the violet flame
Be for the release of that hardness of heart!
Let the mighty heart chakras be cleared!
Let the tributaries be cleared!
Let the points of flow
And the mighty vessels of being be cleared!
Let light flow from our retreat
And from the halls of Luxor,[2]
From the heart of Rakoczy
And that great mansion of light
That is in the Transylvanian foothills![3]

Let light flow from the heart of Kuan Yin
And the retreat of light of the Great Divine Director!
Let light flow from all of the focuses of the retreats
   in the physical and etheric planes
   of the Great White Brotherhood!
Let it come forth from the Royal Teton!
Let it come forth from our retreat over Cuba!
Let light flow from the heart of Angola,
From the heart of Arcturus and Victoria![4]
Let light flow
From the heart of the Violet Planet,
From the heart of beloved Omri-Tas,
   the ruler of the Violet Planet,
And the one hundred and forty-four thousand priests
   of the sacred fire.

"I Demand the Restoration of the Flow of Light"

I call to the priests of the order of Melchizedek.[5] I call for the righting of all wrong. And I demand the restoration of the flow of light of the mighty seven rays from the heart of the mighty Elohim. I call to Almighty God for this preordained release given at the signal of the Elohim and the archangels and the chohans working in consonance now to distribute with the Great Divine Director that new attainment of consciousness forged and won by cosmic service and ratified here below by the chelas of Saint Germain.

Let these energies roll, then! For only by a mighty rolling of the wave of light will all that has transpired that is not of the light be consumed. We will not descend to the levels of argumentation, of undoing the threads, line upon line, of human infamy, of chaos and the spirits of rebellion with their anarchistic philosophies. We will not descend to this level, nor will the beings of nature, nor will the Holy Spirit. When mankind have chosen to go against the law of God and the will of God, they will find that in a moment all of their works are brought to naught as the mighty River of Life flows on and consumes all in its pathway.

What folly it is for mankind to think that they can set up separate systems outside of the Great White Brotherhood and that these will endure forever and that these will produce a utopian society. I say it is not so! Let the archenemies of freedom hear the death knell this day of all of their plots against the Divine Mother! For now with the coming of the Divine Mother and the turning of the ages and the cycles of America's destiny, the very physical manifestation in Mater of the Mother principle is an action which, when counteracted by the fallen ones, will result in an immediate karma.

After the Turbulence and Turmoil Comes the Great Calm

And all that has gone on before in the last century as the programming of the fallen ones to work against the children of light has been the prologue preceding that day, that notable day of the LORD[6] when, by their actions against the hierarchy that is actually manifest, they will have the rebuke of that fire and that energy. And the ensuing cycles will be turbulent and there will be turmoil; and yet, after the turbulence and after the turmoil, then comes the great calm, then come the great liberators marching, then come the hosts of the LORD.

And therefore, let all Keepers of the Flame gird themselves unto the light and unto the victory. Let them hold on to the nearest tree and let them be certain that it is the Tree of Life, for only that Tree of Life will not be uprooted in that notable day of the LORD's coming. Let them hold on to truth and to the branches of truth and to the twelve manner of fruits[7] that are the focuses of God-reality. Let Keepers of the Flame, then, stand fast! Let them plant their feet firmly in this soil, firmly in the physical quadrant. Let them allow themselves to bend, bend gently with the movement of the wind, but never to break in the face of the onslaught of the hordes of the fallen ones.

The key to this God-determination and to the standing when there is the changing of the tide—the key is to go inside, to escape to the sun, as Helios said. The key is to enter into the Within and to know that our God is a consuming fire,[8] to stand and, having stood, to stand again and to know that only that which is real shall endure, that all that passes by will pass into the flame.

And after the long night of the hurricane, when the morning is come and the dawn breaks, you will find the clearing of the skies and the earth and the waters and the mighty flame-fires leaping. And the coming of the golden glow of the sun will see that the birds are singing, the flowers are blooming, the trees are then offering their praises of gladness. And so, after the long night is past, the light will come again.

The Release from the Retreats of the Great White Brotherhood

Let there be the release, then, from the retreats of the Great White Brotherhood in this moment and in this hour! And let it go forth from South America, from the focuses of the Goddess of Light, the Queen of Light and the Goddess of Purity! Let the energies of Helios and Vesta now be as the opening of the retreats, even as the opening of the graves in the hour of the crucifixion of the Lord.[9] So let there be the opening, and let the spirits of just men made perfect by love[10] come forth from their etheric habitations. And let the saints who are robed in white who have said, "How long, O Lord?"[11]—let them also come forth. And let there be the anchoring point in these lifewaves unascended who are abiding in the etheric planes waiting, waiting, waiting for the salvation of souls, souls of light in physical embodiment.

Let all of the energies of the Great White Brotherhood to be released this morning be anchored within the heart chakras of the saints of all ages who are tarrying in Matter for the coming of the Mother flame and for the coming of Lord Maitreya. Let the great heart chakras open wide! I command you now to open your hearts! Feel the doors to your heart open! Feel the freedom of the fire of the mighty birds of light who come and go and enter the heart and are free to be soaring spirits of the Brotherhood.

Open your hearts, America! Open your hearts, people of the world! For by that light of the heart, we will balance the factors of human creation and of the Dark Cycle. And if you close your hearts, your hearts will be then sealed shut, and the energies of the Elohim will not pass into this plane, and there will be the weeping and gnashing of teeth in outer darkness.[12] Let Keepers of the Flame steel themselves unto the victory! Let there not be any more dallying, any more involvement with so many cycles, so many spirals outside of the central theme of life.

"I AM Releasing of the Light of Ten Thousand Suns!"

I AM the light of victory! I AM the light of the Holy Amethyst! I AM Zadkiel, and I stand on the side of the west of the United States of America. I stand in the City Foursquare.[13] I stand on the west side of Los Angeles and I stand facing the east and I behold America. I behold her cities, her plains, her mountains, her open spaces. I behold her people and the hearts of her people.

I stand on the side of the west, and I AM releasing the light of ten thousand suns! And my angels who stand with me in numberless numbers, reinforced by flanks and legions of light who have come forth from the heart of the Ancient of Days and from the heart of Alpha and Omega—they stand with me. And as they stand behind me, their legions arrayed in white and violet and purple flame extend over the entire Pacific Ocean.

They face the land America and they face the diadem in the crown of the Divine Mother. They are facing now the dilemma of America's karma that was begun as the seeds of darkness spawned in other continents. And as this dark cloud of energy has moved over America from Europe, from Africa and from Asia over the last several hundred years, it has begun to coalesce from the East Coast and in the cities of the East Coast, traveling as a plague over the face of the land, moving toward the West. For the goal of that energy is to devour the focus of the New Jerusalem[14] and of the place prepared for the focal point of the Divine Mother and the Ashram of the World Mother.

And so you see Keepers of the Flame and hosts of the LORD who have come—have come to secure the place in the West and to roll back this tide of darkness. And the full-gathered momentum of these legions of light is readied now to be let forth, to roll back that darkness across the continent and into the Atlantic Ocean, where there are other legions of victory and of violet-flame angels who stand to receive our thrust of energy and to catch that residue of darkness that is not transmuted in the rolling of the energies of the violet flame.

A Violet-Flame Carpet for the Coming of the Divine Mother and Her Retinue

And therefore, on one side and on the other of this great continent there are gathered legions of freedom who are determined that every erg of darkness that mankind will surrender into the flame will be taken in this hour of America's freedom. And it will be a mighty violet-flame carpet that will be rolled out for the coming of the Divine Mother and the retinue of the Divine Mother at the moment of the striking of the hour of America's Declaration of Independence on the anniversary, July 4, 1976, at five o'clock,[15] when the release of the Great Divine Director will anchor the changing of the cycles.

And therefore you might say that from an entire cosmos, legions of angels have converged as the cosmic clean-up committee to draw off into that violet flame all of mankind's misuses of the sacred fire. Can you imagine, O people of America, that legions of the cosmos must come forth to clean up that darkness with which you have desecrated this most noble cause of victory from the very heart of Saint Germain?

The Dispensation of a Land and a Free People

People of the world and people of America: understand of what great cosmic moment this dispensation is to hierarchy—the dispensation of a land and a free people   and what it can mean to other systems of worlds. And now, you see, because a people have lost the memory of their inner calling and of their origin, it is required that sons and daughters of God and helpers of God come forth to clean up that which never should have been.

By God's grace we are here. By God's grace you are here. And therefore, we will wipe the tears from our eyes[16] as we behold all that has occurred that is less than the goal of Almighty God. And we will invoke the violet flame that we might have a smile of joy and a solemn expression within the eye of a determined victory, a victory that is a Sirius victory—a victory of the mighty Blue Eagle from the God Star, Sirius.[17]

And therefore, the violet-flame angels are also reinforced by legions of blue lightning, legions who move in the formation of that mighty eagle that is on the seal of the president of the United States, the mighty Blue Eagle that is the sign of that vision, which beholds the enemy and casts out the enemy for the coming of the children of the One.

Release of the Seven Vials of Violet Flame

Now the moment has come for the release of the seven vials of violet flame from our retreat.[18] And these will be released from the side of the west of the City Foursquare, from that point in Los Angeles of the focus of the Mother. We send forth now with a mighty heave and a roll and a ho, ho, ho! We roll that fire! We roll the violet flame, and the seven vials are poured out.

And legions of victory and violet flame now begin their swift movement. And they come from the entire Pacific and they cross America carrying the violet flame, rolling that violet flame, energies of victory over the soil and the land, over the mountains and through the elements and through the hearts of the saints that are open to our message of freedom.

The violet flame rolls across, now, the mighty expanse of the West, across the Rocky Mountains, across the Middle West, coming now into the belts of the great cities and of the great manifestations of the growth of the grain and the abundance of supply of the Mother, rolling back the darkness now, approaching that midpoint and passing it where there is the great concentration of European, African and Asian darkness over the East.

So there is a slowing down of the legions as they are required to consume more and more darkness. And the rolling of the giant wave meeting the wave of darkness is an alchemical action, which you ought to behold with your inner eye. For it is light contacting light and more light, and all of this now bubbling and activating and transmuting the darkness. And it moves on. And the violet-flame angels are holding over the Atlantic Ocean, waiting for the passing of that energy, anchoring the most intense action of the Great Central Sun Magnet, demagnetizing darkness and drawing it into the fiery core of the flame.

A Violet-Flame Glow over America

Legions of light anchoring that flame are using the energies that you have anchored here in the East this day, so necessary for the breaking of the darkness and the hypnotic spell. Now it intensifies and moves on, covering the states of Ohio and Indiana, coming through Pennsylvania and anchoring special focuses of freedom in Philadelphia and in other cities where there are shrines of freedom. So in every focus of freedom throughout the land that is a true focus of light, a portion of this energy has been anchored. And out of the seven vials, a portion of the violet flame surrounds now the chakras of every individual who has a claim to America as a citizen of this nation.

Now the energy is moving; now in this moment it is reaching the shores. It is on the sands of the beaches of the East Coast, and now it is one with the Atlantic Ocean and with the angels of fire. Angels of East and West have converged now, and in this mighty moment of energy and of fire there is the release, there is the sealing, there is the anchoring. And all that has covered the land is now cycling through the etheric, mental and emotional and physical planes, coming right now into the very roots of the earth, into the very physical bodies of the people until there is a violet-flame glow over America that has never been seen before—no, not in the history of the land! No, not since the golden ages of mankind!

A Holding Action for the Absorption of This Mighty Wave of Light

I AM Zadkiel, and Amethyst is with me. We now have a holding action whereby you also, in this moment of silence, might feel the absorption into your being of this mighty wave of light. [Period of silence]

Violet-flame angels are traveling around the borders, across Canada, the borders of the seas, of the Gulf of Mexico, across the Mexican border. And there is a reinforcement of light around this continent, and the same action is taking place in Hawaii and Alaska and all landed surfaces that are under the territorial jurisdiction of America. [Pause] We seal the action of the Panama Canal as the nexus and the flow of the light of Mother of East and West. [Pause] Now the energy is intensified into the soil; it is descending into the heart of the earth. It is expanding high into the upper atmosphere. [Pause] Expansion is occurring in every direction, in every dimension and plane of consciousness. [Pause] Now the crystallization of the violet flame and the amethyst crystals, the anchoring point in the temple in the Rocky Mountains; [pause] and crystalline focuses of Holy Amethyst are an adornment suspended in a violet sea.   [Period of silence]

Keep This Flame of Freedom Pure and Holy!

Now let the thrust for a cosmic purpose that has originated in the Great Central Sun be carried by the return of a people consecrated in the light of the Divine Mother for the action of Omega. Let the fulfillment of this energy begun in heaven be manifest on earth by Keepers of the Flame who will give their lives to keep this flame of freedom pure and holy for America and for every nation upon earth. Let it be done in the name of Saint Germain. We serve him by love. We serve you by his love. We serve you by our intense, great love from the heart of God for your souls, for your hearts, for your life and for the dream of God for earth to become freedom's star.

We are the legions. We are the archangel and the archeia of the seventh ray. We are the feeling body of freedom. We are the desire of God to be free within you. We are that freedom here. Let it be charged now into your feeling bodies, and know the momentum of the archangels and the fervor for freedom that we hold twenty-four hours a day.

Let Victory Be Your Cry!

And therefore, let joy within you be freedom. And let that joy overcome every depression, every failure, every sense that all is lost. Let joy and the vision of the victory and the absolute certainty that God will win be your motto and your strength, your right hand and your banner as you march with the legions of light. So, let victory be your signet! Let victory be your cry! Victory! Victory! Victory!

14

WE EXPECT

A Dictation by Lanello

Hail, Keepers of the Flame! Once again I AM come. I AM come to greet you in the heart of love, in the love that we have shared here below, in the love that I have also consecrated from ascended octaves. I joy to be with you, and I have been with you throughout this conference, singing with you the songs that I love and communing with the hearts that I know.

You may see me here and there, for I have placed my Electronic Presence near to you so that you could converse with me as of old. And to the new Keepers of the Flame who have come since my ascension, I also extend my hand and my heart. And I am with you also that we might converse in the Law and establish that communion of hearts of which worlds are made—the community of hearts beating as one. This is the ineffable light, the indomitable will, the Presence of the Lord. This is the certain victory.

Take heart, precious ones, for the consolation of our flame is nigh, and the Brotherhood of the Royal Teton sends greetings and assurances that hierarchy is continuing to do all in its power to stay the darkness while the lightbearers come into the age of maturity. Take heart, dear ones, for when your soul is heavy and your heart is burdened by the things that seem to be coming upon mankind, know that the Great God, the Great Giver of all, does paint the drama of life in cycles. And therefore, remember the words, The darkest hour precedes the dawn of victory.

If There Is to Be a Dawn, You Must Be the Dawn

We must not rely on these cycles fulfilling themselves, for all cycles fulfill themselves because sons and daughters of God have consecrated to cosmic purpose that very heart of hearts and that life that is the supreme gift of the Creator. And therefore, do not rest in my words knowing that the dark precedes the dawn, but know that because the darkness is here the sun of light must rise—your own Mother flame and your Christ consciousness—and that this rising is the dawn. And unless there is this rising of yourself, there will be no dawn, neither within yourself nor in the world at large.

And therefore, you are the sun and the sun consciousness. And as Gabriel the archangel said, you must become worshipers of the sun[1]— the sun without, symbol of the sun within. You must know that if there is to be a dawn, you must be the dawn.

We expect, therefore, that Keepers of the Flame will retain from this conference a vision, a vision that will not be removed by any form of circumstance, by the pull and the allure of the world, of little projects here and little projects there. We expect—and we have no other consciousness, no other awareness, for there is no other alternative—we expect that every Keeper of the Flame will become totally consecrated to the cause of freedom. We expect that all of the energy that Saint Germain and other masters have placed into dictations and warnings and pleadings will now be fulfilled in the life of each chela who becomes God.

We Expect No Further Compromise

We expect no further compromise with human error, adversities, families that have become tyrants and dictators who have told you, you cannot do this and you cannot do that. We expect that this Fourth of July will be the individual soul's declaration of independence from all encumbrances that prevent the fulfillment of your life on the Path. And we expect that you will keep vigilant in defending that declaration, in refusing to allow any inroads into your world of any force or forcefield, person or impersonal personality coming across your path to take from you your dedication.

Now, you may be called, as a result of this, fanatics or zealots or crazy or queer or peculiar. We do not care. We do not care, and we will not tell you this day how the ascended masters refer to those among mankind who do not come into the Law. I will tell you this: if we were to call them idiots, it would be a mild declaration of the facts of reality.

You ought not to be concerned what the world thinks of you. You ought not to be concerned with your life or the satisfaction of pleasure in this life, for it will all come to naught. And those who have pointed the finger at you, the same who pointed the finger at me and at Saint Germain and Morya—the very same ones will be pointing their fingers a thousand years hence. We trust that as they point their fingers, their feet will have a platform on which to stand.

Archimedes' Lever Is Yours to Use Spiritually

Precious ones, this is the springboard of victory. This is the fulcrum. This is the keystone in the arch. This is the point where the gentle pressure brought to bear by Keepers of the Flame at the right point on the lever will raise the entire earth. Keepers of the Flame, apply the laws of physics! Archimedes' lever[2] is yours to use spiritually. You must understand what concentrated power can do. And as in the use of the pulley, the winding of the cords of light around each soul, connecting each and every one of you, makes this entire movement a giant pulley that can raise millions of souls.

Energy is God. You are God. You are energy. You are abundant resources. You have all that is necessary to change Terra. You have been told this before, but I must say it again because until you do it you do not know, truly know, that teaching which is given. We give it again, then, that you might hear the Word of the LORD and know that as you become one giant pulley for the elevation of earth, so the ascended masters apply the same laws.

Be clever, study, use the principles of science. Apply them to a spiritual physics; apply them to an engineering—an engineering of the design of God for the focus of light that we seek to establish. If at first you don't succeed, then try, try again. Know that all roads lead to Rome, all roads lead to Los Angeles. If you try one way and it doesn't work, then try the next and try the next, and in the course of trying you will become masters in the way of initiation. You will learn the ways of focusing energy in this plane.

If You Make a Mistake, Pick Yourself Up and Try Again

We are not concerned that you make mistakes; we have all made mistakes on the Path. But we are very concerned when you do not pick yourselves up and try again. The crux of the matter is this: that you must keep on trying, keep on moving toward perfection, and do not listen to those who condemn you for your efforts, for your trying, for your faith and hope.

You may do the best and even better than the most intelligent and astute businessmen of the world, but you may find that your plans do not work out because you have an extraordinary opposition of Antichrist that comes forth to thwart what seems to be an airtight plan. Let them point the finger, those who are able to be so clever in business. Were they to try to do the same things on the path of initiation that they do [in business], they would fall flat, flat on their noses, and you would wonder what dolts they were on this path of initiation. For you see, when you are dealing with cosmic energy, all things change.

And therefore, mastery in the world is no guarantee of mastery on the Path. And yet, if it is truly mastery in the world, it is an excellent foundation, for the same laws that you use in any field of endeavor can be translated to the field of the LORD. Which brings me to the subject of the harvest, the harvest of souls where the laborers are few.[3]

Each Morning Establish the Focal Point of the Harvest Sun

Your harvest must be by the action of the harvest sun. What is the harvest sun but the exact frequency of the light, the very light of Virgo becoming the light of Libra. Where the earth merges with the air, there is the appearance of the harvest sun. Let it be in your heart as a gathering sun. We expect, then, that you shall establish each morning with the dawn the focal point of the harvest sun, rich and golden and roseate—a sun that is warm and mellow, a sun center that is the most powerful magnet ever known for the souls of light to come Home.

We expect that you shall rise early in the morning, especially when you are wakened and nudged by your guardian angels, your Christ Self and perhaps a retinue of ascended masters. We expect that you will hear the call, the morning call to keep the flame, and not turn over and put that pillow over your head and draw up the covers and say, "I will rest some more."

We do not desire to see you deprived of your rest;[4] we desire that you shall catch the flow of the tide of light in the morning. Better for you to nap in the afternoon or to retire early than to sleep through those moments in the hours between 5:00 and 7:00 A.M.—when the sun is dawning, when the light is oncoming, when the angels of the dawn circle the planet bringing with them tides of momentum of cosmic energy that can be anchored through your morning rosary, your invocations and your decrees—so that by seven in the morning you have had one or two hours of meditation that has flooded the earth and anchored in every city and nation the momentum of your decrees.

Early Prayer and Early Meditation Combined with the Great Dynamic Power of Decrees

I tell you that early prayer and early meditation combined with the great dynamic power of decrees does more than decreeing in all the hours of the twenty-four because it is catching the tide of the morning light that comes forth from the Great Central Sun. See, then, how if you wait till ten or eleven to decree, you are bumping into the effluvia of the day, the pollution of the air [from] the automobiles of all of those who have been traveling since early morning. You find that the increment of karma that descends upon individuals with the dawn is now heavily upon them and entrenched in their four lower bodies.

Moreover, you find that the farther west you live, the greater advancement the day has had in the East. And therefore your decrees given later do not have the manifestation that they have when they are given earlier and you are counteracting these energies in the East, in Europe and in those countries that see the dawn before you do.

Understand, then, that if you wait, you will have to carve through a great momentum of the astral plane that is not to the fore in the early hours. This is why devotees and mystics and true followers of God in East and West have always risen early, some rising at four, some at three-thirty already ringing the temple bells, already coming to give their mantras. This is for the blessing of earth. This is for the consuming of karma on a world scale and an individual scale.

We desire to see mothers and fathers who have invoked the protection for their children before the day begins, before the little ones arise, so that they, too, may have the opportunity to get up and to give their decrees and to be prepared to face a world, a world of unknowns.

How to Prepare for the Maximum Use of Each Day

Is it not true that when you rise in the morning you have no idea what is going to take place on that day? You may have your plans, your job, your assignments; you may know what you would like to have happen. But life and death and birth and the comings and goings of karmic patterns producing mishaps, accidents and all manner of interruptions—these are all waiting. And they come upon the screen of life quite suddenly—suddenly to your eye but not suddenly to your Christ Self or to the Lords of Karma.

How, then, to prepare for the maximum use of each day is an aspect of the Law that you ought to consider. For if we are expecting you to serve to the maximum potential, then you must know how to get the maximum out of each day.

I suggest that before retiring you give your calls of protection to Archangel Michael.[5] Forty calls to this beloved archangel from your heart enables you to have the knowledge, the certain knowledge that through the night Archangel Michael will be pursuing the protection of the light, of the children of light, of the teachings and of many, many lifestreams who otherwise would be deprived of the blessings of life itself on the morrow. It is the protection of those who must also fight the demons of the astral plane at night, those who are involved in momentums of drugs, of alcohol, of suicide, of death, of all forms of selfishness and sensuality.

The protection in the eleventh hour of victory between 10:00 and 11:00 P.M. fortifies the children of light and the Keepers of the Flame throughout the planetary body against the tail of the dragon—the resentment, the revenge, the retaliation that comes against the victory. And therefore, with the striking of the hour eleven, your calls to Archangel Michael ought to be completed so that he may be standing there to defend you against the dragon of your own human creation and the dragon that is the dweller-on-the-threshold of the planet Earth itself.[6]

Note What You Would Like to Accomplish on the Morrow

I suggest, then, that having concluded these decrees, you take a white sheet of paper, unlined. The white paper symbolizes the soul, the soul that gives itself to God that God might write his word and his will on that paper. Take that sheet of paper, then, and begin to note what you would like to accomplish on the morrow, how you will organize your day, including the time you will arise, when you will give your decrees, when you will eat your breakfast, when you will be at work, when you will be at your desk, when you will be in service, when you will reserve those hours to be not interrupted because you are doing the Lord's work, when you will schedule time for interviews, for seeing people, for discussing the Law, and when you will reserve the time for your family.

If you can set the ritual of your day and have a pattern that is a formula that is used on regular days, then each night you can fill in this pattern. Then there are exceptional days that do not follow the routine, such as your weekend. And we desire and we expect that you shall have no more lost weekends, but that these weekends shall be put to the maximum use for Saint Germain. Therefore the pattern for these days should also be set.

Consecrate Your Day to God

After you have written this at night, put it next to you, go to sleep, consecrate your day to God and ask to be taken to the temples where he desires to have you study. Come back to your body in the morning refreshed, and review your day. See what impressions you immediately have from the masters and from their communication in the retreats. Look at your paper and see if there should be alterations made based on an inspiration, based on an inner direction or an inner key that you have been given.

If it is necessary to throw out the entire plan of the day because God has called you to something different, then do so. Be flexible, be mobile, be pliable—not rigid, but be prepared to be the Lord's instrument. By the same token, do not be movable by the fallen ones and the forces who will come to take from you your requirements, your duties of the hour.

Now see what resistance there is in yourself to completing this divine plan. Is there stubbornness? Is there sloth? Is there lack of organization? Is there lack of the real desire to do the will of God? Is the task so big that you cannot tackle it, and therefore you postpone it for days and weeks and months?

Look at yourself and say, Why am I not fulfilling the maximum for God today? Why am I not doing those things that I know I ought to be doing? And if you see in yourself that which prevents the manifestation, then call to Astrea to encircle it.[7] Call to me and I will run to your side to seize it from you, for I am only too happy to take from you that which hinders your service and to put it into the one flame of life.[8] And if you cannot see that which hinders you, then I say, call to Cyclopea,[9] and call and call and call until every last erg of your own selfishness is exposed.

How necessary this is! It is like polishing windows. Why don't you polish your windows? Why don't you get the proper tools and go and have a day of cleaning windows and feel the action physically of going through your house and making those windows sparkling clean?

And then let that ritual be transferred to the Within, and let your chakras be cleansed and your soul be cleansed and see how you will not be tolerant of the least little smudge or the least little speck of dirt on your soul because you have the momentum now of having accomplished this in the physical plane. It is fun to clean and to make ready and to prepare the house and to have things beautiful in Matter and then to transfer that mastery into the path of initiation.

Have Fun on the Path!

And so, have fun on the Path! Have fun in every day. Make every day a joyous one, and do not be downcast or downtrodden when you meet the heavy energies, the heavy gears of machinery that seem to grind and grind before you until they would grind you to a halt.

Remember that you are here to prove light, light, light, light, light, light! Remember, you have the mastery of the hierarchies of the Sun and the beings of the four elements who come at your behest,[10] who come at your call and who are so very happy to balance with you the four planes of Matter and to enlist millions of elementals to help you in your service.

Some of you neglect to call to the elementals. You forget that they are your servants, yet you have been taught this. All kinds of little gnomes and fairies and undines and salamanders would be with you all the day, making your tasks light and merry and clearing the way for initiation. And they are very, very helpful, these little ones—mighty helpful, I say. They come and they will do almost anything.

If you need something, they will run out to the market to contact someone, to contact a friend. They will tap someone on the shoulder, they will pull the garment until they convince that individual to do the very thing that you need. And then someone comes to the door and says to you, "Oh, I just happened to have this extra book and I thought you might like to read it." And you say, "Why, that's the very book that I wanted to have this day! Isn't that interesting?" And these precious little elementals, perhaps fifty of them, have worked and worked and toiled to make this happen for you, and you do not realize this. Perhaps you take credit, perhaps you give the glory to God, or perhaps you are in that vein of thinking where it is just coincidence.

Elementals Will Mobilize When You Call to Them

Now, if the elementals do all of these things for you without your asking, think how they will mobilize when you call to them. Think how they will mobilize and enter the cities and clean up the pollution and balance the ecology, and think how they will help you to draw the children of God into the light and into the movement.

You see, they are the Mother's helpers in the planes of Matter, whereas the angelic hosts are the Mother's helpers in the planes of Spirit. And so elemental life is often much closer to those individuals who are communing in nature, who are in the flame of the Holy Spirit and who just need to be plucked from where they are and brought to where you are.

And who do you think will do this? The sylphs of the air, the mighty undines; even the fiery salamanders have been known to make things so hot where these individuals are that they leave—they leave because they become so warm they want to change their place. And then the winds blow and perhaps they are caught up in an airplane and they find themselves somewhere on a street corner and there you are, handing out a poster.

The elementals have asked me to be their emissary at this conference and to tell you that they are simply begging and pleading with you to call to them to help in this mighty undertaking, that they are with you 100 percent of the way, and that they know that the four lower bodies of earth will not continue in balance unless people will stop and listen and accept what you have to tell them concerning the Law.

Now, the little elementals are really quite expert at whispering in the ear of individuals. And they do their work so very well and they make people think that their thoughts are their own ideas. Of course we, the ascended masters, are not free of [doing] this either.

But then there are the fallen ones who have come along to imprison elemental life, and they have put them under hexes and in modes of bondage. And then they send forth the little gnomes who no longer can be the instruments of the Mother but they become the instruments of the Great Whore and of Antichrist.[11] And therefore, there are elementals who need to be set free who are also wrongly influencing mankind and following the false teachers. I ask you this: if mankind do not know who they [themselves] are, can you expect that all elemental life know who they [the elementals] are? I tell you, they do not; and these elementals therefore need to be taught.

Elementals Attend Your Lectures and They Love to Decree

And wherever you are teaching, wherever you are lecturing, wherever we have a conference, there are far more elementals in attendance than there are people. And these elementals come and they perch here and there and they have their notebooks and their pencils and they sit with their little hats and they place their chins in their hands and they lean and they watch and they are transfixed. And they love the Mother and they love the slides and they love your singing and they are the sweetest little children.

But they are not all so little, for some of the mighty sylphs are fifty to a hundred to a thousand feet tall, and some of the salamanders manifest twelve feet tall; but they have the ability to expand and contract their consciousness for various needs, and therefore they can also be comfortable attending our conferences. Many times they form a funnel of light or of air or of fire over the place where the Mother is speaking, and so they listen outside under the stars above the places where you are decreeing.

And how they love to decree! And you know, they are imitators; and therefore, sometimes when you are decreeing, they decree after you like little echoes. And so you hear yourself saying, "I AM a being of violet fire!" and then they say, "I AM a being of violet fire!" and pretty soon it sounds like a round, and you find that they are all in different times so that it becomes a cosmic round and every decibel [i.e., degree] of the clock is covered by the repetition of that mantra in increments by these elementals.

Then, of course, there are the fairies, the sprites of nature who work among the flowers; and the devas, the angel devas who teach them to work with the flowers. Well, all of these creatures are simply very, very happy to be in the nation's capital for the celebration of freedom, for they are hoping, hoping so very much that Saint Germain will come and speak to them. And they are hoping that this flame of freedom that you are also calling forth will be like the flame of the resurrection from the heart of Jesus that gave them so much liberation when that decree was sent forth from the heart of the Christ.[12]

Elementals Have Hope in Saint Germain

And their hope in Saint Germain is their hope in freedom from all of these forms—types of animal forms, types of hexes and forcefields—freedom from the drudgery and the burden of the cross of mankind's consciousness. They are not impatient but very much tolerant and accepting of their role. Yet they, too, have a right to the flame of hope, and they look forward with hope to the day when they shall be free to also have the opportunity for immortality.

At this present moment, this opportunity is not given to elemental life. Each little elemental serves his time in space, and when that cycle is concluded, that little elemental as an identity will exist no more but the energy returns to the Great Central Sun. When mankind shall have balanced at least 51 percent of the planetary karma, then and only then will elemental life be given the opportunity to have the threefold flame and the resurrection flame.[13]

Consecrate All of Life and Living unto God

And so you see, if you ever have a moment's hesitation on the Path or in the consecration of your day to light, you may well think of the plight of the elementals: that millions and millions and millions of elemental beings who serve you daily may not know the gift of the ascension until you yourself have earned that gift and have transferred it to others among mankind, raising the entire portion of the planetary home.

We expect, therefore, that every Keeper of the Flame shall consecrate all of life and living unto God. Any other expectation would be unthinkable: the odds are too great, precious ones, the odds are too great. I pray, then, that you will read your newspapers and tune in to the media so that you can know, at least on the surface, what is happening, so that you can have co-measurement with Morya in the understanding of where you are and where the planet is going.

I Drop a Flawless Diamond into Your Heart

I pledge to you my love. I pledge to you my witness. I pledge to you my mantle. I will give you my love, and I will give it to every chela whom you draw into the flame. And now I take a little diamond, but a flawless diamond, and I drop it into your heart. Let it be a treasure there, a point of my attainment. Let it be my smile in your heart. Let it be there as a souvenir of Washington, as a souvenir of the mastery of the throat chakra that God gave to me in the power of the spoken Word. Let it be a souvenir of the moment when we were one in the nation's capital. Let it be a smile and a promise of another oneness—a oneness every day, if you like, a oneness at each conference, a oneness at our retreat in the etheric plane over the Rhine. And "I think of the Bishop of Bingen in his Mouse-Tower on the Rhine."[14]

Children of my heart, I am your father. I will not leave you alone; I will comfort you. But in order to be your true father, it was necessary that I take my leave of this octave to be that focal point in Spirit, that fulcrum in Spirit of which you are the counterpart in Matter, to draw you Home and to draw the earth into the heart of Mother.

I AM in the flame. I AM in your heart forever, Lanello.

15

WE EXPECT

A Dictation by Godfre

Hail, students of the I AM law! Hail, Americans! Hail, Freedom! Hail, light of Victory!

I enter this city—the capital, the shrine of freedom. I come bearing the light of the general and the light of the president. I come bearing the seal of the president, and I anchor the momentum of the first president of the United States in each one of you.[1] For I am determined that that thrust of law and of the will of God that was entrusted to my care should also be in your care and that you should sense the fire and the discipline of those whose destiny it is to forge the light of the nations.

This is not a time for compromise; this is a time for victory! And we look across the face of the land. We see hearts who would be free and yet spirits with not enough strength to manifest that freedom. We see minds that have gone soft and bodies that cannot sustain the vitality of the Spirit that we carried in those days. We would have you be, then, a strong and noble and alive people. We would see America return to that fiery heart of Saint Germain, to the great vastness of the sweep of the land of freedom when purity was known, when causes were clear, when friend and foe were identified.

Shame upon You, Leaders of America!

Now we see a confusion, a great babble of voices. We see leaders who ought to be leaders who are not leading the people in the ways of righteousness. We see the compromise of morality and we cry out,

Shame upon you! Shame upon you, leaders of America! I rebuke you this day! Receive, then, the birthday spanking that is due America, and let these leaders take the responsibility for what they have done with this land. Let it be returned to the people! Let it be returned to the people of light who have the fervor and the dedication to defend the mind, the heart, the soul and the soil consecrated to freedom.

You recall the days in Israel when there were no kings.[2] There were none worthy to be kings, for the people had compromised the law of hierarchy. They had taken down their kings, they had rejected their kings. And so you wonder where is your leadership when the people allow assassination, intrigue, corruption in politics and in the political parties to manifest.

Can the real king of America rise to power? And who is that king? Is not the king the one who has the *key* to the *in*carnation of God *[k-in-g]* within the heart? Is there not anyone who qualifies to be king? I will let you determine that, but I will say this: when the system of the leveling of hierarchy manifests through an ideology of World Communism and all of its ramifications, when there is no hierarchy left, when there is only the proletariat, then there can be no leader, then there can be no king and there can be no queen.

Abomination of desolation![3] Can you imagine a people accepting such a compromise and then crying out, "Where are our leaders?" You have destroyed your leaders, I say! You have given these souls who have been born to be leaders an education that educates them out from being leaders. By the time they have passed through the schools in America today, they have no concept of leadership, they have no concept of responsibility.

Was it not Karl Marx who said of the proletariat: You have nothing to lose and everything to gain. You have a world to gain. Working men of the world, unite![4]

Of course they have nothing to lose—they didn't have any attainment in the first place! Of course they have everything to gain—they have to gain the attainment of the lightbearers whom they cast down, whom they have guillotined, whom they have murdered, whom they have buried with their bulldozers under the soil of Russia and China and Eastern Europe and every nation where they have taken over.

One way or another, they have buried the lightbearers—either by the influences in the mind and the psychological reduction of a people to the position of weakness, or by raw power, by artillery, by armed might. Whatever the consciousness of the people, the fallen ones working through these have an adaptation of their schemes.

Wage Now a Warfare of Light

Now, I say, we expect that lightbearers will adapt the teachings of the I AM and of the Great White Brotherhood to America in this age. We expect that you will not stand still for this holocaust of darkness across the brains, the hearts of the children of light. We expect that you will write to those individuals in the Senate and in the Congress who have behaved like the decadent Romans who caused the fall of the Roman Empire (with their sensuality and their lust and their whiling away the hours) while America goes down and down and down.

We expect that you will wage now a warfare of light that is in absolute God-control, that is not emotional, that is not manipulative, that does not stoop to any tactics that are beneath the level of the Christ. But by the power of the freedoms that you enjoy you will expose the lie, you will expose the truth and you will not lose this torch of freedom and this opportunity of the age.

Do you understand, Keepers of the Flame, why I am fervent this day? Can you imagine going before the Lords of Karma at the conclusion of this life as a body, as a mandala, with heads hanging down, and saying, "We lost the mandala, we lost America"? The Lords of Karma recognize you as the leaders of the people. They recognize your attainment. Why have you not claimed it? Why have you not demanded your voice in these places of power?

Something Has Got to Be Done!

I deplore the separation in politics and religion of the children of light. And I am determined to release that flame of intense, fiery love this day that those who are truly of the light can be set free from these pockets and sockets of consciousness that are absolutely diabolical. It is diabolical that the people of the world who understand freedom will deny the science of the spoken Word that is the key to freedom, that they will persecute and condemn the lightbearers.

This must not be! I tell you, Keepers of the Flame, something has got to be done! And when I take my leave of you, I am going straight to the Royal Teton to address the Lords of Karma. And when I go and I tell them that I am coming to demand change, they will say to me, "Well, who is supporting you, and who is giving you a vote of confidence, and who is pledging to you, Godfre, anew that energy of light that is necessary to give that dispensation?" When I go and they ask me this question, whom shall I say sent me unto them?

[Audience responds: "I do!" "We do!"]

Hosts of light, friends of light, I will take your pledge and I will say to them, I will say the words of the LORD: "I AM hath sent me unto you"[5]—the I AM Presence and the fire of the Christ in the chelas of the Law.

Chelas on the Path in the I AM Movement

And what about those chelas on the Path who are a part of the I AM movement so dear to my heart.[6] Why have they rejected this messenger? Why have they failed to come when I have appealed to their hearts? I ask you to pray for them. I ask you to pray for those children of the light who must understand that the nature of [the relationship between] the chela and the guru is obedience, but it is also understanding. The chela must also weigh the Law and weigh the principles of the Law and come to his own conclusions. The chela must understand that a certain teaching given through the messengers may change because of changing conditions in the world.

Saint Germain had a great plan for America, and if the children of light had responded to that plan there would not be a need to have further messengers. But the need is great. Hierarchy has acted. Hierarchy is not limited by doctrine or dogma or prophecy or even its own previous statements on the Law.

The Ascended Masters Must Work with the Needs of the Hour

Some law is unchanging, but there are rulings, there are dispensations, there are interpretations that come forth that, according to the times, may have an alteration. Take, for instance, the law that was given at the time of Jesus and Paul that there should be no divorce.[7] This was a very necessary law in that time because of the sensuality of the people, because of the need to establish the Holy Family matrix and for souls to work out their karma and not to be allured, one to the other. We do not advocate divorce in this day and age, but we recognize that two thousand years later there is a different situation on earth.[8] That situation is the acceleration of the balance of karma.

With the acceleration of these cycles, therefore, it sometimes becomes necessary for individuals to change partners, as you say, for a higher purpose, for a higher calling and for the working out of that manifestation of light within them, especially in the case of lightbearers, where past associations do not lead to the victory of the soul or to the path of initiation. It becomes necessary, then, to cut those ties, to go on and to know that you can balance karma on a universal basis. And so you see, it was Jesus himself who gave this teaching; yet Jesus today standing before you would [in some cases] give you the opposite teaching.

Do you not understand, then, that the ascended masters are here because we must work with the needs of the hour? We must work with the current manifestations of free will. As free will responds to God's will, then there is created a new dispensation and a new requirement for an interpretation of the Law.

The Supreme Court Affirming the Death Penalty

You will see, then, how your own Supreme Court has gone back and forth on many issues over the years, and only today has come forth the announcement of the Supreme Court affirming the death penalty in the United States.[9] There has been great discussion concerning this.

I am here to tell you that I ratify this decision, and the reason is this: it comes more closely into the reflection of cosmic law. You understand that cosmic law also provides for the death penalty in the second death before the Court of the Sacred Fire on Sirius[10] where there are those souls who are absolutely incorrigible, who will not glorify God, who have spent all of their energy on darkness. When their time is up, they pass through the second death. They stand on the dais where the currents of Alpha and Omega are manifest, and there that identity is canceled out.

Now, what do you think this does to the rest of the evolutions of the cosmos? It is the same goad to righteousness that you find in your own death penalty. As you sit here knowing the Law, knowing that you do not have forever and a day to while away the hours and to waste God's energy—knowing that there is a judgment—then you are spurred to righteousness.

And some among mankind likewise need that threat (much closer, of course, in their own lifetime) that if they commit these heinous crimes against the Mother and her children, against the body of God upon earth, that they will have to give an accounting. We see, then, that justice at work in this hour of turmoil and chaos necessitates this court decision being implemented by the states.

You see, the Lords of Karma realize that the soul that goes through that ultimate punishment will be given very quickly an opportunity to reincarnate. And on the record of that soul will be that record of the judgment and that knowledge: "If you fail, this is what happens." We desire to see that recorded. And, therefore, we repeat with Christ, Fear not those who kill the body, but those who are able to destroy the soul in hell.[11]

And I tell you, many souls who have committed these crimes who are in the prisons today are rotting away because they have not had that edict of the descent of their karma. And so the bodies are preserved and the souls rot away. Would it not be better if the reverse were so? And therefore, this is that explanation.

I would also tell you that it is, in our opinion, a manifestation of far too great a leniency when those who are in prison for life are allowed to leave on good behavior—hardened criminals, those who have committed mass murders. I bring these things before you so that you will understand that ours must be a total victory, and that total victory must manifest in justice, in the law and in every area of life that is lived in America.

Dispensation for the Release of Lightbearers

I say, then, I am going to the Royal Teton and I am going to ask for a dispensation for the release of the next band of lightbearers and of children of the Mother who are caught in various psychic activities. And many of them are caught with those who are the [false] gurus.

These individuals [the lightbearers and the children of the Mother] are highly sincere and highly motivated for America, but they have been plunked down into a teaching and a forcefield that is a half-truth and sometimes a whole error.

Once they have accepted these errors, precious ones, it becomes a part of their own mind, their own ego, their own identity. To surrender these patterns is difficult for them, for it demands a surrendering of a portion of their own self-consideration, their concept of their own ability to assess religious principles, to make decisions, to see the truth and to not see the truth. And therefore, if they are told that they are in a movement that is entirely wrong, it is an insult to their consciousness and they are not so quick to admit that they have made an error as the human consciousness goes.

And so you see, it is vital that the souls who are uncommitted, who have not found the true teaching, be drawn into the teachings of the ascended masters. For it is far more difficult to find them once they have been swallowed up in one of these houses or centers or forcefields of teachers who do not represent our Brotherhood. Therefore, it is indeed high time that these teachings and these books were made universally available.

Conflicting Desires in the Subconscious

I AM Godfre! I AM a God-free being, and I have willed to be free! I tell you that those individuals who are living for freedom yet who are encamped in the right and the left wing—one and all, there is something, *something* within them that resists freedom at the same time it desires freedom. I will tell you something very interesting and perhaps curious: that there are many such as these, and if they really desired to be free, if they truly wanted to be free, they would accept the teachings of the ascended masters.

Therefore, there are conflicting desires in the subconscious. There may be involved a desire for recognition. There may be a desire that is a fear molecule. There may be a desire for wealth, for family, for gain, for some other commodity, and this desire then presents the conflict. And when they encounter the teachings of the ascended masters, they are not able to let go.

Even the desire for righteousness itself, the desire to be saved, the desire to be free from sin is a selfish desire in one aspect because it is an attachment, it is the desire to get something for a reward. This desire for the reward, then, tends to make people be bound to doctrines and dogmas. And therefore, really, when they are in the churches or when they are fighting for America, in many instances their motive is based on self-preservation. And self-preservation is a binding force. It eclipses the light of the all-seeing eye.

Understand, then, that the only legitimate love of God is to love God merely for the sake of loving him and loving him alone, and not for the consequences of his return love, his reward, his elevation of your soul, et cetera. Only this freedom, this freedom to be God and to love God, will secure for the soul of light the true path and freedom from error and compromise due to his own pride and ambition.

In Each and Every Nation There Are Lightbearers Whom We Have Called

I give you this key so that you can pray for the American people. Many of them are eight-tenths motivated in the right direction. But there is something holding them back from coming into the light; and once that something is transmuted, then there will be no stopping this people. For this people is a mighty people. This people is of old from the temples of Atlantis and Mu, from other systems of worlds. Among this people are the legions of Sanat Kumara and the volunteers who came forth, the disciples of Jesus, the multitudes to whom he spoke on the hillsides, those who lived in the catacombs in Rome. This people is the drawing together of some of the most noble and stalwart souls of the ages of this entire system of worlds.

And the Lord has placed many of these souls in other nations. In each and every nation there are lightbearers whom we have called, and we do salute those representatives at this conference who have come from lands afar, who have come at the behest of freedom. We will send you home with our love and freedom, with our rod of power, with our energy that you might also be the electrodes for the rolling back of the darkness. And as you give your violet flame in your home bases, you will reach a crescendo of light where the legions of violet flame from the Great Central Sun can also come to your nation and roll back the karma of the Dark Cycle.[12]

Understand, then, that the reason that this was given to America this day is solely because Keepers of the Flame and other students of the I AM have been diligent in giving their calls to the violet flame in this past year. We need many souls in every nation to create that mandate whereby the solar lords will send these millions of violet-flame angels to a nation. And so you have the challenge, Ghana has the challenge, Africa and Europe, Sweden and Canada and every place where Keepers of the Flame rise up.

We Expect Victory!

Yes, I AM God-free! But I will never rest until you are God-free, until America is God-free! Precious ones, if you will but take that fervor of the early patriots who knew that all of the future and all of life and the future of freedom on the earth depended upon their staying power—if you will take that fervor, you will save America and we will win for God together. *We expect victory!*

16

THE ANTAHKARANA OF POWER

A Dictation by El Morya

Now comes the will of God!
Now comes the will of God!
Now comes the will of God!
And see how the energies roll
Into the inner blueprint,
Into the matrix of the law
Of each one's Christed being.
I kneel before the altar of the will of God
And I say, O God, thank you for thy law!
O God, thank you for thy will!
In this is salvation still
For earth, for elemental life,
For the angelic hosts and blest humanity.

I AM Morya, your friend old and new,
Known forever unto you,
You who are in the diamond of God's will.
Do you remember when
We swam in the sea of cosmos together,
Souls aborning,
Souls putting on skeins of the cosmic will?
Do you remember
How we said to one another,

"How glorious is this mighty blue fire!
We will stay in this fire forevermore"?

And as the cycles rolled
And others of the seven rays began to enfold the soul,
Some of you chose to follow the way of wisdom
And of love, of purity, of truth,
Of service, of science, of healing, of freedom.
And so you chose your path to Christhood
And to Buddhahood on one of the seven rays.
But you remembered your friend Morya,
Who tarried in the will of God
Forever and a day,
Who was created to say,
"I love thy will, O God. I love thy will, O God.
I love thy will, I love thy will, I love thy will."
And here I am with you,
With you in this joyous moment of freedom,
Saying still, "I love thee, O my God,
In the eternal will."

Now in the very core of the atoms
Of the flame of freedom
Which the magnificent violet-flame angels
Have spread across the land this day,
I consecrate the diamond of my will
And my attainment on that path,
Path to Hercules' retreat,
Path to Half Dome which I have walked
So many, many times that my feet
Have carved a path in the rock.
Perhaps one day you will find my footsteps
To the retreat of my own Guru
And you will remember the one
Who was enamored by the Elohim
Because of his cosmic consciousness of will.

And so I consecrate
And I add my own flame
In support of Saint Germain,
And I lay out the royal blue carpet
For the coming of the God of Freedom to this city.
And I proclaim him president of the nations,
Master of ceremonies, guardian of the flame!
He is my master also.
And when I worship at the shrine of freedom,
It is to his heart that I come—
To the heart of blest Joseph,
Father of the Christed One,
Father of the Manchild within you.

Angels of the will of God, come forth!
Come forth now
With a mighty sealing action of freedom's ray!
And now let us see what we will do this day—
We who are devotees of fire—
What we will do for freedom,
For victory, for America.
We will place our focuses of God's will;
We will put them here and there
And in the hearts of people,
In the rocks and in the flowers,
In the streams and in the mountains,
In the cities and in the towers,
In the skyscrapers.
And we will publish it abroad,
Even in the newspapers.

The will of God will come forth!
Let it come forth!
Let it come forth to tell,
To tell of the magic and the moment
And the miracle of the Mother

And of Maitreya
And the magnificent followers of God
Who in this moment of a cosmos rejoicing,
Inundating waves of light,
Do stand in the foam, on the sand,
One with the shore and with the sea,
As hand in hand these devotees know
That the will of God is a poetry and a song;
It is the meditation of the heart all day long.
It is the light,
And it is the void of the night
Into which we project
Cosmic consciousness of Virgin pure,
Womb of God and fiery stars
All inside becoming children,
Children, children of the heart of love.

The will of God is marching on.
The will of God is marching!
Legions of the will are marching,
And we bring the banner of the victory
Of the turning of the tide.
Let those who have joined
The light revolution
Know that the rod of power
Is thrust into the hand of the Mother
And the electrodes of power are placed
Within the hearts of her children.
Now let us see what darkness and deceit,
What degeneration and deception
Can stand against the moment
Of the coming of the light of God.

And with the turning of the hours
And the dawning of the day
And the moment of the beginning

Of the Fourth of July,
The Mother light will begin to flow
And to glow and to flow and to glow,
And all of Earth and all of her evolutions
Will have a new cycle and a new moment.

I AM Morya,
Morya in love with the Divine Mother!
I AM Morya,
Come to proclaim the mighty mantle of that Mother
That is large enough to enfold evolutions
And lifewaves of all systems of worlds.
I AM with the Buddha
In the heart of the Mother,
I AM with the Mother
In the heart of the Buddha.

I AM in you the perpetual reminder
That God is ever new.
And I AM the new friend also,
For I AM not in any moment
The Morya you have known.
For life is transcending life.
And where I stand and where I serve
And from that point in Darjeeling
Where I project the light
Of God-government to the nations,
God as law, as principle, as science
Is transcending himself.

Day by day, we are renewed
And transformed from glory unto glory.[1]
So is the coming
Of the will of God
In our hearts.
And the Elohim have pronounced

The writing of the light in the sky,
And by the rainbow of their consciousness
They have carved an ark of a covenant
Of God and man.
Lo, this is the Word of thy Maker!
Children of Israel, children of reality,
This is the Word!

In the will of God,
In the will of God is the commandment.
In the will of God is the covenant.
And in the will of God is the compassion of the Lord,
Who sends his hosts and his legions
To the children God adored.
This is the Word, this is the Word
That God writes in the azure blue,
The celestial dome,
This is the Word:
O chelas, come home,
O chelas mine, into my heart!
Come now for the thrust,
And in sacred trust take my hand
And let me show you the power and the glory.[2]
Let me show you the light within.

I give to you now my mentor,
The flaming one, Hercules.

17

THE ANTAHKARANA OF POWER

A Dictation by the Elohim Hercules

Did you think, O mankind of earth, that we would stand by and see the desecration of the will of God? Did you think that you would not hear from the Lords of Flame and from the beings of the first ray of the dawn? Did you think that we would remain silent?

So long as we exercise the power of the spoken Word, so long as there is a messenger dedicated to that will of God, we will speak out! We will let it be known that the grids and forcefields of the mind of God are being lowered into this planetary body as the antahkarana of power. Let mankind try, if they will, to go against these rods and cones and forcefields of our love of that will.

That will comes forth and the antahkarana descends now! It is the edict of the Almighty, and we are but his emissaries—as you are. We are the servants of the will of God, and there is but one God and one LORD and one Maker of heaven and earth.

We come to serve these evolutions, for we have long ago chosen the path of Christhood. O silly and foolish mortals, you think because you have come lately into the path of Jesus Christ that no one before you has ever known his name and no one before you has ever attained to the ascension in the light.

Well I tell you, Jesus Christ and Gautama the Buddha have lived forevermore* in the will of God, and therefore by our communion in the Christ, we won our victory aeons ago. Have we not also the right

---
*forever, eternally

to be, as you have the right to be? Will you deny our existence?

Try and see, if you will. I can assure you in this moment that your denial of the reality of the ascended masters can only mean the denial of yourself. For we will not accept that energy; we will allow it to return to you. And you will find that there is, after all, only one Great Self, and if you deny that Self in manifestation anywhere in the sons and daughters of God, then, so, you pronounce the edict and the judgment of your own being.

Therefore I say, choose wisely what thoughts and what feelings you send my way. For I am an Elohim and I encompass stars and galaxies in my awareness of God. This you may also do. And this is not blasphemy, for in your devotion unto God, God is most willing, I assure you, to give unto you the allness of himself.

A Focal Point for the Crystallization of Will

See, then, what God hath wrought! He hath brought forth now in this hour that focal point for the crystallization of will in earth as you have not seen will in aeons of lifetimes. I tell you, the coming of that will, will present an obstacle course for those who are not able to surrender to that will each day. I tell you that those who are the rebellious generation, who have the laggard consciousness and who constantly thwart that will, will find themselves extremely confined. For by the antahkarana of power, there will be a swift return of their rebellious consciousness.

Let the warning go forth, then, that those who resist the will of God will find that the very rebellion that they have projected upon the cosmos will return to manifest within their own microcosm. And they will find their own cells in rebellion, their own molecules and atoms, the organs of the body, and then they will find the tearing asunder and the splitting of the four lower bodies. What do you think is the cause of insanity? What do you think is the cause of darkness and of the diseases that plague mankind? It is rebellion that they have sent forth, and it is the boomerang of karma.

Learn this, O mortals: The light is oncoming! Either you will preserve your identity in that light, or you will find yourselves—by your own edict and none other—canceled out by that very light that you have misqualified. I AM indeed Hercules, and none may question that individualization of the God flame! For to question the identity of the Christed One is to question the source of the Christ, *God himself!* This indeed is the blasphemy—not the claim to Sonship, not the claim to Godhood, but its denial!

I am a scientist, and my invention comes forth from the will of God. By the invention, you know that the scientist exists. So by your presence in the universe, I hope, by God, that you also know that God exists as the inventor of your manifestation. And by my presence here, may you determine once and for all that God is very, very real, and there are octaves of light and levels and planes of consciousness that you know not of.

Standing in my presence, then, see how you can be that awareness, for a moment, of the Elohim. See how you can feel *consciousness* expand, *reality* expand—*light* and new dimensions and hope of transcending this mortal coil, this mortal frame.

Love Impels the Masters to Chastise Their Chelas

O beloved, O beloved, I release the power of God to *shake* you, to *quicken* you, to *roll* that energy through your grids and through the density of darkness that you have chosen to hang upon your grids! As wash upon the clothesline, so you have hung all of the substance of your subconscious on the precious grid of light that God has given you, the place prepared where you can be the energy of Christ.

O beloved, I come with such intensity because of only one, *one* concept. It is love and love alone that impels the masters of the will of God to chastise their chelas, to quicken, to shaken, to goad, to spur you on, to keep you working day and night in the victory so that you can lose all of the pettiness of your self-concerns and come to the place where you can truly run, rejoicing, to greet your Lord who has said, "He that will not take up his cross daily is not worthy of me. He who seeks to save his life shall lose it."[1]

We desire that you should preserve life, integrity and the things that count! After all, what counts in life but loving, but being free, but being whole, but knowing that you can walk Home to God and knowing that he will receive you, knowing that you are acceptable in his sight.

Let the words of my mouth and the meditations of my heart be acceptable in thy sight, O God, my redeemer![2] This is the prayer of the one on the path of Christhood. This is the imploring of the soul to know this one, this one hope: that effort is worthy of grace, that consciousness is worthy of being in the presence of God!

Hercules Opens His Retreat to Chelas of the Will of God

I am also opening my retreat to chelas of the will of God who have made their way to the Will of God Focus,[3] who have given the calls to the blue ray consistently day by day. If you will undertake a novena of invocations to Hercules, then by cosmic law I am compelled to draw you into the fiery core of my devotions to that will. And then you can look forward to an even greater stripping of your consciousness of that human will that you thought you had surrendered long ago.

Precious ones, this is the key: If you would be a chela of a master, an archangel, an Elohim, of Helios and Vesta, then make it your life to give daily invocations, extensive invocations to that master. Do not be surprised if that master will make you wait two years, three years, five years. But then suddenly, when you have given those calls faithfully without fail, you will find yourself in the presence of the Guru and you will hear the word, "Welcome, my son. Welcome, my daughter. Thou hast been faithful over a few things, I will make you ruler over many. Enter into the house of the Lord."[4]

The Sealing of the Antahkarana of Power

Now is come the moment for the sealing of the antahkarana of power by the legions of Hercules who are gathered now at certain key points: at the North Pole and the South Pole, along the equator, along certain lines of longitude and latitude. And now the grid of light is moved into place and sealed by the seven mighty Elohim.

Now let the earth respond and come into conformity with the will of God in every aspect of life! Now let the chelas of the will of God accelerate the blue ray! And let us see if the air and the fire and the water and the land and the souls of a people can be brought into inner alignment with the law of God. This is the first step of the light revolution!

In the sun of the light of Alpha and Omega, I AM and I remain Hercules of the will of God!

18

WE ARE ONE IN THE FLAME OF EAST AND WEST

A Dictation by Gautama Buddha and Jesus Christ

Hail in the AUM of the Buddha and the Christ!

We are one in the flow of Mother. We are flowing in the light of Holy Spirit. We are fire and earth and air and water. We are the converging of the caduceus of East and West. Out of the East comes the principle of Father. Out of the West comes the personality of Mother. The intertwining creates the culture, the government and the civilization of the lightbearers.

With the turning of the cycles of the light on this 200th anniversary of the Declaration of Independence, we come to announce the dispensation of the Lords of Karma that a free people throughout the world, by their stand for the light of freedom, have magnetized the gift of the principle of unity, of the light of God interpreting to all hearts by the love of Mother the essential oneness of the brothers and sisters in the family of God.

It is by the unguent and the oil—the very balm of Gilead itself and even the precious ointment of spikenard, which the Mother uses to anoint her children preparing for the crucifixion—that the Mother softens the barriers.

Mankind Will Come into the Orchestration of the Spirit in This Age

The Mother shows all life that, in reality, all who love light are in one accord, in one place as on the day of Pentecost when they were found in that accord[1] that is the chord of cosmic law that touches all hearts.

Are there not many notes that compose the great symphonies of life and the harmonies and the fullness of orchestration? Do these notes quarrel with one another and tell each other, "You should be my tone; you should be my frequency. Because you are not, you are wrong"? Mankind will come into the orchestration of the Spirit in this age.

We are the guardians of the shrine of the Mother flame and of the Christ and the Buddha in every heart. We have some say in this world, after all. There are millions of devotees who pray to us daily asking for God's will, asking for salvation, asking for healing and comfort. By their prayers they give us the authority to enter this world, and so we come. According to cosmic law, the call compels the answer. But the answer that is given is the answer of God, and it is not the answer of man.

Let mankind be humbled. Let them understand that the ways of this world are foolishness with God,[2] that the interpretation of scripture, whether East or West, will always be brittle, will always be intellectual until the surrender of that carnal mind to the Christ and the surrender of the adulterous Great Whore[3] to the Mother.

Let all, then, read scripture infilled with the Holy Spirit and let the Holy Spirit give utterance.[4] Let the Holy Spirit proclaim the truth and the grace of that Law which is immutable and inviolate.

The Flame of Freedom Consumes Every Form of Tyranny over the Mind of Man

We stand in the presence of the hierarch of the Aquarian age. We stand in the presence of a universal flame of freedom. That flame of freedom is the consuming of every form of bondage, every form of tyranny over the mind of man. Let all patriots this day stand and declare that eternal hostility over every manifestation of the tyranny over the mind and the heart and the soul![5] Let them swear on the altar of Almighty God that rejection of the lie of the fallen ones! And by this courage, this conviction and this fiat of souls, there will be the crumbling of the dragons of the tyrants that, after all, were only paper dragons to begin with. And like children, mankind have feared the specters in the night, which are the specters of their own creation.

Do you not understand that at every point when World Communism is challenged and checked, it recedes? It is the very philosophy inherent in the [Communist] system to press on where people are weak, where there are the marshlands. And when they contact steel and the light of truth, they are told to withdraw and to proceed on other lines of battle. And so the West, the lightbearers retreat and retreat and retreat, giving away the land that is the abundance of the Mother, the very abundance of light.

The Buddha Consecrates All Space to the Coming of the Mother and Her Children

I AM Buddha! I AM space! I have consecrated all space to the coming of the Mother and her children! I have consecrated these worlds in the name of Almighty God to the fulfillment of the sons and daughters. This is hallowed space. Will you allow the fallen ones who deny the Buddha, who deny Maitreya and the great teachings of the Eastern masters—will you allow them to usurp the holy ground?

I say with the God of Moses, who stood in the presence of the living flame: "Put off thy shoes from off thy feet, for the place whereon thou standest is holy ground!"[6] This city is holy ground. All cities that are the chakras of the nation are holy ground. The plains and the mountains, the seas—all of this holy ground, holy Mother, holy God, the cradle provided for the evolution of the Christ Child within you.

Will you allow yourselves to be rocked in the cradle of the fallen ones who rock their sheep to sleep, fast to sleep, *fast to sleep?* Will you be rocked to the lull of materialism? Will you be rocked to the lull of Communism? Will you be rocked to the lull of a false ideology and a false religion that promises you salvation, whether through the acknowledgment of the state or the acknowledgment of the Saviour?

Attain Salvation by Becoming the Saviour

Understand, precious hearts, that it is by becoming the Saviour that is within you, by merging the flame of your Christ Self with the flame of Jesus, that you attain salvation. Another cannot do it for you. And this is the dialectical materialism that has infiltrated Communism, that has infiltrated Christianity since its inception.

Two thousand years ago the lie of materialism and mechanization was already spawned to compromise the teachings of the law, the law of Incarnation. What is the law of Incarnation? It is the law of the Word made flesh.[7] Where is the Word made flesh? Where is the Word incarnate? Is it in Jesus alone? I tell you, nay! Right where you are the Word is incarnate. Christ has come into your temple and Christ lives; and if you did not have this spark of God within you, you would not be children of the Most High.

The law of the Incarnation, then, must be set aright and the lie concerning only *one* Incarnation must be refuted. And so the same lie concerning a one-world government [must be refuted]—that only in a one-world government by the fallen ones can you have salvation in the form of peace. You will notice that they never promise you freedom, but they only promise peace.

We are the masters of peace of East and West! *We* know the flame of peace and we know the power of peace and we know those who cry out, "Peace, peace!" and there is no peace.[8] There is a false peace. It is the peace of the flesh. It is the peace of the kine on the hillsides. It is the peace of the rocks and the inert matter. It is the peace of those who sit in front of the TV set who consider an evening of peace a pizza and a can of beer and a TV program. This is peace while the world crumbles, while the path of hierarchy is made the subject of negotiation!

Can you imagine the Christ and the Buddha sitting at the table with Satan, with the fallen ones, with the archdeceivers of mankind and negotiating peace? I tell you, on whose terms? Do you not remember Christ in the wilderness?[9] Was there any negotiation, was there any compromise? By cosmic law he refuted every temptation of the Fallen One. And it is the temptation for the power in this world to which the Communists and the capitalists have succumbed.

Let us understand, then, that only in absolute conviction that Christ is the way, that Buddha is the way, that the light within can conquer the planes of Mater by the law of cosmos—only in this will you earn that point on the path of initiation, that ultimate victory that was given to Jesus in the final hours of his mission when he declared before all mankind and before the ascended hosts of God, "All power is given unto me in heaven and in earth!"[10]

Does this not prove that you do not have to go to the fallen ones for power, you do not have to follow the philosophy of the end justifying the means, you do not have to secure power from those who have sided in with the archdeceivers?

They have not the source of power or the source of energy, but they seek to claim it. I tell you, they seek to control the oceans and the landed areas and the sources of oil, the pipelines from the Middle East. They seek to cut off Europe and America and every free nation, and thus you see their pursuit of the control of the continent of Africa and the Cape of Good Hope and Angola and the Persian Gulf and the Suez Canal and the Panama Canal. These people who have never even had an access to the sea now have the open door, opened wide by the negotiators.

We Negotiate with the Councils of Almighty God

We are the ones who negotiate, and *we* negotiate with the councils of Almighty God. We sit at the Darjeeling Council table. We sit in the chambers where God-government is planned and its application to these nations and to this system of worlds. Negotiation is the negotiation of light and law and its application to an evolving humanity. *This* is the only place for discussion. And our compromise is never a compromise of the Law, but it is the compassion of the Christ meting out to an infant humanity their daily requirements through the best form of government and the best form of an economy that we can evolve given their present state of selfish, sensual evolution.

If you do not think that this is a dilemma for the ascended masters, well I tell you: to know the perfect forms of God-government and of the flow of abundance and then to have to work through a people who cannot take the pure forms but must have a stepping down of those forms, which is always extremely dangerous—this is indeed God's challenge to his ascended sons and daughters. For when you have a stepping down of the pure forms of the geometry of God, you have a greater opportunity for the overthrowing of these forms; for they are inherently less strong, less secure than if they were founded solely and totally upon the Rock of Christ and the Christ consciousness.[11]

But you see, even the highest of the evolutions of mankind, even those you find among the greatest people, have not understood the path of initiation as the path of Christ and Buddha. And therefore we must rely upon the soul, the inner light of the soul and its knowledge of inner spheres, to interpret the Way, the Truth and the Life.[12] Inasmuch as mankind's religions have become so watered down that they [mankind] cannot even distinguish good and evil based on the moral principles they are taught, we must rely on the soul memory of the Ancient of Days.[13] We must rely on the soul's contact with Reality and not upon its outer indoctrination.

Do you not see, then, that the conspiracy is not confined to the realm of politics or religion? It is not confined, whether to the manipulation of the media or to the educational systems. But the conspiracy is overall and all-encompassing, and it manifests wherever there is the inherent weakness of compromise within the human soul. Where there is compromise with the energy veil, this is the beginning of slavery, human slavery. Oh, wretchedness of the spirit! Oh, wretchedness of life! Not life but death—death and a slow dying, a slow rotting away of an identity until few among mankind today actually remember who they are, who I AM, who and what is Reality!

Mother's Manifesto—And the Truth Shall Make Them Free

Now I proclaim the coming of the flame of the Mother to the rescue. And I announce to her and to you this day that there shall go forth from the heart of Omega through the heart of the Mother a document for all children upon earth, a document that shall be a refutation of these entrenched lies, the lies of the fallen ones cleverly put forth in the *Communist Manifesto* and in various publications that have fomented darkness in every area, every field of endeavor in every corner of the globe. And so it shall be known as a divine document, as the gift of Omega, the Divine Mother, to her children. And it shall be called *Mother's Manifesto!*[14]

And it shall be distributed far and wide over the face of the earth through your very hands, and it shall be read by those who have not understood the battle lines or the forces of light and darkness. And they will read the word, and the flame will leap from the very pages to the heart, and they will have the illumination of my crown, my crown chakra, and they will have the illumination of the heart of Christ. And they will know the truth, and *the truth shall make them free!*[15]

19

MEDITATION IN THE MOMENT OF THE BIRTH OF A NATION

A Dictation by the Great Divine Director

Good afternoon, ladies and gentlemen. I am come in the light and the fire of the lineage of the House of Rakoczy. I thank you for your tribute to this heritage that descends even from the Ancient of Days, your tribute in your meditation on the "Rakoczy March."[1] Truly it was inspired from the very core of my own causal body; and the intricacy of the flow, the timing and the spaces are as the cosmic intervals of initiations that move step by step quickly, quickly as notes up and down on the piano of a cosmos and of a soul.

And so you see what mastery is required of those who would hold the balance for a mandala of so many forces and forcefields and integrating spirals and energies that crisscross throughout a cosmos. This is the meaning of divine direction. For the consciousness of divine direction holds within itself an awareness of cosmic cycles, cosmic moments when out from the Sun* come forth sons and daughters of light to be born, to be victors, to ascend, to liberate a planet and a people and to rescue the downtrodden, to set the captives free.

There are those among the cosmic beings whom I represent who are entirely responsible for focusing the Cosmic Christ consciousness of divine direction. And we must have the accuracy of the timetable of a cosmos available to us and therefore we must contain it within our own consciousness. When you call to me, when you call to the

---
*the Great Central Sun, the point of all physical-spiritual creation

Great Divine Director, I would like you to know that there are many cosmic beings who answer to this call, for they serve in the mandala of this divine direction.

The Moment of the Consecration of Your Own Soul's Declaration of Independence

And so you see, cosmos is interdependent and we are all complements of one another's victory. And therefore I even bow most humbly before your own Christ Self and your own souls who have responded to my flame as you have given the novena of invocations to the Great Divine Director, and this in answer to the request of my own beloved chela Saint Germain.[2]

Because you have faithfully given these calls, spirals of divine direction have entered into your worlds and you have embarked upon a new flow. Because you have given the calls, spirals of divine direction have been sent forth into America, and, what's more, spirals of divine direction have accrued to my own cosmic consciousness. It was because of this, because of the devotion of the chelas of Terra, that I so desired to be with you in that moment of glory, which is the glory unto God for all that we accomplish together in these planes of Mother and in these planes of Father. I am with you now in the moment of the consecration of your own soul's declaration of independence.

While others rally for lesser causes, you have come to the city, to the city Washington, to celebrate the cause of the Great White Brotherhood, to celebrate the cause of freedom in the human spirit. Freedom—the opportunity to have free will, to choose rightly or wrongly, but the opportunity to choose.

We defend the freedom of those who are meeting elsewhere in the city. We champion their rights as God does and as you ought to also. For only in manifesting a stand—whether to the right or to the left of God's law it does not matter—will individuals understand the rightness or the wrongness of that stand. It is the same with karma. Until you take the contemplated action, you do not have the return of karma, which is the instrument of the Lord's teaching and never of punishment.

The Lords of Karma Deliberate
the Flow of Energy Back to the American People

And therefore the Lords of Karma are meeting even now to deliberate the flow of energy back to the American people, which the American people have given unto their Lord and their God and their nation in this week of celebration. What a pity it is that the media have been used to spread abroad the concept that Washington would be so filled with people that there would not even be room to move or to have vehicles. And all of the nation has been hearing these reports for so many months that people made other plans and went other places, and therefore they did not come to the throat chakra [of the nation][3] to be liberated in the hour of the dedication of the will of God.

Fortunately, you have come. Fortunately, the Mother of the Flame had the foresight to insist upon the conference in this city despite all reports that it would not be possible. And so you see, to the lightbearers is given the key to the city, for you are here in person, in physical person.

And you see, hierarchy must select the most qualified this day among all who have come to this city, for it is the key that we will give—the key to the city, the key to the capital of the United States of America. The *key* is the key to the incarnation of God. The key is the key to the initiation of the spirals of the Mother's consciousness. The key is the integration of the flow of Buddha and of Mother. The key is to the next 100-year cycle and to those who will come to power and who will take embodiment and who will help to uplift this nation through the light of the teachings of the Mother flame within you.

The Mandate to Move to the City of the Angels

Precious ones, we have hope. We have hope this day, for we have seen your *consecration,* we have seen your *determination,* we have seen your *love.* I come representing the Lords of Karma. Therefore, you may count my words as the words of that body of seven beings[4] who determine the flow, by God's grace and by God's direction, of karmic cycles in Terra.

We have heard the ratification by Keepers of the Flame of the mandate of Jesus Christ to move the Mother and her children to the

City of the Angels. We have joyfully received your contributions and your pledges given at the Keepers of the Flame Fraternity meeting. We joyfully and gratefully accept your commitment, Keepers of the Flame, in the amount of fifty-nine thousand dollars given by you in this very conference, pledged by your hearts. This is the confirmation, this is your vote of confidence. And we of the ascended hosts now have a turn to applaud our chelas!

The Beacon of the Lighthouse and the White Stone of the Mother

There is a light that comes forth from the beacon of the Lighthouse. And as the beacon turns, the light shines upon a world and it enlightens and illumines the dark night. And by that beacon, souls will take flight and will come Home to the center of the I AM THAT I AM.

Keepers of the Flame, *we* will also commit our causal bodies, as you have laid your lives, your fortunes and your sacred honor[5] upon the altar of Saint Germain. So we also will place upon that altar a multiplication factor that is as the white stone[6] of alchemy, the very philosophers' stone, that stone that is the action of the Mother for the multiplication of Mater. And you will see how the LORD God will take up this substance, will consecrate it, and will use it now, even now, for the victory.

I call to Keepers of the Flame, then, to intensify your invocations to me and to Cyclopea for the locating of that property in Los Angeles.[7] I ask you to give your invocations so that we might see what can be done by God and man to bring our activity and the flame of the Brotherhood to that city in this year. We make no promises, yet we set forth opportunity and the certain promise of the Lord: The call compels the answer!

You must have the faith, the absolute God-conviction that by your decrees and your fervent calls that place should come into manifestation even by precipitation, even if it did not exist at all before you made your invocations. This indeed is the faith of the chelas of the Master Alchemist.

And speaking of the Master Alchemist, he is here! Ladies and gentlemen, Keepers of the Flame, I give to you the Knight Commander!

20

OUR SERVICE IN THE NEXT HUNDRED YEARS OF AMERICA'S DESTINY

A Dictation by Saint Germain

Most beloved Keepers of the Flame, with a tear of joy in my eye, I thank you for your love. I thank you for your life that for an ascended being makes life worth living. I tell you truly, many are the memories in my soul of others who have failed the cause of freedom as we have tried again and again over the centuries to draw souls of light together. How I remember our desire to form the United States of Europe and how, by the selfishness and the sense of blame and the vendetta consciousness and the separatist consciousness, they would not listen. They would not listen.

In a Moment's Hesitation, the Victory Has Been Lost

Again and again the master plan of the ages has been brought forth. And in a moment, a moment's hesitation, a moment being off guard, supply, light, and the projects of the Brotherhood have been lost. In that moment when the Western powers gave way to the black magician Stalin, gave to him Eastern Europe, in that very moment when the West was victorious and when we saw the opportunity once again to unite Europe and to build a new Germany, a new freedom, a new place of refuge for that unique flame of the House of Rakoczy, for my very own Guru, the Great Divine Director—I can tell you that in that moment when I saw the spell of the fallen ones reaching out, even on Churchill and Roosevelt and on those who assented to that appeasement, I cried, precious ones.[1]

I cried for mankind and I tell you, Mother Mary cried. You think that ascended masters do not weep. I assure you that we weep, and our tears are shed as the tears of a cosmos. I can assure you that that which is done in a moment of weakness may take many, many cycles to undo. And therefore, those who acknowledge and understand the forging of a new world and a free world must realize that day by day decisions are being made and day by day there is the requirement of the flame.

The armies had withdrawn. America was in celebration for a victory. People were off guard. They were too anxious, too anxious, and not at all in the vigil. And therefore, from the very light of victory there came the greatest defeat to freedom that has ever been known. And now, the retreat of the Guru and of the cosmic forcefield of the Great Divine Director must be compromised and eclipsed by that darkness.

Need I tell you how we wept when Soviet tanks entered Budapest and Hungary? The people, the people in their love of my flame, in their love of my Guru, were willing to give their lives for freedom—to attack tanks! And America would not come. America would not hear. America would not respond to defend them.[2]

The Flame of the Original Signing of the Declaration of Independence

O Lord Sanat Kumara, I am here with these souls who have declared the freedom and the victory. I am here, Sanat Kumara, and they have responded, and they will not betray America. I know they will not! I implore you, Sanat Kumara, to release now into our hearts the flame of the original signing of the Declaration of Independence as we meditate upon Independence Hall and go there to the very cradle of our liberty.

So we assemble as the early patriots. We assemble together as statesmen ascended, unascended. We come in consciousness. We come to hear the call, "Sign that document!"[3] We come to ratify the original thirteen. We come to declare that this nation ought to be and is indeed a free people, a sovereign nation, one that is conceived in liberty.[4]

Saint Germain's Prayer before the Altar of Freedom

Ancient of Days, O Sanat Kumara, let us be one, then, in this moment, and let our hearts' energies be multiplied by the powers of a cosmos, by their wisdom, and by their love that we might not surrender this blessed earth.

I kneel before Almighty God this day. I kneel before the altar of freedom and I ask once again for those dispensations of freedom. I beg you, Almighty God, not to say no to me, for I am your son of freedom and I have brought with me to your altar sons and daughters of freedom. And if, O God, all dispensations that I have called forth have been misused by mankind and if, O Lord, you will not hear my plea, then I say, Hear the plea of these embodied souls! Hear their cry, O God! Receive their causal bodies and know that I no longer stand alone on earth, but there are those with me who will not surrender to the tyrant's will, who will surrender only to God.

And I know, O Lord, by thy name and by thy flame, these too can conquer in Christ's name. These too can go forth as we went forth of old. These too can cast the writing on the wall that is not a spell of darkness but is the writing of the victors bold. O Lord, I implore you by our fervent cry, Send forth the instrument! Send forth the light-bearers! Send forth the army! Send forth the light that will crystallize, crystallize the mind of God and the heart of God and turn this nation into a miracle of joy and light ascending.

I thank thee, O God. I thank thee for the opportunity to pray this day. I thank thee for the opportunity to stand on earth and to come to this glorious city where the saints have walked, where the pilgrims have known the inspiration of Mother Liberty. I thank thee, O God, for Opportunity, my own twin flame, who has extended that flame throughout a cosmos. And in the moments of discouragement when freedom seemed lost, I thank thee for her aspiration of the feminine consciousness of opportunity whereby I could try and try again to work with mankind for the victory.

I thank thee for the Mother on high and the Mother below. I thank thee that there have been many ascended masters who have taken their stand with me and who have pledged their love. I thank thee, O God, in thy name, in the name of the Father and the Son and the Holy Spirit and in the name of the Blessed Virgin.

Ladies and gentlemen, thank you for your tribute. Won't you be seated.

Saint Germain Received a Mandate from the Lords of Karma and from the Cosmic Council

Precious ones, I will tell you why I sent forth my dictations to you concerning the manifestation of self-concern and of selfishness. I will tell you that it was I who received a mandate from the Lords of Karma and from the Cosmic Council. And they said to me again, "See here now, Saint Germain, we have given you dispensations for your chelas and for your Keepers of the Flame, and look at what they are doing. Look at the record." And once again I was called upon the carpet and once again I heard the words, "Unless your chelas, unless some among mankind will show that they can take their stand, we cannot give you dispensations on the Fourth of July, we cannot sponsor you, we cannot back you in your continual programs for this land and this people."

And so I said to myself, "I cannot go to Washington under such circumstances. I cannot come to the Keepers of the Flame. I cannot appear unless I can appear in the light of our joint victory, our one victory, our victory of service together that proves to an entire cosmos that ascended and unascended beings can work hand-in-hand together and can create that wonder of wonders, that golden-age society, that God-government on earth, that reign of peace, that freedom in the Mother, that culture that comes to its very height under her aegis and with the light of the Holy Spirit."

And therefore, you see how hierarchy goes: when the master is called on the carpet, then the master calls his chelas on the carpet. And so it goes. And it is handed down until there is a response in the other direction. And as the chelas are victorious, so the master is victorious. And so the Great Central Sun releases paeans of joy and cosmic love. And opportunity comes again.

An Electrode for the Turning of the Tide

Now from the heart of my own Guru who stands with me—also backing me in this cause and therefore backing you—he stands now with me, his hand upon my shoulder. And I have the good joy to announce to you that this great dispensation given unto the Great Divine Director[5] is a dispensation whereby this cosmic sphere, this mandala, may release in this very moment, this very moment of the cycles turning, an energy field—a light and a will and a truth and an electrode—for the turning of the tide, the turning of the tide that is a vast turning of the cosmic computer. And this turning will affect all lifewaves in these systems of worlds. And it is a slow turning; but as it turns, it will alter the flow of energies and the manifestation of energies through the quadrants of Mater.

The Great Divine Director and Saint Germain Place Their Momentum of Attainment and of Victory upon the Altar of Freedom in Terra

And therefore on this anniversary that this nation has endured two hundred years, the Great Divine Director and I with him place our combined momentum of attainment and of victory upon the altar of freedom in Terra, upon the altar of the heart of the Mother of the Flame—for we must have a living altar—upon the altar of the heart of each Keeper of the Flame. Upon that altar we place the mantle of our momentum as opportunity for you to anchor in these planes that which we can anchor only thus far.

Only at the highest point of the etheric plane may we anchor this momentum. And from that point, the point of the light of the fire in your heart, the point of the threefold flame, we count on you to lower our momentum through the entire memory body of the race that they might also remember their origins in God and the days of the golden ages when man and woman walked and talked with God in the Garden of Eden, in the paradise consciousness.

Let the Chelas Reach Up and Pull It Down by Their Fiats

So let the memory body of earth be saturated with our fire! And let the chelas reach up to the etheric plane and pull it down by their fiats, by their love, by their devotion, by their hope and joy and love and singing and the music that they make in tribute to our presence. Let them pull it down into the mental plane and let that fiery momentum of our causal bodies be for the throwing out of all philosophies and ideologies that were spawned by Antichrist long, long before the current cycles of history.

These aspects of dialectical materialism were not brought forth in application to the times. They have been present in the minds of the fallen ones for thousands of years. They are not so timely as they appear to be, for the timeliness of this dispensation is the coming of the teachings of the Great White Brotherhood.

Seize the Bag and Run with It!

Let it be understood that the archdeceivers of mankind have a bag of tricks. But it is only a bag, and there are only a limited number of tricks within that bag. I say, *Seize* the bag and run with it and put it to the torch! Beloved ones, as Abraham Lincoln said, "You can fool all of the people some of the time and you can fool some of the people all of the time, but you cannot fool all of the people all of the time."[6]

Finally, on the replays of their tricks, mankind will suddenly awaken, and they will awaken because you are awake with Gautama Buddha,[7] because *you are awake! You* will be the spark that flies! *You* will be the fireworks on the Fourth of July! *You* will be the flame and the torch that ignites *the world!* You will be the victory!

Now the Lords of Karma open the Book of Life.[8] And it is their desire that I should read to you from the pages of the Book of Life. And so I read to you from page 4689:

The Reading from the Book of Life:
The Coming of the Woman Clothed with the Sun

The prophecy has gone forth from the altar of Alpha and Omega, the prophecy of the coming of the Woman clothed with the Sun.[9] And she shall come forth and she shall be enshrined in that haven of light, in that new nation which is and shall be called the New Jerusalem.[10] And in the center of that nation, her shrine shall be erected, and she shall give birth to holy children, and these holy children will occupy the four quadrants of Mater, and these children will take dominion in fire and air and water and earth. These holy children will come to show the way of the Law and the light appearing.

And in that day there shall be turmoil in the land and there shall be a clamoring of voices, and there shall be wars and many wars taking the life and the blood of other children of the Mother who will come from many shores to rally at the focus of freedom. And yet some will not arrive at the focus of freedom, for they will be taken abroad and apart from the Mother by the warfare of the dragon and the archdeceivers of mankind.

The Deliverer, Michael the Archangel, Will Defeat the Dragon

And in that day I, the LORD God, will send forth my deliverer, Michael the archangel, who will go forth and who will defeat the dragon and the seed of the dragon who also go forth to make war with the remnant of the seed of the Mother.

And there shall be a crown of twelve lights, and the lights shall be the energy of our altar and the energy of the mastery of the feminine ray in this people. And there shall be the opportunity for the people to take the Mother's crown and to also be blessed by the action of her attainment. And the crown shall be for the victory, and the opportunity shall be for this people to elect to serve under the light of her protection.

Within the Forcefield of the Mother, They Will Know the Victory

And all who by free will do not elect to serve under the light of her protection will be outside of the circle of the thirteen, of the Mother and her disciples. And these will be outside of the consciousness of God where there is weeping and gnashing of teeth. And those who remain within the forcefield of the Mother, they will know the victory, and they will be an electrode to galvanize many of mankind unto the light.

And there will be others who will come, who in seeing the Mother, will recognize that their opportunity is spent and that judgment draweth nigh. For they, too, know the law of God, that the coming of the Mother is the coming of the judgment. And therefore, they will join the armies of the fallen ones to make war against this light and against the persons in the sons and daughters of God who espouse the light.

Then it is that there will come with the armies of heaven The Faithful and True, the Lord Christ, leading the armies of the saints and ascended beings, leading them across the face of this mighty land.[11] And all who are caught up unto God and his righteousness in the affirmation of the law of the science of the spoken Word will be delivered by the hosts of the Lord.

And this is the end of the reading from the Book of Life.

Americans Have Lost the Power of the Word

Now let it be understood that on this day, Americans as a whole have lost the power of the Word. By their hearkening unto the fallen ones, their speech is not the speech of God and their mouths have become the instruments of the fallen ones as they express the rebellion of the fallen ones that is not even their own. Precious ones, it is not even their own! Yet they think it is their own because they rise up in that sense of injustice. I will give you now certain remedies for this manifestation.

The Turning of the Dark Cycle April 23, 1977

Injustice is abroad in the land as a dark and dense manifestation of returning karma. And with the turning of the Dark Cycle[12] next April 23, that manifestation of injustice that is already upon the earth will intensify as a flood rising even to the roofs of the houses, and people will find themselves inundated by the emotional energies and their impact upon society and government of this gross sense of injustice. And of course, their sense of injustice is that the lightbearers and those who have attainment ought to give away their attainment and their light. And they think that it is injust that they should be the recipients of their own individual karma, that they should have to work out that karma.

And therefore you see, their rebellion is against Almighty God directly and against his law. They camouflage the rebellion in social causes, rebelling against this and that and this and that, against each other, against the Church, against the State. But they are rebels to the core, and you see, their rebellion is against the white-fire core of being. This energy shortly coming to the fore must be transmuted before it is precipitated, for its precipitation will cause further spiritual and material blindness and the coming to power of those individuals who are in no wise capable of running the affairs of state.

Doubt and Fear—Your Greatest Challenge

Therefore, I am repeating the call of Ray-O-Light and the legions of fearlessness flame who came at the turn of the year.[13] And now a half turn later I come and I say, Indeed, doubt and fear are your greatest challenge! For doubt and fear are the manifestation of a consciousness of injustice that is based on human curiosity and human questioning. Let us see, then, that the students of the Law concentrate on the transmutation of all misuses of the sacred fire under the hierarchies of Pisces and Virgo. For Virgo is Mother Earth, Opportunity, Justice, my very own beloved keeping the action and the flow of Christ-mastery for you in your own cycle of return to the heart of Omega.

Let it be, then, that you work diligently with the fearlessness flame, that fiery white light tinged in emerald green, which will cut through all of the mob consciousness, the mass consciousness, the emotional fervor that the fallen ones attempt to generate among the people. And let your calls be to me and to the Divine Director to lower our momentum of mastery in the third quadrant that is the quadrant of the Mother and that is the quadrant of the hundred-year cycle of America's destiny. Let it also be seen that, in addition to the manifestation of the utter transmutation of this line of the Great Divine Director's mandala, that there is a need for you to clear these lines within and to apply yourselves to the study of what is happening in government.

In a Moment When Harmony Is Forsaken,
In Comes the Riptide

As I mentioned, when mistakes are made, when there is the slip 'twixt the cup and the lip[14] and the torch is dropped, it is always in a moment, a moment when, by pride or insecurity, harmony is forsaken. And with a sudden thrust of emotional energy that catches all off guard with the opening of the door, then, of the solar plexus, in comes the riptide! And the riptide is a mass energy, and the fallen ones are waiting to project that mass consciousness through those who are near the Mother and the children of the Mother that, in the riptide and in the maelstrom and the havoc that follows, there will be a teetering and a tottering of the soul and of the state.

And all of a sudden the vote goes through! The Federal Reserve is given excessive powers. America is sold away—her technology, her secrets, her grain, her life. In a moment, the signing away of Vietnam, of Cambodia, and what next? In a moment, a moment's decision, millions of lives are committed to death.

Upon You, America, Is the Burden of This Karma!

Listen to my question: Who decided the death of thousands and thousands of Vietnamese after America pulled out?[15] Who decided the death of a million Cambodians who have been lost in the past year?[16] You say, "The Communists decided their death. *They* murdered them."

I say, nay! Nay, it is the free people! It is the people to whom is passed the torch of initiation. You who were not there keeping the flame. Upon you, America, is the burden of this karma. For you knew the intent of the enemy. You knew the doctrine of the enemy. You knew the avowed doctrine of world takeover and world conquest. And you knew the writing of history—that every nation that has been taken over by Communism has murdered the life, the light of the leaders in government, in the military, and in the professions.[17]

Who Made the Decision?

Therefore, who made the decision? According to cosmic law, the people who have the highest level of initiation have a much greater commitment and responsibility. Given two lifestreams, the one with greater attainment makes greater karma for the same mistake. This is the Law. To them to whom is given much, much is expected.[18]

But then, who did? Who did make the decision? The American people who have the light? The Christed ones? The children of God? No. The handful of rebels and demonstrators supporting one or two individuals in your government who manipulated these decisions, chief of which is Henry Kissinger. And I repeat the judgment of Archangel Michael![19] Let it be upon him, and let it be upon this nation, and let it be upon every individual in government who makes the decisions for the lightbearers, yet has neither the light nor the authority of the Brotherhood to make such decisions.

And Still They Have No Compassion, No Fervor

What about the people who do not know the law of reincarnation, who have no sense of an afterlife, who know not where the soul departs when the body is no more? For us, we see another day and another opportunity for these souls who have been lost. And many of them, the most beautiful children of light in Russia and in China, have been received into incarnation in this land of America. Many of these are here, and they bring with them a great light of the ages.

We, then, have hope, even after death. But those who do not and who see life as only in this life, more callous are they when they allow the decision to be made for these ones to be abandoned. And so you see, according to their own understanding, they have a greater karma. For, for them, in their minds, this is the ultimate death; and still they have no compassion and still there is no fervor.

Come out from among them and be ye a separate people.[20] Be that people! Be that one and that whole and that nation!

Study Carefully What Is Happening in the Government

Let us then study carefully what is happening in the government. Whether or not you are studying government or political science, you have an opportunity and a responsibility to be informed, to vote, to know the candidates, to study the platform. And if you do not understand, then see that you are instructed. You cannot afford to not know the issues because when you study the issues, you will also see the intertwining of the plots of the fallen ones.

The Equal Rights Amendment

Take the women's rights amendment.[21] The ascended masters are for women's rights. Who is not? Who is not? But can you say whether that amendment secures those rights or whether it tears down those rights? You ought to know by having studied not only the amendment, which is very short and therefore deceptive, but you ought to study the minds who framed it. You ought to study what their intent is and what the intent of the fallen ones is behind them. And behind them still, the archdeceivers.

Trace, then, the plot and realize that the intent of those who move the radicals and the rebellious ones for the same causes that we move you—those who move them have other designs and other goals, and they will manipulate those who are uninformed and at the same time who have even just a little bit of rebellion.

The Goal of the Archdeceivers Is the Suppression of Woman

The goal of the archdeceivers is not equality for women, it is the fall of woman, it is the suppression of woman, it is the tearing from her of her spiritual office. Woman is placed on a pedestal by man, where she ought to be; for the feminine aspect of himself is his aspiration, his upward pulling energy, his light in the center of the sun. Therefore, man naturally looks up to woman as he looks up to the light of the Mother within himself.

After all, man is the child of woman, therefore he must place her as the Source of life. And so you see, this is to tear from woman her spiritual opportunity, her right to be woman, to push down her energies, to tear them from the crown and drive them to the base chakra and then to cause these energies to be dissipated, putting woman in closer and closer proximity to man in all the armed forces and in places where men, by their caste and their calling, ought to be free to be men.

We Also Defend the Rights of Men

We also defend the rights of men to be free from the entanglements of women who come not with the flame of Mother, but with other designs to tear down the integrity and the honor and the life force of men. And so you see, the liberation of woman in sex, in short skirts, in all manner of the desecration of the body of the Mother including abortion is not for her freedom, it is for her enslavement!

You see through this. Will you please tell me why mankind cannot see through this? Why are they so dense when the writing is on the wall, when God has spoken for thousands of years? I, too, scratch my head and I say, "How is it that they cannot see?" And then, of course, the cosmic Mother reminds me, "They are blinded by their own selfishness."

Because I Love You So Much, You Are the Ones Who Get the Spanking

And so I come again and I speak to Keepers of the Flame and I talk to you about this selfishness, for you are the only ones who will understand. I cannot get these people to put aside their selfishness. It is ingrained from birth! They are indulged from birth! But *you* will listen, *you* will hear, *you* will make the sacrifices that they cannot make. And so I come and I chastise you. And some are not worthy of the chastisement, and so I chastise you for all of the American people. And because you are so close to my heart and I love you so much, you are the ones that get the spanking. [Laughter and applause]

With every ascended master and cosmic being I say, I love you, I love you, I love you! And when you hear from me, no matter what I say, no matter what it is, know that sometime, somewhere you will have an understanding of why I say what I say. And therefore, no matter what it is, no matter what the dictation that you suddenly receive in the mail, know that that dictation is saying, "I love you, I love you, I love you!"

Share with Me My Heart Chakra

Children of my heart, rise to the level of equality. Share with me my heart chakra. Though it is said the servant is not greater than his Lord, I say, You whom I have called servants, I call you friends.[22] I elevate you to that position that one expects of a friend: responsibility, understanding, friendship. I can confide in you, I can open up my heart to you. I can cry with you, I can laugh with you. I can let you know what is happening and know that you will understand and you will do something—that of a certainty.

O God, O Mother, when I have called, they have acted. Keepers of the Flame have acted. This, then, is a promise, a hope. It is a prayer. It is a prediction and a prophecy. It is the power of the Word fulfilled. I say then, from your throat chakras, Let the lightning and the thunder go forth! And let those American people who have become as the dumb ass,[23] let them now be opened and let them speak.

I AM Casting Forth My Flame to Shatter the Spell upon the Throat Chakras

For I am casting forth my flame to shatter that spell that has been placed upon the throat chakras, and I desire that this people should speak the Word of God, should speak the fiats of freedom, should give forth the mandate for God-government, for light, for Christ, for Mother. And so my word goes forth and I say, This people shall no longer be as dumb animals! And as the LORD God gave it unto the ass of Balaam to speak,[24] so I touch these people and I say to God, "Speak through them, for they do not even know the words to speak!" And I send my guardian angels to guard the throat chakras of the American people that they will no longer utter the blasphemies, the condemnation, and the words that are unholy and ungodly and unfit to pass through the mouth of the Mother or to rest upon the gentle ears of her children.

Let these people be silent no longer, Omega! This is my call. But let them join in the decrees, and let us hear those decrees roll with a mighty thunder and with the thrust of Zadkiel and his bands. And with a roll, "a thrust and a roll and a ho, ho, ho,"[25] we come! Lightbearers come! Lightbearers come in the march of freedom!

By the victory of this day, blessed ones, I will be with you on the morrow. And with joy in my heart, I will walk the streets of this nation with those who have the authority and the right to rule this nation, who are the patriots, who are the sons and daughters of liberty.

By the Flame of Mother, We Shall Conquer!

O Liberty, we thank thee, our Mother, for holding high the torch! We thank thee, we thank thee, and our gratitude is unto thee this day. O Liberty, O Mother, O Woman clothed with the Sun, O Woman with the crown of twelve stars, we salute thee, we salute thee, we salute thee! For by the flame of Mother, *we shall conquer!*

I AM in you forevermore, Saint Germain of the flame of freedom and of the House of Rakoczy! [Applause]

21

"GOD HAS DECIDED TO SAVE THE EARTH"

A Dictation by the Goddess of Liberty

The new cycle has begun, and the sign of the cycle is balance: balance in heart and mind, balance in soul and Spirit, balance in thought and feeling, balance in the inner and the outer manifestation. For every yin, a yang. For every yang, a yin. And in this, the mighty scales of Libra will preserve that nation whose fire is sent into the air as a display to all nations,* as the outer confirmation of the inner consecration of the sons and daughters of liberty.

Let those who would be instruments of the LORD know that all, *all* leads to the cycling at the point of the nexus and the Now. The center of the scales is the pillar for transition. It is a cross of fire and gold and the promise God holds for you and for me. Under the sign of Libra, let the personality of a nation mature to God-reality.[1] As the moon has been seen in Libra, so by the Law will this hierarchy initiate a new age.

And do you know, God has sent forth a light. God has said: "I will save Terra. I will save freedom. I will save all through my people, through my own. Through my instrument on earth, I will save a fiery destiny." These words are the sign to the Cosmic Council and to the Lords of Karma for a new release. And yet this release is a tempered release that you might become like tempered steel and that we might temper the great winds of the Holy Spirit to the shorn lamb of mankind's identity.[2]

---

*refers to the spectacular fireworks displays throughout the United States during the bicentennial celebration

A Storehouse of Energy to Be Given at First to the Few

There is a great holding of the reins of power by the Elohim on behalf of the Lords of Karma. There is a great holding action, and it is of a mighty tide of light. It is in order that these focal points of energy might be released not so abundantly that they are taken for granted and easily misused because there is such plenty. No, it is a storehouse of energy, an energy pool and a resource that has great momentum. But it would be given at first to the few, the few who have the balance of God-control in God-reality.[3]

Let the heart chakras, then, of those who are bold in the flame, of those who carry the torch with me and the book of the Law, be strengthened. Let these strengthen the heart, and let our heart become one great heart of love. Let the heart be the orifice. Let it be the great opening into the lens of the mind of God. Let it be the means whereby God reaches through and touches humanity through you. Let it be for the flow.

Let Your Bodies Become the Ritual of the Rhythm of Cosmos

And as you open your heart to receive our dispensation, remember the creative tension of the Lord. Remember—that each point of energy you release be a disciplined one, be one that has purpose and measure, honor, momentum, ritual in freedom. Let your bodies become the ritual of the rhythm of cosmos. Let the T'ai Chi flow through you and let the postures of the holy ones be known to you. As you establish flow in your chakras, so establish flow for the maximum anchoring of God's light in physical atoms.

Let these cups be filled. Let the cups of Matter be consecrated. Let them be filled with the holy wine and let them be touched by the hem of his garment.[4] Come into alignment with the promised ones who have gone before and mastered these planes. So many are they! They are hope that what man has done, man can do.

Heaven Confirms Its Love for You

When you feel homesick for our bands, when you feel joy, when you hear our footsteps in the way but it seems that you cannot quite reach us, rise up on your tiptoes and reach a little farther. For we really are no farther than your highest aspirations, your innermost dreams, your prayers to God, your hope for the children, your love for America and her people.

We are in your dreams and in your loves. We are in your longing. We are in your decrees. We are very much a part—and so when light as cosmic lightning strikes upon your soul with the blessing of the Comforter and of celestial sons and daughters, feel touched and know that heaven is very near. And heaven by so many manifestations confirms its love for you.

I stand on that island waiting for those who would walk through the open door of my heart. I have sent joy and love and the promise of freedom to generations—so many who have had the dream, the dream of the Great White Brotherhood. All love me, all place their trust in me. And yet the sternness of my face reveals the discipline of grace, of feminine principle and the seriousness of the hour.

"God Has Decided to Save the Earth"

I come from the God Star, Sirius, this night. I come where the deliberations of the Four and Twenty Elders[5] concerning all manifestations of earth are underway. And one and all, I hear them say: "God has decided to save the earth." Simple words—words given to a child.

I am that child. I am the child of liberty. I adore liberty, I live in liberty, and I send forth liberty to all. Before the almighty ones, I am but a child and so these simple words are enough for me. I live in the comfort of the LORD God of hosts. I am nestled in his cosmos. I am secure in starlight, in sunshine, in the wind and in the rain. I am secure because God made me and because I know he is in me.

Let these lessons be taught to young and old alike. Let them be spread abroad throughout the land. Let them be repeated as the report from the Lords of Karma. We could tell you of the intricacies of the plan, but then if you would gaze upon the rose and enjoy the rose, you would really rather not know, for the moment, the intricacies of the plan.

Someday and somewhere you will know, but suffice it to be that God has decided to save the earth. And when you ask how and why and where and who, the answer is: "Through you!"

My love to you. My wisdom to you. And all of my power, yours to command. Let us see now what the Lords of Karma can do to draw you into that starry light, that focus of the Son of God. Let us see what the Lords of Karma will do as we see once again what you will do when you go forth in the flame of victory.

Children of the Sun, We Are Indeed One!

Take the torch from my heart. Will you carry it for me on the morrow through the city? For you see, I must be at my focus releasing certain cosmic energies. I will arc them to you, but for the march you must carry the torch for me. And I will carry my torch for you. And I will place my torch in a very secret place, in a very, very secret place. And I ask you to come and find that place, a very, very secret place. And perhaps when we meet again, I will tell you that place.

And now the curtain is drawn on the bicentennial celebration of the ascended masters and their chelas. And now all is sealed within you by our love. Go forth in love. Live in the love of the Mother and the Spirit, the Son and the Father. Be sealed, be healed, be made whole! And through you, see how America and the world will also be made whole.

Children of the Sun, children of the Sun, children of the Sun, we are indeed one!

NOTES

FOREWORD
1. Acts 10:9–16.

CHAPTER 1
1. Ezek. 1:16; 10:10.
2. Mark L. Prophet, November 10, 1968, "The Exhalation and the Inhalation of the Breath of God."
3. John 4:34.
4. John 15:13.
5. I Cor. 13:3.
6. II Cor. 12:2–4.
7. John 14:6.
8. II Cor. 12:15.
9. Matt. 16:25; Mark 8:35; Luke 9:24; 17:33.
10. Matt. 10:33.
11. Matt. 28:18.
12. Matt. 28:19, 20.
13. El Morya, *The Chela and the Path,* chap. 10, p. 77.
14. I Cor. 15:47.
15. The twelve sons of Jacob were the ancestors of the twelve tribes of Israel: Reuben, Simeon, Levi, Judah, Dan, Naphtali, Gad, Asher, Issachar, Zebulun, Joseph, and Benjamin. Joseph, the eleventh and most favored son, was an incarnation of Jesus Christ. His sons, Ephraim and Manasseh, were blessed by Jacob as his own, thereby forming two half-tribes. The seed of Ephraim and Manasseh reincarnated in the British Isles, then the United States, and are to be found generally among the English-speaking peoples of the world. The other eleven tribes reincarnated to form the European nations, including Russia, and many were scattered to the four corners of the earth, embodying today in every race and nation. See Gen. 41:50–52; 46:20; 48.
16. II Cor. 12:9.
17. Rev. 1:8.

N.B. The publications listed in these notes are Summit University Press publications unless otherwise noted.

18. John 5:17.
19. II Cor. 3:18.
20. Col. 3:9–10.
21. Dan. 7:9.
22. Exodus 3:14.
23. Paul Foster Case, *The Great Seal of the United States: Its History, Symbolism and Message for the New Age* (Santa Barbara, Calif.: J. F. Rowney, 1935).
24. Gen. 3:21.
25. Eph. 5:26; Serapis Bey, *Dossier on the Ascension,* p. 6.
26. John 10:17.
27. Paul the Venetian, October 11, 1975, "The Revolution of Love," *Pearls of Wisdom,* vol. 62, no. 42, November 8, 2019.
28. John 3:16–17.
29. Prov. 14:12.
30. Rev. 13:8.
31. El Morya, *The Chela and the Path,* p. 77.
32. Mark L. Prophet and Elizabeth Clare Prophet, *The Path of the Higher Self,* p. 7.
33. Ezek. 18:4, 20.
34. Rev. 20:13.
35. Rev. 20:15.
36. Rev. 20:6, 14; 21:8.
37. Rev. 1:6.
38. Rev. 7:9, 13.
39. Rev. 5:11.
40. Gen. 3:20.
41. Luke 7:38.
42. Luke 7:47.
43. Luke 7:50.
44. John 8:3.
45. John 8:4.
46. John 8:5–8.
47. John 8:9.
48. Heb. 5:6, 10.
49. I Pet. 3:4.
50. John 8:10–11.
51. John 3:17.
52. John 8:12.
53. Matt. 12:39; 16:4.
54. Rom. 3:23.
55. Job 19:25.
56. John 1:14.
57. John 20:16.

58. John 20:17.
59. Rev. 12:10.
60. John 11:50.
61. Rev. 12:1–6.
62. Isa. 1:18.
63. John 13:34.
64. Matt. 10:34.
65. John 8:32.
66. Jer. 31:33.

CHAPTER 2

1. Dan. 7:9. The prophet Daniel recorded his vision of Sanat Kumara in the book of the Bible that bears his name: "I beheld till the thrones were cast down, and the Ancient of days did sit, whose garment was white as snow, and the hair of his head like the pure wool: his throne was like the fiery flame, and his wheels [chakras] as burning fire."
2. *Mater* (Latin for "mother"). The spiritual universe is identified as masculine (Father) and the material universe is identified as feminine (Mother). The physical world is the mother because matter is the womb or chalice into which Spirit descends.
3. I Cor. 15:54.

CHAPTER 3

1. Matt. 10:41.
2. John 8:32.
3. Prov. 29:18.
4. According to tradition, the apostle Peter was fleeing Rome to escape persecution when he encountered the ascended Jesus Christ as our Lord was entering the city. Peter asked, "Domine, quo vadis?" (Lord, whither goest thou?) He answered, "I go to Rome to be crucified again." Realizing that the Master could be crucified only through him, only through his own sacrifice of the human will, Peter turned back to Rome, where he was later crucified.
5. Exod. 13:21; Num. 14:14.
6. Matt. 13:33; Luke 13:21.
7. Ps. 91:7.
8. Matt. 6:6.
9. See Mark L. Prophet and Elizabeth Clare Prophet, *Saint Germain On Alchemy: For the Adept in the Aquarian Age.*
10. Rev. 19:11.

CHAPTER 4

1. On November 23, 1975, Saint Germain came with Portia and cosmic evolutions for "the enshrining of freedom, . . . the quickening of a flame that has not been quickened in ten thousand years." Saint Germain said:

"I come—the bearer of gifts, of dispensations, of fires of freedom.... Let now the cycles roll from the causal bodies of these ones and from freedom's scroll... to implement the fire of freedom!... It is a dispensation of light sent forth to all the nations that souls of light... might respond to the teachings of the I AM THAT I AM.... I select the monument, the focal point for the enshrining of freedom; and I place that focus of freedom in the heart of America, in the very heart chakra of the Goddess of Freedom reigning over the Capitol building of the United States. And there the heart chakra of the Divine Mother shall broadcast the fires of freedom from the crystal of the heart, from the twelve fiery focal points of the mandala of her crystal. So shall freedom from the twelve hierarchies of the Sun go forth and beam that arc of light to the heart of the Statue of Liberty. And I place that flame of freedom in the heart of the Statue of Mother Russia.... Now let the angels of freedom who have taken their places across the planetary body raise the taper of fire! And at the moment of the invocation of the Elohim given forth by the devotees assembled here in consonance with the angelic hosts, ... feel the fire flow from your heart as you participate in this sacred ritual of igniting the earth for the victory of the age. [Audience chants *Elohim* three times.] In the Christ of Cuernavaca, in the Christ of the Andes and the Christ of Corcovado, in the Great Pyramid of Egypt, in the heart of the statues of the Buddha in the East, in the Taj Mahal, in the great cathedrals, and in the statues of great patriots, in the obelisks, in the monuments, so the light of freedom has been implanted as a flame from our hearts." See Saint Germain, "Enshrining the Flame of Freedom in the Capitals of the Nations," in *The Greater Way of Freedom*, pp. 41–43.
2. Rev. 12:1.
3. II Pet. 1:10.
4. William Ross Wallace, "The Hand That Rules the World," stanza 1.
5. I Cor. 3:13–15.
6. I Cor. 13:1.
7. Gen. 10:8–10; 11:1–9.
8. The Club of Rome is a nonprofit, nongovernmental global think tank concerned with the future of humankind. Its members include scientists, economists, businessmen, international high civil servants, heads of state and former heads of state from all five continents.
9. See Arnold Toynbee, *A Study of History*, abridgment by D. C. Somervell, 2 vols. (Oxford: Oxford University Press, 1987).
10. See Rev. 12.
11. Rom. 8:31.

CHAPTER 5

1. Jonathan Elliot, ed. and comp., *The Debates in the Several State Conventions on the Adoption of the Federal Constitution...*, 2d. ed., 5 vols. (Philadelphia: J. B. Lippincott & Co., 1866), 3:137.

2. James M. Mead, "Heartbeat of the Republic," in *Our Bill of Rights: What It Means to Me,* ed. James Waterman Wise (New York: Bill of Rights Sesqui-Centennial Committee, 1941), p. 99.
3. Gen. 3; Ezek. 1–3.
4. Ps. 91:1.
5. John 10:30.
6. Gen. 1:26.
7. I Pet. 3:4.
8. Luke 24:32.
9. Phil. 2:5.
10. Jer. 31:33.
11. John 8:58.
12. I Cor. 13:12.
13. John 6:68.
14. James Winthrop, "The Letters of Agrippa," in *Essays on the Constitution of the United States, Published during Its Discussion by the People 1787–1788,* ed. Paul Leicester Ford (Brooklyn: Historical Printing Club, 1892), p. 113.
15. Elliot, *The Debates in the Several State Conventions,* 2:80.
16. Cecelia M. Kenyon, ed., *The Antifederalists,* American Heritage Series (New York: Howard W. Sams & Co., Bobbs-Merrill Co., 1966), p. 187.
17. Abraham Lincoln, Address at Gettysburg, 19 November 1863.
18. Matt. 14:15–21.
19. Girouard v. United States, 328 U.S. 61 (1946), quoted in Milton R. Konvitz, *Fundamental Liberties of a Free People: Religion, Speech, Press, Assembly* (Ithaca, New York: Cornell University Press, 1957), p. 227.
20. Gen. 11:1–9.
21. Adrienne Koch and William Peden, eds., *The Life and Selected Writings of Thomas Jefferson,* The Modern Library (New York: Random House, 1944), pp. 311, 312, 313.
22. William Allen White, *The Editor and His People: Editorials by William Allen White,* comp. Helen Ogden Mahin (New York: Macmillan Co., 1924), pp. 348–49.
23. In 1960 atheist activist Madalyn Murray filed a lawsuit against the Baltimore City public school system in which she asserted that it was unconstitutional for her son to be required to participate in Bible readings at Baltimore public schools. The lawsuit reached the Supreme Court, which in 1963 ruled in Murray's favor. Her son, William, went on to become a Baptist minister.
24. Archangel Michael, "In Defense of the Mental Quadrant," *Convocation of the New Birth in the City of the Angels* conference, Los Angeles, California, April 11, 1974.
25. Aleksandr I. Solzhenitsyn, "America: You Must Think About the World," address given in Washington, D.C., 30 June 1975, in *Solzhenitsyn: The Voice of Freedom* (Washington, D.C.: AFL-CIO, n.d.), p. 18.

26. Ibid., pp. 16–17.
27. Gen. 3:21.
28. Rom. 7:23; James 4:1.
29. Rev. 6:1–8; 9:17.
30. Luke 21:26.
31. Elizabeth Clare Prophet, *The Greater Way of Freedom*, p. 6.
32. Luke 22:42.
33. Gen. 1:26.
34. Matt. 28:18.

CHAPTER 6

1. Saint Germain, November 23, 1975, "Enshrining the Flame of Freedom in the Capitals of the Nations" (see p. 295 n. 1, this volume).
2. Thousands of years ago, mankind's departure from cosmic law became so great that all light had gone out in Earth's evolutions and cosmic councils decreed the dissolution of Earth. Sanat Kumara, the Ancient of Days (Dan. 7:9, 13, 22), volunteered to come from his home star, Venus, to embody the threefold flame on behalf of the evolutions of Earth—who had willfully ignored and forgotten the God flame within their hearts. One hundred and forty-four thousand souls from Venus volunteered to come with him to support his mission. They vowed to keep the flame with him until the children of God on Earth would respond and turn once again to serve their mighty I AM Presence. See Sanat Kumara, *The Opening of the Seventh Seal*, pp. 11–15.
3. Matt. 10:28.
4. Abraham Lincoln, Speech to the Republican State Convention, Springfield, Illinois, June 16, 1858.
5. The retreat of the Elohim Arcturus and Victoria is located in the etheric plane near Luanda, Angola, Africa. This retreat focuses the energies of the seat-of-the-soul chakra of the planet and is dedicated to the freedom of all mankind through the alchemical action of the flame, the mercy of the great law, and the love of the Father-Mother God. For more on this retreat, see Mark L. Prophet and Elizabeth Clare Prophet, *The Masters and Their Retreats*.
6. Communist takeover of Angola. In November 1975, Portugal granted Angola its independence from colonial rule. A fierce civil war ensued as rival groups sought control of the nation. Thousands of Cuban troops, with logistical support from the Soviet Union, backed the left-wing MPLA (Popular Movement for the Liberation of Angola) in its successful military campaign to gain power. By mid-1976, the Marxist MPLA government had received official recognition by the Organization of African Unity and the United Nations.
7. II Thess. 2:11, 12.
8. The term Watergate is used to describe a web of political scandals between 1972 and 1974. The word refers to the Watergate Hotel complex in

Washington, D.C., where the office of the Democratic National Committee was burglarized on June 17, 1972. The investigation of the burglary and subsequent cover-up eventually resulted in the indictments of some 40 government officials and the resignation of President Richard M. Nixon on August 8, 1974.
9. Exod. 3:13, 14.
10. Gen. 22:17; Heb. 11:12.
11. Rev. 20:12, 15.
12. Maldek, once a planet in our solar system, was destroyed when its lifewaves waged a war ending in nuclear annihilation. For further teaching on the laggard civilizations, see Mark L. Prophet and Elizabeth Clare Prophet, "The Coming of the Laggards," *The Path of the Higher Self*, pp. 74–85, paperback; the Great Divine Director, *The Mechanization Concept, Pearls of Wisdom*, vol. 8, nos. 3–26; and "The Future of a Planet Read from the Scroll of Cosmic History," *Pearls of Wisdom*, vol. 17, nos. 5–6; Elizabeth Clare Prophet, May 4, 1980, "Anti-Life Begets Anti-Life—a Conspiracy of Absolute Evil against Absolute Good," on album *Life Begets Life*, available from AscendedMaster Library.org.
13. Abraham Lincoln, Gettysburg Address, November 19, 1863.

CHAPTER 7

1. See Sanat Kumara, "Raising the Consciousness of the Mother Flame," *Pearls of Wisdom*, vol. 42, no. 24.
2. Luke 1:38.
3. Two lines from "The Prayer of Saint Francis."
4. The test of the ten is the test of selflessness, the test of the ten-petaled solar-plexus chakra; On the tenth station of the cross, Jesus is stripped of his garments.
5. I Sam. 15:23.
6. Rev. 12.
7. Matt. 27:46; Mark 15:34.
8. Rev. 22:1.

CHAPTER 8

1. Matt. 7:14.
2. Matt. 18:2–3.
3. John 5:30; 14:10.
4. Luke 2:42–47.
5. Isa. 11:6.
6. Acts 17:28.
7. Matt. 13:45–46.
8. Serapis Bey, *Dossier on the Ascension*.
9. Matt. 11:30.
10. The Dark Cycle. See chap. 20 n. 12.

CHAPTER 9

1. Ezek. 1:4.
2. Matt. 12:45; Luke 11:26.
3. John 5:14.

CHAPTER 10

1. The Keepers of the Flame Fraternity was founded in 1961 by Saint Germain as an organization of ascended masters and their chelas who vow to keep the flame of life on earth and support the activities of the Great White Brotherhood. Members of the fraternity receive monthly lessons on cosmic law. To find out more about the fraternity, go to www.keepersoftheflame.org.
2. Published in *The Human Aura*, by Kuthumi and Djwal Kul.
3. Ibid.

CHAPTER 11

1. Rev. 22:1.
2. Vine and fig tree. I Kings 4:25; Mic. 4:4; Zech. 3:10. The vine is the Holy Christ Self; the fig tree is the I AM Presence and the causal body bearing the fruits of God consciousness through good works.
3. Tree of Life. Gen. 2:9; 3:22, 24; Rev. 2:7; 22:2, 14. The Tree of Life is the I AM Presence and the causal body. See *Saint Germain On Alchemy*, glossary, s.v. "Tree of Life."
4. I Pet. 3:4.
5. Mark 4:39.
6. Exod. 3:14, 15.
7. See Matt. 24.
8. Matt. 21:12, 13.
9. Matt. 10:34.
10. Rev. 12:1.
11. Matt. 10:26.
12. Dan. 12:1; Rev. 12.

CHAPTER 12

1. Isa. 40:31.
2. I Cor. 15:52.
3. See chap. 20 n. 12.
4. Matt. 13:30.
5. *Master R* is an appellation of the Great Divine Director. The *R* stands for Rakoczy, the royal house of Hungary that he founded.
6. Rev. 1:8.
7. I John 2:18.
8. "As ye deal with my contemners..." Julia Ward Howe, "Battle Hymn of the Republic."

CHAPTER 13

1. John 13:34–35.
2. "Halls of Luxor." The Ascension Temple, etheric retreat of Serapis Bey, Chohan of the Fourth Ray, is located in the etheric octave, superimposed over the physical Temple of Luxor on the Nile.
3. "Heart of Rakoczy... in the Transylvanian foothills." The Great Divine Director, known as the Master R, founded the royal House of Rakoczy of Hungary and established a retreat of the Great White Brotherhood, the Rakoczy Mansion, in the Carpathian Mountains in Transylvania. It was the Great Divine Director who carried the flame of freedom, the violet flame, from the altars of Atlantis to safety in the Carpathian foothills. The focus of the flame of freedom is there and in other retreats of the Great White Brotherhood.
4. "Heart of Angola,... heart of Arcturus and Victoria." The retreat of the Elohim Arcturus and Victoria is located in the etheric plane near Luanda, Angola, Africa.
5. Ps. 110:4.
6. Acts 2:20.
7. Rev. 22:1, 2.
8. Heb. 12:29.
9. Matt. 27:52–53.
10. Heb. 12:23.
11. Rev. 6:9, 10.
12. Matt. 8:10–12.
13. Rev. 21:16.
14. Rev. 21:2.
15. Since 1987, Elizabeth Clare Prophet has explained to her audiences that, according to El Morya, the United States of America was conceived at 5:13 p.m. on July 4, 1776, when Congress adopted the Declaration of Independence. (See Elizabeth Clare Prophet, *The Astrology of the Four Horsemen*, pp. 141–47; 1988 *Pearls of Wisdom*, Book II, Introduction, pp. *30–35;* 1989 *Pearls of Wisdom*, pp. 725–30; and 1990 *Pearls of Wisdom*, pp. 122–24.)
16. Rev. 21:3, 4.
17. The God Star is the ascended masters' term for the binary star Sirius, which is the galactic seat of God-government and focus of the Great Central Sun, representing with its companion sun the guru-chela relationship. It is called the "Dog Star" by astronomers.
18. In a dictation in 1975, Archangel Zadkiel prophesied the future release of these seven vials of violet flame for the transmutation of the seven last plagues (Rev. 15:1, 6–8; 16). He said, "I hold in my retreat over the island of Cuba seven other vials given unto my keeping by the Lord God of hosts. These are the seven vials of the concentrated energies of the violet flame that will be poured out over the earth by the archangels of the seven rays when mankind

have invoked enough of the sacred fire to warrant the release of these concentrated energies of the sacred fire. I stand on the side of the west of the City Foursquare. I stand on the West Coast of the United States of America, and I face the East and the kings and queens of the East to gather them to the battle of that great day of God Almighty. I raise my hands for the release of the momentum of the violet flame that shall reverse the tide of darkness and roll it back from the West unto the East. And it shall be as the rolling-up of a mighty scroll, and it shall be the rolling-up of that darkness which has covered the land. And it shall be the rolling-up of the unclean spirits that, like frogs, have been sent forth out of the mouth of the dragon and out of the mouth of the beast and out of the mouth of the false prophet." (See Archangel Zadkiel, "The Joy of Judgment in the Flame of Transmutation: The Seventh Vial," in *Vials of the Seven Last Plagues*, chap. 13.)

CHAPTER 14

1. "Become worshipers of the sun." On October 12, 1975, Archangel Gabriel said: "Children of the sun, I would that you would become worshipers of the dawn and of the sun. For in your meditation upon the rising orb of Helios and Vesta, you face the East and behold the rising Christ and the consciousness thereof illumining a darkened world. And you see in the fire that pierces the night with the morning light the image of your own I AM Presence. You glimpse the brilliance in physical, tangible manifestation of the I AM THAT I AM." See "The Judgment of the Sun," chap. 7 in Elizabeth Clare Prophet, *Vials of the Seven Last Plagues*.
2. "Archimedes' lever." The ancient Greek scientist, mathematician and inventor Archimedes (287–212 B.C.) formulated the principle of the lever. He is credited with the saying, "Give me the place to stand, and a lever long enough, and I will move the EARTH!" (E. D. Hirsch, Jr., et al., *The Dictionary of Cultural Literacy* [Boston: Houghton Mifflin Company, 1988], s.v. "Archimedes.")
3. Matt. 9:37, 38; Luke 10:2.
4. "We do not desire to see you deprived of your rest." The ascended masters have often recommended that their students pace themselves, balancing their service to life with sufficient sleep and exercise as well as proper nutrition. Elizabeth Clare Prophet has also recommended that each person set the ritual of the day as his or her schedule, responsibilities, health, karma and dharma dictate. For more, see Archangel Gabriel, *Mysteries of the Holy Grail*, chap. 18 n. 16.
5. See "Lord Michael," decree 10.00, and the decrees for protection in the blue section of *Prayers, Meditations and Dynamic Decrees for Personal and World Transformation*.
6. Rev. 12; Isa. 27:1.
7. "Decree to Beloved Mighty Astrea," decree 10.14 in *Prayers, Meditations and Dynamic Decrees for Personal and World Transformation*.

8. Elizabeth Clare Prophet has explained that "Lanello has a very special personal work to do for chelas who give their Astreas. When you give your Astreas, Lanello can enter in at that moment, hour and day and work with you very personally on all of the things that you are working on and things you know not of whereby he can bless you." She has said that if we can spare the time to sing a song to Lanello before or after giving Astreas, we might even see him literally walking into the court—or wherever we are—in his white suit. Song 514, "To Our Beloved Lanello," decree 10.14, "Decree to Beloved Mighty Astrea," and song 516, "Hail to Thee, Lanello!" are available from www.AscendedMasterLibrary.org.
9. "Beloved Cyclopea, Beholder of Perfection," decree 50.05 in *Prayers, Meditations and Dynamic Decrees for Personal and World Transformation*.
10. "Beings of the four elements who come at your behest." The hierarchs of the Nature kingdom, the elements they govern and the elemental beings who serve with them are: Oromasis and Diana, fire element, salamanders; Aries and Thor, air, sylphs; Neptune and Luara, water, undines; Virgo and Pelleur, earth, gnomes.
11. The Great Whore: Rev. 17; 19:2. Antichrist: I John 2:18, 19, 22; 4:3; II John 7.
12. In a dictation given March 29, 1964, Jesus Christ announced that he was endowing elemental life with the flame of his momentum of the resurrection and that, from that day forward, the elementals would "never again have the sense of death." Jesus said: "They shall feel my flame always. A portion of that flame resting in them shall remove for all time... all fear that they have outpictured."
13. Since Lanello's dictation, additional dispensations have come forth from hierarchy on behalf of elemental life. In a dictation on June 30, 1988, the Elohim Heros and Amora promised the elementals that they could earn a threefold flame by assisting the sons and daughters of God. Addressing the elementals, Heros and Amora said: "Those whom you... serve who do attain the ascension... shall in turn endow you with a threefold flame.... The hour draws nigh when those to whom you have given so much may turn and give to you what they have long desired to give." (See *Pearls of Wisdom*, vol. 31, no. 60.) In their April 11, 1998 dictation, Virgo and Pelleur said: "Elementals will not have a threefold flame, the gift of immortal life, unless they are endowed with that flame by service to life and by a tremendous effort on their part. It is Jesus who does sponsor elemental life. And now we ask you to take substance of your own Christ consciousness from your heart and transmit it to elemental life. In so doing,... you will begin the spiral wherein these elementals may one by one enter into immortal life. This is something that Jesus has spoken of, but today is the day and the hour when the opportunity begins and the clock does strike." (See *Pearls of Wisdom*, vol. 41, no. 18.)
14. "I think of the Bishop of Bingen / In his Mouse-Tower on the Rhine." See

Henry Wadsworth Longfellow, "The Children's Hour," stanza 7. Lanello was embodied as Longfellow (1807–1882).

CHAPTER 15

1. The ascended master Godfre was embodied as Gen. George Washington (1732–1799), the first president of the United States.
2. Gen. 36:31; Judg. 17:6; 21:25.
3. Dan. 9:27; 11:31; 12:11; Matt. 24:15.
4. "The proletarians have nothing to lose but their chains. They have a world to win. Working Men of All Countries, Unite!" (Karl Marx and Friedrich Engels, *Manifesto of the Communist Party.*)
5. Exod. 3:13, 14.
6. I AM movement. In his final incarnation, the ascended master Godfre and his divine complement, Lotus, were embodied as Guy and Edna Ballard (1878–1939 and 1886–1971 respectively). In the 1930s Saint Germain contacted the Ballards and trained them as his messengers. Through them, the master founded the I AM Activity and released the dispensation of the violet flame.
7. Matt. 5:31, 32; 19:3–9; I Cor. 7:10–17, 39.
8. On July 5, 1982, Elizabeth Clare Prophet gave the following teaching on divorce: "The teachings of the Bible on divorce are for the dispensation of Pisces and the Arian dispensation which preceded it.... When we come into the Aquarian age, we actually come into a new dispensation regarding divorce laws. There is a reason for this. [Although] the masters have never approved divorcing a spouse on the basis of simply tiring of a plaything and... finding a better sexual partner,... the Brotherhood understands... that in one lifetime we are expected to balance many areas of karma, and some of these conditions of karma can only be balanced through marriage. And at the end of that marriage, whether it's two years or fifty years, the karma is satisfied.... The Brotherhood... tells us that each one must search his soul and discover whether or not one has done all in one's power to bring harmony to a marriage and a home, to make a go of it, and whether there is such disagreement and such discord that it would be more costly to the partners to remain together than it would be to go... their separate ways.... The ascended masters... are concerned... that you do not walk out on your responsibilities and... your karma.... We have to beware of self-righteousness in marriage, of condemnation of the spouse. We have to beware of intolerance. Our spouses don't have to be the same religion as we are. They may be very devout and holy people in their own vein. What is important is that there be harmony, and, if there are children in the family, that they see a unity of the parents, a proper and dignified representation of the Father-Mother God and not continual strife and self-degradation." (For more on relationships and marriages, see Elizabeth Clare Prophet, *Soul Mates and Twin Flames: The Spiritual Dimension of Love and Relationships,*

pp. 85–102; and Elizabeth Clare Prophet and Patricia R. Spadaro, *Karma and Reincarnation: Transcending Your Past, Transforming Your Future,* pp. 88–107.)
9. U.S. Supreme Court affirms constitutionality of death penalty on July 2, 1976. In 1967, while awaiting a U.S. Supreme Court ruling on capital punishment, the states put a hold on all executions. Before that time, few individuals in the U.S. had challenged the constitutionality of capital punishment. In 1972 *(Furman v. Georgia),* the U.S. Supreme Court ruled 5–4 that the death penalty as then administered, without standards or guidelines for trial juries to follow, was "cruel and unusual punishment in violation of the Eighth and Fourteenth Amendments." This was the first case in which the Supreme Court had ruled against the death penalty. Significantly, the Court did not rule on the constitutionality of the death penalty itself but rather on the sentencing procedure. The decision created three options for individual states to employ: a mandatory death sentence for certain offenses, development of standardized guidelines for juries, and outright abolition of the death penalty. Subsequently, the legislatures of at least 35 states revised their statutes to provide for the death penalty for at least some crimes that result in the death of another person. Then, on July 2, 1976, in *Gregg v. Georgia,* the Court voted 7–2 to uphold the constitutionality of the death penalty, stating that "punishment of death does not invariably violate the Constitution." The Court approved a number of the revised capital punishment statutes. Six months later, in January 1977, the first person to be executed in the U.S. in ten years was executed by a Utah firing squad. In a 1988 decision *(Thompson v. Oklahoma),* the Supreme Court ruled 5–3 that the "Eighth and Fourteenth Amendments prohibit the execution of a person who was under 16 years of age at the time of his or her offense."
10. Second death. Rev. 2:11; 20:6, 11–15; 21:7, 8. "You can think of the divine spark as pure Spirit. It can never die. But the soul can be lost; she can self-destruct by her own actions. If the soul does not exercise her free will to realize her potential, she may ultimately lose that potential and cease to exist." (Elizabeth Clare Prophet with Patricia R. Spadaro and Murray L. Steinman, *Kabbalah: Key to Your Inner Power,* p. 102)
11. Matt. 10:28.
12. See chap. 20 n. 12.

CHAPTER 16

1. II Cor. 3:18.
2. I Chron. 29:11.

CHAPTER 17

1. Matt. 10:38–39.
2. Ps. 19:14.
3. Will of God Focus. Hercules is referring to a small sanctuary dedicated to the will of God on the grounds of the Motherhouse in Santa Barbara, California.

This focus was established in response to Saint Germain's dictation given September 19, 1969, at the Motherhouse, where he announced, "El Morya is walking upon the very soil [of this property] in order to establish here a focus of the will of God, not only for Santa Barbara but for all of California, for all of America and for all of the free world, extending, then, beams of hope into... the countries behind the iron curtain." This focus of the will of God was consecrated on October 10, 1973. Subsequently, in 1979, a will of God focus was established at the Ashram of the World Mother in Los Angeles. Other Summit Lighthouse centers have also established focuses to the will of God.
4. Matt. 25:23.

CHAPTER 18

1. Acts 2:1.
2. I Cor. 3:19.
3. Rev. 17:1; 19:2.
4. Acts 2:4.
5. "I have sworn upon the altar of God, eternal hostility against every form of tyranny over the mind of man." Thomas Jefferson to Benjamin Rush, September 23, 1800.
6. Exod. 3:5.
7. John 1:14.
8. Jer. 6:14.
9. Matt. 4:1–11; Luke 4:1–13.
10. Matt. 28:18.
11. I Cor. 10:4.
12. John 14:6.
13. Dan. 7:9, 13, 22.
14. The messenger later explained that Mother's Manifesto includes two aspects. The "Spirit cup" is "the presentation of the real teachings of God pertaining to your identity, your I AM Presence, your Christ Self and the homeward path. It is the whole body of ascended masters' teachings that have to do with your spiritual life." The manifesto on the "Matter cup" is the "examination of the entrenched forces of darkness that seek to undo the path of the soul." She said there are perversions of truth in every field, including education, government, the economy, science and religion, that must be exposed. Among the messenger's exposés and lectures given in response to Gautama and Jesus' announcement are *Mother's Manifesto on the Manipulators of Capitalism and Communism; Psychotronics: "The Only Way to Go Is Up!"; The Religious Philosophy of Karl Marx; The Economic Philosophy of Jesus Christ; The Psychology of Socialism; The Right to Live in the New Age—Marijuana, The Death Drug*. Go to AscendedMasterLibrary.org to order.
15. John 8:32.

CHAPTER 19

1. "Rakoczy March" is Hungarian Rhapsody no. 15, by Franz Liszt.
2. For the novena to the Great Divine Director, see Saint Germain, "Divine Direction for the Path of Your Choosing," *Pearls of Wisdom*, vol. 13, no. 32.
3. The messenger has explained that certain major cities in the United States represent the chakras of the nation. The throat chakra of America is focused in Washington, D.C. She said that the city that focuses the throat chakra is always the seat of government and of God-government of the people. It is where the voice of the people and the blueprint of the nation is to be manifest.
4. On December 30, 1993, the Dhyani Buddha Vairochana announced that he had become the eighth member of the Karmic Board. The other members are the Great Divine Director, representing the first ray; the Goddess of Liberty, representing the second ray; the ascended lady master Nada, the third ray; the Elohim Cyclopea, fourth ray; Pallas Athena, the Goddess of Truth, fifth ray; Portia, the Goddess of Justice, sixth ray; and Kuan Yin, the Goddess of Mercy, seventh ray. Vairochana explained that his role on the Karmic Board would be "to assist those who have light who are sincere but who have strayed from the track of reality, considering that their karma was too hard to bear." (*Pearls of Wisdom*, vol. 37, no. 3)
5. Thomas Jefferson, Declaration of Independence, July 4, 1776.
6. Rev. 2:17.
7. The move to Los Angeles. In 1976 the messenger moved the international headquarters of The Summit Lighthouse and Church Universal and Triumphant to a campus in Pasadena, California. She also established the Ashram of the World Mother and the Los Angeles Teaching Center in downtown Los Angeles. In 1978 the headquarters moved to a 218-acre estate in the Santa Monica Mountains near Malibu (Camelot). The headquarters is presently located in Corwin Springs, Montana.

CHAPTER 20

1. Prior to the Allied victories in 1945 that brought World War II to a close, Prime Minister Winston Churchill, President Franklin Delano Roosevelt, and Premier Josef Stalin met at Yalta (February 4–11, 1945). The decisions made at Yalta permitted the Soviet occupation of East Berlin and East Germany, and the creation of the Communist governments in the eastern European countries of Poland, Czechoslovakia, Yugoslavia, Hungary, Romania, and Bulgaria. In short, Roosevelt and Churchill entrusted the security of eighty million eastern Europeans and hundreds of millions of Chinese to the Soviet Union, resulting in the murder of millions of freedom-fighters in those countries.
2. A student uprising in Hungary in 1956 led to the fall of the Soviet-backed regime and the formation of a new government under Imre Nagy, which

declared its intention of withdrawal from the Warsaw Pact and reinstituting free elections. The Soviet Union initially appeared to be ready to negotiate the withdrawal of their forces from Hungary, and the Hungarian people thought they had succeeded in winning their freedom. However, on November 4, a large Soviet force invaded Budapest and other regions of the country in order to crush the revolution. Hungarian freedom fighters took to the streets to defend their nation against Soviet tanks, and thousands of civilians were killed. Nagy appealed to Western nations for help, but none was forthcoming.

3. On July 4, 1776, following a stormy debate by members of the Second Continental Congress meeting in the State House (Independence Hall), Philadelphia, Pennsylvania, a fiery, impassioned speech by an unknown man broke the deadlock and inspired the delegates to sign the Declaration of Independence. "SIGN! if the next moment the gibbet's rope is round your neck! SIGN! if the next moment this hall rings with the echo of the falling axe! SIGN! By all your hopes in life or death, as husbands—as fathers—as men—sign your names to the Parchment or be accursed forever! Sign—and not only for yourselves, but for all ages. For that Parchment will be the Textbook of Freedom—the Bible of the Rights of Man forever!" See George Lippard, *Washington and His Generals: or, Legends of the Revolution* (Philadelphia: G.B. Zieber and Co., 1847), pp. 391–97.
4. Abraham Lincoln, *Gettysburg Address.*
5. See chap. 7.
6. To a caller at the White House. *Lincoln's Yarns and Stories,* Alexander K. McClure, p. 24.
7. *Buddha* means "the Enlightened One" (from the Sanskrit *budh,* "awake," "know," "perceive").
8. Rev. 3:5; 20:12, 15.
9. Rev. 12:1.
10. Rev. 3:12; 21:2.
11. Rev. 19:11–14.
12. The Dark Cycle of the return of mankind's karma began on April 23, 1969. It is a period when man's misqualified energy, held in abeyance for many centuries, is being released for balance in the period of transition into the Aquarian cycle. According to the cycles of the cosmic clock, the misqualified energies of mankind's karma were released under the hierarchy of Capricorn in the first year and in subsequent years under the hierarchies of Aquarius, Pisces, Aries, Taurus, and Gemini. April 23, 1975, commenced the seventh year of the Dark Cycle under the hierarchy of Cancer. Saint Germain refers to the Dark Cycle in Virgo which commenced April 23, 1977, returning the momentums of planetary injustice requiring transmutation by the flame of divine justice focused by his twin flame, Portia, the Goddess of Justice, also known as Opportunity. Subsequent cycles were under the hierarchies of

Libra, Scorpio, and Sagittarius, at which time the cycle recommenced with Capricorn. Each year the respective hierarchies release the light whereby mankind may redeem the energies misused in past cycles when they have failed the initiations of that particular hierarchy. For more about the Dark Cycle, see Elizabeth Clare Prophet, "Prophecy for the 1990s," Part 3, *Pearls of Wisdom*, vol. 33, no. 6, February 11, 1990.

13. Ray-O-Light, December 28, 1975, "Keep Moving!" *Pearls of Wisdom*, vol. 25, no. 29, July 18, 1982.
14. Palladas, *Greek Anthology*, bk. X, epigram 32.
15. Following the United States' withdrawal from South Vietnam in 1973 and the takeover by the North in April 1975, it is estimated that the Communist government sent up to 300,000 South Vietnamese to reeducation camps, where many endured torture, starvation, and disease while being forced to perform hard labor. Another 750,000 fled as refugees.
16. Marxist insurgents overturned the Western-backed Lon Nol government of Cambodia in April 1975 after nearly five years of fighting. Although there is no way of accurately counting, it is estimated that as many as three to four million Cambodians out of a population of some seven million were murdered or died from disease, malnutrition, or forced labor during the four-year Khmer Rouge regime.
17. No precise enumeration of the number of deaths worldwide caused by Communism since 1917 is possible. This is the result of the loss of (or inability to keep) records due to civil war, state-organized famines, forced relocations, collectivization, terror, political executions, disease, malnutrition, and the general hardship that accompanies the takeover and process of consolidating power by the Communists—and the suppression of such information as a matter of state policy. However, estimates are that the total number is in excess of 100 million. See R. J. Rummel, "How Many Did Communist Regimes Murder" https://www.hawaii.edu/powerkills/COM.ART.HTM.
18. Luke 12:48.
19. See Archangel Michael, December 28, 1975, "The Glory of the Word," *Pearls of Wisdom*, vol. 63, no. 17, May 1, 2020.
20. II Cor. 6:17.
21. From the 1960s to the early 1980s, women's rights groups were seeking ratification of the Equal Rights Amendment, a proposed amendment to the U.S. Constitution that read: "Equality of rights under the law shall not be denied or abridged by the United States or by any state on account of sex." The Equal Rights Amendment was not ratified by the required number of states and did not become law.
22. John 13:16; 15:15.
23. II Pet. 2:16.
24. Num. 22:28.
25. See chap. 13.

CHAPTER 21

1. God-reality under the sign of Libra. On the cosmic clock, the quality of God-reality is charted on the 9 o'clock line under the solar hierarchy of Libra. The perversions of God-reality include dishonesty, intrigue, treachery and deception.
2. "God tempers the wind to the shorn lamb" [Dieu mesure le froid à la brebis tondue"]. Henri Estienne, *Les Prémices* (1594).
3. The balance of God-control in God-reality. On the cosmic clock, the qualities of God-control and God-reality are charted respectively on the 3 o'clock and 9 o'clock lines under the solar hierarchies of Aries and Libra. The perversions of God-control, on the 3 o'clock line, include conceit, deceit, arrogance and ego, intellectual and spiritual pride. These lines correspond with the heart chakra.
4. Matt. 9:20–22.
5. Four and Twenty Elders. Rev. 4:4, 10; 5:5, 6, 8, 11, 14; 7:11, 13; 11:16; 14:3; 19:4.

298 pp   ISBN 978-0-916766-17-7

COSMIC CONSCIOUSNESS
One Man's Search for God

Mark L. Prophet, compiled by Elizabeth Clare Prophet

Mark L. Prophet walked before mankind as a friend on the spiritual path. He illustrated Truth as a day-to-day experience of God that could come to all. For him, the path of Truth led to cosmic consciousness. This book captures Mark Prophet's rare compassion and deep sensitivity. The author, a twentieth-century mystic, shares teaching on the Divine Mother, the presence of love, the eternality of being, and the aura as an expanding egg of cosmic consciousness. Includes a guided meditation for nourishing the heart and the soul.

212 pp   ISBN 978-0-916766-21-4

DOSSIER ON THE ASCENSION
The Story of the Soul's Acceleration into Higher Consciousness on the Path of Initiation

Serapis Bey

   A profound look into the life of the soul, her purpose and destiny. Serapis Bey shows that the soul's reunion with God through the ascension is the goal of life for all. He gives practical keys for spiritual growth that can lead to the attainment of the ascension. The author answers the ultimate questions about life after death.

ELIZABETH CLARE PROPHET is a world-renowned author, spiritual teacher, and pioneer in practical spirituality. Her groundbreaking books have been published in more than thirty languages and over three million copies have been sold worldwide.

Among her best-selling titles are *The Human Aura, The Science of the Spoken Word, Your Seven Energy Centers, The Lost Years of Jesus, The Art of Practical Spirituality,* and her successful Pocket Guides to Practical Spirituality series.

Printed by Libri Plureos GmbH in Hamburg, Germany